Mental Spaces

Mental Spaces: Gilles Fauconnier

Aspects of Meaning
Construction in Natural
Language

CAMBRIDGE
UNIVERSITY PRESS

PUBLISHED BY THE PRESS SYNDICATE OF THE UNIVERSITY OF CAMBRIDGE
The Pitt Building, Trumpington Street, Cambridge CB2 1RP, United Kingdom

CAMBRIDGE UNIVERSITY PRESS
The Edinburgh Building, Cambridge CB2 2RU, UK   http: //www.cup.cam.ac.uk
40 West 20th Street, New York, NY 10011-4211, USA   http: //www.cup.org
10 Stamford Road, Oakleigh, Melbourne 3166, Australia

First published in 1985 by The Massachusetts Institute of Technology
First published by Cambridge University Press 1994
Reprinted 1995, 1998

Typeset in Times

A catalogue record for this book is available from the British Library

Library of Congress Cataloguing-in-Publication Data is available

ISBN 0-521-44499-3 hardback
ISBN 0-521-44949-9 paperback

Transferred to digital printing 2003

"Why, how long you been on the island, Jim?"
"I come heah de night arter you's killed."
"What, all that time?"
"Yes-indeedy. . . . How long you ben on the islan'?"
"Since the night I got killed."

Mark Twain, Huckleberry Finn

. . . and even now I can hear the sweet little health and welcome in the singing language of Acadia which once was French and now is itself.

John Steinbeck, Travels with Charley

Contents

Contents

Foreword

George Lakoff and Eve Sweetser

An Overview

This book is a major advance in the study of reference, descriptions, and coreference—topics that have long been at the center of research in linguistics and the philosophy of language. The more traditional theories assume that natural language semantics can be adequately studied with the tools of formal logic. Fauconnier has, however, recognized that the tools of formal logic fail when confronted with the full range of natural language phenomena. He has realized that what is needed instead is a cognitive theory—a theory that is based on the capacities of the human mind rather than the capacities of the mathematical systems that happen to be used by logicians.

Fauconnier posits a theory in which reference has a dimension of structure all its own, which is simply representable using mental spaces, connectors across the spaces, and a few general principles. The complexity lies largely in the interaction between the principles, and in the contextual structures that feed into the principles for interpretation. With such a simple structure, Fauconnier can handle examples that are beyond the capacities of complex logical theories. Here is a salient class of such examples.

The Split Self

There are sentences whose meaning requires splitting the self in two parts:

If I were you, I'd hate me.

If I were you, I'd hate myself.

These do not mean the same thing, and the problem is to represent both meanings. The first problem is: *Me* and *myself* refer back to two different people. But since they are both first person, they both should refer to the speaker. The second problem is: How can the self be split into two parts, one identified with you and one remaining me? Formal logic has apparatus for indicating coreference, but not for indicating coreference for parts of an entity that has been split up in this way. As you will read below, the problem is easy in the theory of mental spaces.[1]

Split Coreference

There are other sentences in which a single referent splits into two:

If Woody Allen had been born twins, they would have been sorry for each other, but he wasn't and so he's only sorry for himself.

The word *twins* here is a nonreferential predicate nominal, which, being nonreferential, cannot serve as an antecedent. That leaves *Woody Allen* to serve as the antecedent of both *they* and *he.* Again, the logical theories do not have the capacity to deal with split antecedents, whereas Fauconnier's cognitive theory does.

We will shortly bring up a wide range of phenomena that are dealt with equally simply within the theory of mental spaces. But first, we should say something of the theories using formal logic to which Fauconnier's theory is a successor.

The Theory of Logical Form

Russell ([1905, 1919] 1971, pp.167–80), in proposing logical forms, separated the representation of descriptions from indications of reference and coreference, which were indicated by variables. His idea was to give a single logical formula containing information about coreference, quantification, predicate-argument structure, and logical operators, all in one structure. Fauconnier's innovation was to separate out referential structure as a separate domain of structure that works by principles of its own.

Within cognitive semantics, referential structure is indicated by mental spaces, whereas conceptual structure is indicated by *Idealized Cognitive Models* (or ICMs) and *frames*, which structure the mental spaces. The entities in the mental spaces are (1) the roles defined by ICMs and frames and (2) values for those roles. The ICMs themselves are not entities in the mental spaces; rather, they provide relational structure linking the roles, which are entities in the spaces.[2]

Possible Worlds and Situations

A *possible world,* in formal logic, is a state description—a set of entities and the properties and relations that hold of them in that state. A *situation* is a partial state description—some entities and some properties and relations that hold of them. A possible world semantics (or, equivalently, a situation semantics) is a formally stated relationship between expressions in some formal language (like predicate calculus) and set-theoretical models of possible worlds or situations.

These are objectivist models, models of the actual world, or a possible world, or an actual or possible situation. Possible worlds and situations are not models of the human mind, but models of the world as it is assumed to be or might be.

Discourse Representation Theory

This theory, developed after Fauconnier's, is similar to situation semantics in that it includes partial state descriptions. It adds one important thing: the ability to augment a state description as one goes through a discourse.[3]

None of these theories are cognitive theories. They attempt to account for the meaning of natural language sentences using only the mechanisms of formal syntax and set theory, without permitting any cognitive mechanisms. As we shall see shortly, each of them handles a certain range of phenomena, and each falls seriously short of handling other important phenomena. What Fauconnier accomplished was to show how the full set of recognized problems of reference could be handled with ideas and principles that make sense from a cognitive perspective: *mental spaces* (separate domains of referential structure), *connectors* between referents (within and across spaces), the distinction between *roles* and *individuals,* the ability to extend spaces in a discourse.

The other major accomplishment of Fauconnier's theory is that it demonstrates that the problem of presupposition inheritance is the same as the problem of reference, and that the same theory works for both.

The Phenomena

To get an idea of how profound Fauconnier's idea is, let us consider some of the crucial puzzles it solves. Among the phenomena that have posed problems for logicians and researchers on semantics is the following apparent contradiction:

I am taller than I am

is a contradiction, whereas

John thinks I am taller than I am

has a noncontradictory reading.

This kind of example can be handled by Russell's theory of logical form. It can be assigned a logical form like:

[(The degree x) (John thinks that I am tall to degree x)] is greater than [(The degree y) (I am tall to degree y)]

This can be paraphrased by:

The degree to which John thinks I am tall is greater than the degree to which I am tall.

What makes this analysis work is the occurrence of the propositional attitude verb *think,* which has the degree variable x bound within its scope, whereas the degree variable y is not bound within its scope. This kind of solution however does not work for cases like Jackendoff's (1975) celebrated example:

In this painting, the girl with the brown eyes has green eyes.

In this painting is neither a logical operator nor a verb of propositional attitude, and thus cannot introduce a similar scope difference. This problem for the Russellian account is handled straightforwardly in mental space theory. *In this painting* is a *space-builder:* It sets up the mental space of the painting, *P,* which is distinct from the mental space of the real world, R. The girl who has brown eyes in R has a counterpart in P who has green eyes. Fauconnier's Identification Principle (his ID Principle) permits the description of the girl in R to be used to name the girl's counterpart in P. Thus the description "the girl with the brown eyes," which holds in R, can be applied to the girl in the painting. Therefore, the clause *The girl with the brown eyes has green eyes* is not contradictory because the two descriptions hold in different mental spaces. Fauconnier shows that this simple kind of solution can be extended to the full range of known problems of reference.

One of the most impressive things about Fauconnier's theory is that it unifies the treatment of reference and the treatment of presupposition. Consider the classical problem of presupposition cancellation:

John's children are blond.

presupposes that John has children, whereas

If John has children, John's children are blond.

does not presuppose that John has children. Placing the presupposition in an *if*-clause has the effect of canceling it.

In Fauconnier's theory, *if* sets up a conditional mental space C, separate from the reality space R. *John has children* holds in C, but not necessarily in R. *John's children are blond,* as the second clause of the conditional construction, holds in an extension of C, but again not necessarily in R. Thus, the presupposition that John has children holds in C, but not in R. On the other hand, where there is no conditional construction setting up a separate mental space, *John's children are blond* will be taken as holding in R and hence as presupposing that John has children in R.[4]

Fauconnier's solution to this problem also accounts for the classic problem of donkey-sentences, which can stated as follows:

A man owns a donkey

can be represented in classical logical form with existential quantifiers: $(\exists x)\ (\exists y)\ ((\text{Man } x)\ \&\ (\text{Donkey } y)\ \&\ (x \text{ owns } y))$. The existential quantifiers are seen as representing the meaning of the indefinite article *a*. But, in the following sentence,

If a man owns a donkey, he beats it.

the indefinite articles have the same meaning, but cannot be represented in classical logical form by existential quantifiers, since such quantifiers would not bind *he* and *it*. What is required instead are universal quantifiers, as in: ($\forall$ll x) ($\forall$ll y) ((If ((Man x) & (Donkey y) & (x owns y)), then (x beats y)). The problem is how to get a uniform meaning for the indefinite article, while solving the problems in the last three sets of examples.[5]

In Fauconnier's theory, *if* sets up a conditional mental space, *C*, in which *a man owns a donkey* holds. The indefinite article has the function of setting up a referent for the first time in a discourse. Referents *d* for donkey and *m* for man are thus set up in *C*. When *C* is extended to include *he beats it*, *he* refers back to *m* in *C* and *it* refers back to *d* in *C*. Having an anaphoric referent is thus parallel to having a presupposition, and the same principles apply to both. General operations on the relevant spaces will then give you the required inferences in both cases.

Since the publication of the first edition of *Mental Spaces*, a number of new phenomena have been found that support Fauconnier's theory. We will conclude with one example that is indescribable within any of the competing theories based on formal logic: logical form, possible world semantics, and discourse representation theory. Consider the following example:

If the Ile de la Cité is the heart of Paris, then the Seine is the aorta.

Here, the *if*-clause states a metaphor and the *then*-clause extends it. The problem for the theories based on formal logic is that they cannot deal with metaphor at all, because metaphor is a cognitive phenomenon and the logic-based theories are only suited to talking about objective reality rather than imaginative constructions. Logic-based theories simply treat all metaphors as the same: necessarily false statements from which nothing can follow. That view doesn't differentiate the above sentence where the *then*-clause extends the *if*-clause in a sensible way, from the following sentence, where the *then*-clause is not such an extension of the *if*-clause:

If the Ile de la Cité is the heart of Paris, then Harry's theory is an apple.

Cases like these are straightforward in Fauconnier's theory, since it is fully compatible with contemporary cognitive theories of metaphor (see Sweetser (to appear)). This is but one example of the many ways in which the theory of mental spaces not only solves classical puzzles, but solves new ones as they arise.

This book goes through the most difficult known problems in reference and presupposition, and solves them all with equal ease. It also meshes with all the research done on conceptual systems within the field of cognitive semantics. Fauconnier's theory is truly elegant. It has become the standard account for these problems within cognitive linguistics. This reissue of Fauconnier's already classic work is most welcome.

Notes

1. For a fuller description of the complexities of the split self, see Lakoff (to appear).
2. Fauconnier does not explicitly discuss ICMs in *Mental Spaces,* although it is clear that such mechanisms will be needed. For a fuller discussion of how generic structure interacts with specific spaces, and other such issues, see Fauconnier (in press). At a higher level, there is the possibility for ICMs that include mappings between mental spaces structured by ICMs; for example, we might want to say that our understanding of Marriage as a Joint Journey (Compare Lakoff and Johnson, (1980)) was a complex ICM of marriage, involving a set of mappings between a space structured by a simpler ICM of marriage and one structured by an ICM of a shared journey.
3. Compare Kamp (1984).
4. This is merely the bare bones of Fauconnier's approach, which naturally has to deal with more complexity in the relevant data than we have treated here; readers are directed to the present volume, and to Fauconnier (in press).
5. Fauconnier's more fully developed treatment of these issues, including his concept of generic spaces, can be found in Fauconnier (to appear).

References

Fauconnier, G. (To appear). *Cognitive Mappings for Language and Thought.* New York: Cambridge University Press.

Fauconnier, G., and E. Sweetser, eds. (To appear). *Spaces, Worlds, and Grammar.* Chicago: University of Chicago Press.

Jackendoff, R. (1975). On belief contexts. *Linguistic Inquiry* 6:1.

Kamp, H. (1984). A theory of truth and semantic representation. In J. Groendijk, T. Janssen, and M. Stokhof, eds., *Truth, Interpretation, and Information.* Dordrecht: Foris.

Lakoff, G. (To appear). Multiple selves. In Fauconnier and Sweetser, eds.

Lakoff, G., and M. Johnson. (1980). *Metaphors We Live By.* Chicago: University of Chicago Press.

Russell, B. (1905). On denoting. [*Mind* 14, 479–493.] Reprinted 1956, in Bertrand Russell, *Logic and Knowledge: Essays 1901–1950.* R. Marsh, ed. London: George Allen and Unwin.

Russell, B. (1919). *Introduction to Mathematical Philosophy.* [London: George Allen and Unwin.] Reprinted 1971, New York: Simon and Schuster.

Sweetser, E. (To appear). Reasoning, mappings, and meta-metaphorical conditionals. In M. Shibatani and S. Thompson, eds., *Grammatical Constructions: Their Form and Meaning. (A Festschrift for Charles Fillmore.)* Oxford: Oxford University Press.

Preface
Backstage Cognition

When language, mind, and culture are the object of scientific study, the investigator is no longer a mere spectator. He or she is one of the actors, part of the phenomenon under study: The thinking and talking that need to be demystified are also the thinking and talking used to carry out the demystification. The investigation that will reveal backstage secrets is also part of the main show, and clearly we are on intellectually perilous ground.

The promising development of cognitive semantics in the last fifteen years has given us wonderful insights into some of the backstage organization of language and thought. But such insights do not come easily. Many traditional, respected, well established ways of viewing and interpreting empirical phenomena need to be reassessed, questioned, or abandoned. Commonsense views that have been worked into scientific theories may constitute a misleading context for scientific communication.

Cognitive science is beginning to flourish. Powerful new computational techniques are available. Neurobiology is destined to play an important role. Sophisticated accounts have been developed for mental representations, the nature of consciousness, and the mysteries of learning and cognitive development. Language plays an important role in much of this work, either as a direct object of study or as an indirect implicit means of accessing other information. Yet, too often, the sophistication of the techniques and experimental procedures is not matched by a corresponding awareness of the hidden, counterintuitive complexities of cognitive construction linked to language. The commonsense, folk-theoretic picture of speech, thought, and communication is easy to import uncritically into general cognitive science research.

Mental spaces—the connections linking them, the linguistic, pragmatic, and cultural strategies for constructing them—are a significant part of what is happening backstage, behind the scenes, in the cognitive background of everyday speaking and commonsense reasoning. The principles governing the operations are, in themselves, simple and general. They appear to be universal across languages and cultures. When combined and applied to rich pragmatic situations, the principles are able to yield unlimited numbers of meaning constructions and unlimited nesting. Generativity is fundamentally a property of meanings, only derivatively one of syntax.

Grammar plays a major role in this overall scheme because it is the visible link between mysterious backstage cognition and the superficial apparent behavior of human thinking organisms. The reason for this is broadly as follows: In order for thinking and communicating to take place, elaborate constructions must occur that draw on conceptual capacities, highly structured background and contextual knowledge, schema-induction, and mapping capabilities. Expressions of language do not in themselves represent or code such constructions—the complexity of the constructions is such that the coding, even if it were at all possible, would take very large amounts of time and be extremely inefficient. Instead, languages are designed, very elegantly it would seem, to prompt us into making the constructions appropriate for a given context with a minimum of grammatical structure. Language does not itself do the cognitive building—it "just" gives us minimal, but sufficient, clues for finding the domains and principles appropriate for building in a given situation. Once these clues are combined with already existing configurations, available cognitive principles, and background framing, the appropriate construction can take place, and the result far exceeds any overt explicit information.

This fundamental property of language is counterintuitive: In our folk theory, it is the words that carry the meaning: We "say what we mean," we "put meaning into words," and so on. The difference between the folk-theoretic conception and the actual (backstage) reality goes unnoticed for very interesting reasons. Not only are we not aware of the constructions we perform (any more, say, than we are aware of chemical reactions in our brain or other biological operations), but we do not suspect the extent to which vast amounts of prestructured knowledge, selected implicitly by context, are necessary to form any interpretation of anything. We notice only the tip of the iceberg—the words—and we attribute all the rest to common sense. This fiction is wonderfully convenient in everyday life, where we need notice only what is different, not what is shared, but we must resist the temptation to import it into scientific theory.

The theory of mental spaces was developed in reaction to mainstream views of meaning. It recognized the importance of phenomena such as quantifier scope, referential opacity, presupposition projection, and counterfactuals singled out by logicians, philosophers, and linguists, while placing in doubt the semantic foundations, analytical tools, and empirical methods that had been routinely assumed in the investigation of such phenomena. The new approach has proven fruitful: In recent years, many aspects of language and reasoning that were not initially linked to mental space construction have been studied by scholars of different disciplines and integrated into a more general powerful theory of connected domains. Section 0.4 of this Preface contains a brief review of this research, its authors, and future prospects. I will begin with a general overview of the ideas that have guided our work and attempt in doing so to clarify issues of method and theory.

0.1 Methodology and Empirical Base

There is long tradition in grammar and in philosophy (of the noncontinental variety) to take the *sentence,* in isolation, as the basic object of study. In many ways, this tradition would seem eminently reasonable. If the conditions for sentences to be well-formed (syntax) are understood, and if their meanings (semantics) can be operationally characterized, then surely we will have a firm handle on the structure of language. Furthermore, some sentences are more "simple," "typical," and "probable" than others. It makes sense to study these first, build a theory for the core fragment, and worry later about extending the analysis to complex, outlandish, marginal, constructions.

The work on mental spaces and on other areas of cognitive semantics challenges those reasonable assumptions. We have found time and time again that unusual cases reveal the general nature of the operations at work, whereas the typical cases do not, and that the "typical" cases are then straightforwardly accounted for as simple, particular instances of the general mechanism. The reverse does not hold: Theories developed for fragments seldom extend to the general case, and, what is worse, they lead to improper partitioning of the data.

Take for example the case of referential opacity. This is a phenomenon that has justifiably been considered important and revealing for natural language semantics. It is commonly apprehended as a property of sentences involving propositional attitudes (Quine (1960)), in which substitution *salva veritate* does not seem to hold unproblematically. Cases like the following are considered typical: Jack is the son of Philip, and also, secretly, the leader of the Black Brigade. Then *Philip believes his son is a genius* and *Philip believes the leader of the Black Brigade is a genius* are not equivalent, even though the underlined phrases refer to the same person. It has been customary to ask how the representation of sentence meanings might reflect such data. This formulation of the problem predetermines in many ways the type of investigation and data that will appear relevant for its analysis and leads to the familiar approach in terms of scope, sense and reference, and intensional contexts. In Chapters 1 and 2, the same data is viewed somewhat differently, as a special instance of a much wider range of cases arising from general properties of discourse construction and conceptual connection. The key methodological point is that although classical cases such as Quine's follow straightforwardly from the construction of mental spaces and connections in discourse, the reverse is not true: Considerations of sentence logic and scope of descriptions will not provide adequate theoretical notions to frame, let alone solve, the general discourse problem.

With hindsight, one can see where Quine went wrong (which didn't prevent him from saying many interesting things). By assuming like everyone else that natural language sentences, although endowed with fairly bizarre logical properties, were still in principle objects of the same *nature* as the formal sentences of logical systems, he transposed to the former, queries appropriate for the latter. In the meantime, we have found that this reasonable assumption about the nature of natural language sentences was untenable. They are in fact a very different kind of thing. Sentences bring together, in one linguistically homogeneous form, heterogeneous and incomplete information as to the cognitive constructions to be performed within a context for the purpose of constructing meaning. Meaning ensues when such operations are performed, but is not itself directly assignable to sentences.

It follows that meanings assigned to sentences in isolation, such as the above *Philip believes his son is a genius,* are obtained in reality by building local, maximally simple contexts in which the sentences can operate. What a logician like Quine will really be studying are these minimal contexts, not inherent separable logical properties of the linguistic form. Of course, it could turn out that such minimal-context properties are in fact all we need (semantically) to account for the interpretation of the sentence in other circumstances. In that case, the minimal contexts would indeed reveal an inherent logical form, and the classical Quinean view would be saved.

The work on mental spaces, and in other areas of cognitive semantics, shows unequivocally that this is not the case. The minimal context observations do not generalize to larger ones. Rather, in scientifically unsurprising fashion, it is the principles applicable to the general case that also explain the minimal one as a special instance under special circumstances.[1] So, in the example of referential opacity, the minimal case involves an explicit linguistic marker (*believes*) of propositional attitude, an explicit description (*his son*), and a fixed number of readings. In the present work, abundant evidence is offered that none of these features are characteristic of the general phenomenon, sometimes called *space accessibility* in later work.[2] Access, guided by the Identification (ID) Principle (Chapter 1, sections 1.1 and 1.4.2), allows elements in mental spaces to be accessed in terms of elements connected to them, and situated in other mental spaces. The corresponding interpretation possibilities will therefore depend on the available spaces and connectors in the configuration where a sentence operates. This information in turn may be available to the discourse participants from the existing discourse configuration when the new sentence is added, or from grammatical features of the new sentences, or from nonlinguistic pragmatic factors, or any combination of the above.

Readers will have no trouble checking that the minimal contexts constructed for the Quinean sentences automatically restrict Access, by allowing only mental spaces that are explicitly signaled linguistically (the speaker's Origin or Base, and one Belief space), and only one space-connector (Identity). Any account that restricts itself to a logical distinction between transparent and opaque readings is really only reflecting this minimal-context situation, without reflecting the deeper principle behind it and the richer interpretation possibilities in other configurations. Although observationally accurate, such an account is not theoretically useful. And it is empirically misleading because it obscures the link between opacity for propositional attitudes and general accessibility for mental spaces set up for many other kinds of domains, such as pictures, time, reality, and physical space.

Our methodology, then, is a classic scientific one: Aim for the most encompassing generalizations; bring together theoretically superficially diverse empirical data; try not to prejudge theoretical outcomes with premature descriptive classifications.

0.2 Subject Matter

Theoretical advances have nontrivial consequences for empirical observation: Questions can only be asked from a particular theoretical standpoint; they cannot be theory-neutral. One strong finding of mental space research, repeatedly borne out in studies of different language phenomena over the last fifteen years, was evoked in the previous section: Language does not carry meaning, it guides it. As Mark Turner felicitously put it:

Expressions do not mean; they are prompts for us to construct meanings by working with processes we already know. In no sense is the meaning of [an] . . . utterance "right there in the words." When we understand an utterance, we in no sense are understanding "just what the words say"; the words themselves say nothing independent of the richly detailed knowledge and powerful cognitive processes we bring to bear (Turner (1991), p. 206).

The same fundamental tenet is expressed in *Cognitive Mappings for Language and Thought:*

Language, as we use it, is but the tip of the iceberg of cognitive construction. As discourse unfolds, much is going on behind the scenes: New domains appear, links are forged, abstract mappings operate, internal structure emerges and spreads, viewpoint and focus keep shifting. Everyday talk and commonsense reasoning are supported by invisible, highly abstract, mental creations, which grammar helps to guide, but does not by itself define (Fauconnier (to appear)).

And more specifically, concerning the status of linguistic forms, such as *sentences,* a sentence that appears at some stage of the discourse construction will contain several kinds of information, indicated by various grammatical devices:

information regarding what new spaces are being set up, typically expressed by means of *space builders;*

clues as to what space is currently in focus, what its connection to the base is, and how *accessible* it is; this information is typically expressed by means of grammatical tenses and moods;

descriptions that introduce new elements (and possibly their counterparts) into spaces;

descriptions or anaphors or names that identify existing elements (and possibly their counterparts);

syntactic information that typically sets up generic-level schemas and frames;

lexical information that connects the mental space elements to frames and cognitive models from background knowledge; this information structures the spaces internally by taking advantage of available prestructured background schemas. Such prestructured schemas can, however, be altered or elaborated within the constructions under way;

presuppositional markings that allow some of the structure to be instantly propagated through the space configuration;

pragmatic and rhetoric information, conveyed by words like *even, but, already,* which typically signal implicit scales for reasoning and argumentation.

A natural language sentence is cognitively complex, because it incorporates information and building instructions at all these different levels. What kind of meaning will actually be produced depends on the mental space configuration (generated by earlier discourse) that the sentence actually applies to.

This view of language and meaning has received considerable support from other work in cognitive linguistics, in particular Lakoff's research on conceptual metaphor and idealized cognitive models, Fillmore's frame semantics and construction grammar,

Langacker and Talmy's cognitive and conceptual theories of grammar, and Sweetser's analysis of modality, conditionals, and diachronic semantic change. It has some deep consequences for the very formulation of problems relative to meaning and form, which I now outline.

0.2.1 Meaning

One notable consequence of our findings about linguistic forms is that a *sentence* is not the kind of thing that expresses a *proposition* (or even a quasi, or semi, or pragmatically incomplete proposition). Regardless of whether propositions play a role in semantic theory or natural language logic, *sentences are not carriers of propositions*. This follows directly from the characterization reported above of the sentence as a semantically heterogeneous and highly underspecified form that gives simultaneous information relative to widely different aspects of the discourse-building and contextual insertion process of meaning construction.

Now, as it happens, a considerable body of work on meaning, reference, and truth is predicated on the contrary assumption—that sentences *do* express propositions, and that our mission is to find out what they are and how the pairing is achieved. It is often taken for granted that without such an assumption, semantic theory could not even get off the ground, and so the study of meaning itself, and not just a particular theory, comes to be dependent on the assumption. The consequences are broad and, as it turns out, unfortunate, because the formulation of key questions is prevented, and highly relevant kinds of data are kept out of bounds.

The study of mental space phenomena, as reported in this book, and in later research by scholars working on a variety of other problems, attempts to break out of this mold by focusing on linguistic *generalization*, showing that the same principles operate in grammatically regular ways far beyond the confines of prototypical, minimal, "literal", sentence meaning. In that light, the following are some of the generalizations obtained in the course of the present study.

Access through conceptual connections is a powerful component of meaning construction that language reflects in general, regular, and systematic ways, independently of its particular domains of application. Accordingly, we find the same language and interpretation mechanisms at work in mappings between source and target domains (literary, conceptual, and conventional metaphor) (Fauconnier and Turner (1993); Lakoff (1987); Lakoff and Johnson (1980); Lakoff and Turner (1989); Turner (1991)); in reasoning and talking about images, pictures, and representations (Jackendoff (1975, 1983)); in the use of pragmatic functions of reference (with the special cases of metonymy and synechdoche) (Nunberg (1978)); in talk about propositional attitudes (beliefs, desires, . . .); in discourse involving time, viewpoint, and reference points; in the construction of hypothetical and counterfactual situations.

In all these cases, cognitive domains are set up and connected. Uniform linguistic operations for access can apply: The Access Principle (also called here the Indentification [ID] Principle); cross-space (or transspatial) connection signaled by a copula (*be* in English), multiple connecting paths (giving rise to surface ambiguities of the isolated forms), grammatical markings (tense, mood, anaphora, space-builders) for keeping track of the dynamic progression through spaces as discourse unfolds; general default optimization strategies for structuring these domains, and grammatically marked ones, such as presupposition "float."

The generalizations obtained bring together types of data that are widely considered in traditional treatments to differ not just analytically, but in their very nature:

The subset of mental space phenomena involving propositional attitudes, time, and hypotheticals in prototypical "minimal context," single-sentence situations is classically assumed to be in the realm of core semantics (literal, truth-conditional, model-theoretic interpretations), the larger set is relegated to pragmatics;

Metonymy, novel metaphor, synechdoche are consigned to rhetoric, literary embellishment, and the like;

Conventional metaphor is largely ignored and is attributed to the vagaries of language change and etymology;

Pragmatic functions, needless to say, are in pragmatics;

Analogical mappings are viewed as higher-level reasoning processes, not at the core of direct language interpretation;

The difficulties with reference in pictures and representations have gone unnoticed, but would presumably also be considered pragmatic, and not relevant to basic truth-conditional semantics.

0.2.2 More about Method

In a slightly circular fashion, changes in theory trigger changes in relevant types of data, and new kinds of data lead to changes in theory. Changes in method of investigation follow.

The strong, and in many ways fruitful, focus on the *sentence*, both in semantics and syntax, carries with it methodological choices that will be altered when this focus is shifted and expanded. In linguistics, the theoretical outlook by Chomsky in the 1950s became deeply associated with a simple, elegant, and broadly applicable method of investigation, "the wonderful stars." The idea was that native speakers had intuitions about strings of words: whether they were well-formed sentences, whether they were meaningful or not, how many meanings they had. Native speakers' judgments reflecting those intuitions could be obtained at little cost, and yet they constituted powerful evidence for or against theories, with a status comparable to experiments in science. The *star*, *, and its graded and semantic variants such as ?, ?*, **, %, were the symbols used in linguistic science to indicate the negative outcome of such experiments on particular sentences (for example, *Apple the eating for about higher., *What did Max read the book about?). An entire generation of investigators came to see their goal as ultimately accounting for the distribution of stars in linguistic forms. The method was powerful, ingenious, and often fruitful: An hypothesis initially based on observed data could be tested extensively by checking the predictions of stardom it made for forms that had not been observed, and which the investigator had little statistical chance of finding positive evidence for in a corpus, and absolutely no chance at all of finding negative evidence against in attested behavior. This in turn would lead to refinement, extension, generalization, and integration of the hypothesis, and others like it, and concurrently, or subsequently, to development of the theory itself, in the best scientific tradition.

In an article titled "Galileo, Stars, and the Great Syntax," and written in response to important critical comments made by N. Ruwet (1991) in regard to current aspects of generative theory, I suggested some reasons of principle as to why the "star system" would not apply methodologically to properly conceived investigations of cognitive linguistic constructions. Simplifying greatly, one reason is that native speakers' judgments in isolation do not inform us about meaning and form per se, but rather about the subject's ability to construct appropriate minimum contexts of the kind mentioned in section 0.2.1. Even though speakers (and hearers) have the cognitive capacity to map a cognitive configuration plus a linguistic form (at stage *n-1* of discourse) onto the "next" cognitive configuration (stage *n*), they do not have the cognitive capacity to map forms onto pairs of successive configurations.

It follows that data obtained in isolation will reflect the minimum context construction process (and this of course may be scientifically useful), but will not necessarily provide information as to the general construction process. The investigator will depend heavily also on attested productions in attested context, in which cognitive constructions (often unexpected ones) have actually taken place. This scheme by no means dispenses with native "intuitions": They are called upon to assess hidden aspects of analyzed discourse such as plausible inferences, context defaults, and so on.

In practice, empirical investigation supports this abstract argument. In the present book, single sentences *are* studied, not as self-supporting, meaning-bearing forms, but as steps in the complete meaning construction process. Accordingly, we may consider one invariant *form,* and vary experimentally its conditions of use: the previous configurations in which it might 'appear, the available background frames and knowledge, the relevant pragmatic functions or connectors, and their number. We invent context (acceptable to subjects) or find it in attested conversation, literature, and so on. Once we start paying attention in everyday life to instantiations of connectors, frames, induced schemas, conceptual connections, and metaphor, counterfactual mental spaces, . . . the real world discloses far richer and more revealing configurations than our feeble efforts as linguists or philosophers have been able to produce. There is an abundance of such data that goes largely unnoticed despite its obviousness, mainly, it would seem, because it does not fit the observational categories of our established academic practice. "Discovering" bodies of data that were staring us in the face, and yet were invisible to us (the black holes of science, the blind spots of the scientist), is a common feature of the evolution of scientific inquiry. An analogy in linguistics might be the sudden explosion of syntax in the 1960s: Grammatical phenomena that had been in plain view all along suddenly became "visible" through the new lens of transformational grammar (extraction constraints, raising, anaphoric binding, . . .).

0.2.3 Form
The explosion of syntax just alluded to was surely the single most important factor in making us aware of the immense complexities of language structure and organization. Even though grammar had been studied diligently, and insightfully, through the centuries, it was not until Zellig Harris, Noam Chomsky, and their students gave us an explicit program for the formal study of syntactic structure that the awesome intricacies of word combination were fully perceived to be the scientific challenge that they are.

It is also true, and this is itself an important scientific result, that in many ways this explicit program did not work out as expected (Fauconnier (1992); Gross (1979); Lakoff (1987); Langacker (1987, 1992); Ruwet (1991)). The reasons for the failure are nontrivial, and as it turns out, they are closely tied in some respects to the problems of meaning construction addressed in the present work.

Although syntax as we know it was invented by Zellig Harris, it was his student Noam Chomsky who most clearly articulated its place in the intellectual realm, pointed out its devastating implications for behaviorist psychology, and gave it the streamlined *generative* look that links it to axiomatic, logical, and computational algorithmic systems. Chomsky offered a general framework for asking questions relating to form that was elegant and conceptually simple: Just as mathematical well-formedness had become a scientifically tractable problem in the twentieth century through the detailed study of recursive algorithms, linguistic well-formedness could be approached with the same techniques and with the same goals.

It is worth noting that once the analogy with formal systems was perceived, Chomsky's position appeared eminently reasonable. Clearly, users of a natural language have a strong, by and large reliable and reproducible sense of what counts as "well-formed" in their language, and what does not, and this capacity to tell the difference is one they can apply to any number of novel exemplars, never heard or never produced before. Such knowledge is equivalent to the (procedural) mastery of a complex recursive algorithm. What is more, the position advocated by Chomsky was put to the test, and in the early days of generative syntax, rule systems were developed that indeed met the goal of accounting (in explanatory ways) for fragments of natural languages. There was every reason to hope that the scheme would work. It was conceptually simple, operationally sound, and made use of successful techniques developed in mathematics. It yielded initial analyses that were sophisticated and encouraging. And as mentioned above, it revealed new phenomena that had been impossible even to observe in the absence of proper theoretical and classificatory constructs. Finally, as mentioned also in the previous section, it brought with it a powerful new method of investigation, the "wonderful stars."

The puzzling aspect of the algorithmic approach was its lack of concern for meaning—the so-called autonomy of syntax view, inherited from American structuralism. Could it be that the fundamental combinatorial principles of language had little to do directly with cognitive, communicative, or social function? Few researchers in the 1960s really believed this. There was a widespread feeling that syntax was not just syntax, but also a good way of doing semantics. Meaning would show up at the level of deep structure; some transformations might be motivated by principles of discourse organization, involving notions such as topic, focus, new and old information, and anaphoric links. Even pragmatics could perhaps show up at deep syntactic levels, as in Ross's celebrated performative analysis. This interesting conception of an extended and deeper syntax produced much insightful work, but did not work out theoretically.

Another source of disappointment was the realization by those who carried out systematic empirical research, that grammar was not *generative* in the way it was supposed to be. Exhaustive studies, like Gross (1975),[3] irrefutably documented that language users had knowledge of patterns in great numbers that differed from one lexical item to the next in such a way that no category assignment and sensible generative rule system could account for the observed productions and judgments. This result does not preclude that the patterns in question may be constrained to fit formal structures characterized by a generative algorithm, but it does entail that such algorithms will considerably overgenerate. This in turns weakens the initial appeal of the generative enterprise: accounting for vast bodies of data in terms of economical, innately constrained, recursive procedures.

The nongenerativity of grammar, in this sense, is a negative but nevertheless very interesting property. It is counterintuitive, both within the modern computational paradigm and within our folk theories and commonsense views of language, which represent the combination of words as "logical" and nonproblematic. It raises some deep questions. Are the endless idiosyncrasies of patterning and distribution an accidental and nonsignificant effect of arbitrary choices that emerge in language communities, get reinforced statistically, and are culturally disseminated and transmitted? Or do they reflect central aspects of semantics and pragmatics? Or is it a combination of both?

Clearly, a theory of form without a comprehensive account of meaning will not do (for natural language). The next step in filling this considerable gap was the development in the 1970s of model theoretic accounts that would interpret syntactic form in the same general way that logical forms are truth-conditionally interpreted in mathematics. This Tarskian approach was especially popular among some logicians and philosophers who had a very definite idea of what semantics *ought* to look like. It was instantiated most explicitly in Montague's work (1974). The reason why this approach also backfired takes us back to our discussion of subject matter. Like Quine, Kripke, and others, and in the general spirit of commonsense views, Montague assumed uncritically that sentences, with their grammatical structure, were the sort of object that lends itself to literal truth-conditional interpretation. Because of this assumption and a lack of concern for the wealth of relevant empirical data, his work encountered the same difficulties that had plagued sentence-oriented semantics before him. Here too, the reasons for failure are nontrivial and Montague, like Giovanni Saccheri, who came close to "proving" Euclid's fifth postulate, deserves credit for pushing a worthwhile, if ultimately untenable, line of research. Still, it should be noted that the narrow notion of semantics adopted in much of this philosophical work has the drawback of excluding from consideration highly relevant empirical evidence. It fosters the misleading impression that semantics is a matter of finding the appropriate formalization, when in fact the subject matter remains poorly understood and circumscribed.

It is also unfortunate that this paradigm for the study of meaning came to be known as *formal semantics*. Formalization does not inherently carry with it the strong and specific (and arguably erroneous) assumptions linked to the paradigm in question. I return to this issue in section 0.3.

The cognitive linguistics framework that was elaborated in the 1970s and considerably developed in the 1980s abandoned many of the central assumptions just outlined, in particular the algorithmic approach to syntactic form and the literal meaning, truth-conditional, sentence-oriented view of semantics. The work on mental spaces is part of this reassessment. It provides what we take to be massive evidence for the role of grammar in constructing discourse configurations and at the same time, for the strongly underspecified nature of such constructions. As I have stated, it brings together phenomena that had been assigned to different realms of language or reasoning and studies principles that apply throughout.

0.3 Substance and Formalization

At one level of scientific inquiry, "mental spaces" and related notions examined in our work are clearly theoretical constructs devised to model high-level cognitive organization. In that sense, their status is that of usual scientific notions, whether in the physical, social, or cognitive sciences: Magnetic fields, social habitus (Bourdieu (1979)), syntactic structures, and mental models all have a connection to the "real world" that is necessarily mediated by the theories of which they are part. Such theories come with (socially agreed upon and at the same time, hotly disputed) procedures for linking the notions with other aspects of our interaction with the world—the physicist's experiments, the astronomer's recordings, the linguist's grammaticality judgments, the sociologist's surveys, the economist's accounting.

How real a notion is felt to be depends on many factors, such as the degree of our commitment to the theory, its usefulness for apprehending the world, whether it gains wide acceptance, and so on. In that sense, folk theories, religions, paranoia, and science, all produce strong feelings of reality. We need not debate the "reality" (in that sense) of mental spaces (or syntactic structures, or black holes, or charms and quarks).

In cognitive science, another reality issue that often comes up is biological plausibility. The biological is understandably felt to be more real than the purely mental. It is in principle highly desirable to tie together the biological substrate with higher-level organization, and there are a number of ways in which this might happen. Neural architectures might provide a good computational implementation of the theoretical constructs but still be equally well suited for alternative theories, thus providing at best a weak compatibility argument. A stronger result (in fact a very strong one) would be that mental spaces are naturally emergent, given, independently discovered properties of neural organization. This would clearly yield a strong feeling of "reality" for such mental representations, in spite of their abstraction. Conversely, any computational incompatibility would count (perhaps decisively) against the higher-level constructs. A different scenario is produced by eliminative reductionism: A better understanding of the biological allows direct explanation without appeal to the high-level constructs. In the worst case of this scenario (for the present work), notions like "mental space" undergo the same fate as "phlogiston" or "epicycles": They turn out to be wrong, and in fact irrelevant. In a preferable subscenario, they are comparable to "heat" or "energy" and retain some validity derivatively from more primitive notions, but thereby become less real and less useful. Finally, it can turn out that we have been victims of a "first-order isomorphism fallacy," and that the regularities discovered, although valid, are not mental properties of the organism, but structural properties of the organism's (and the scientist's) interaction with the world, fallaciously attributed to the organism alone.

There is at the time of writing no biological evidence of which I am aware strongly supporting one or another of these alternatives. The reason, of course, is that in spite of spectacular research in neurobiology, there is nothing remotely close to explanation of higher-level phenomena such as the ones discussed in the present work. There is, however, suggestive work on convergence zones (Damasio (1989)), neural group selection (Edelman (1992)), mappings linking cortical areas (Sereno (1990)), which highlights dynamic aspects of binding and meaning construction.

Another issue is that of formalization. Because generative grammars are formally axiomatic systems, it was natural, and in a sense inevitable, that accounts of syntax would be formalized in the fashion of twentieth-century mathematics. The same was true of model-theoretic accounts. It does *not* follow that this type of formalization is intrinsically preferable, useful, or desirable. This point is widely misunderstood, for reasons that appear social rather than intellectual. Advanced formal and empirical sciences such as mathematics and physics have reached the stage where such formalisms are useful, efficient, and insightful. "Math envy" spreads easily to other domains of inquiry that will "look" (and feel) scientific by virtue of employing a "mathematical" apparatus. But any formalization is only as good as the theory it formalizes. Theories evolve dynamically, groping through the ages for the best concepts, laws, and operations, and there is no example, and presumably no possibility, of scientific inquiry that starts off with a full-blown formalism, simply because such a formalism, if successful, cannot help but incorporate many of the notions that have yet to be discovered.

There is some irony for those who have a deep interest in mathematics, in being rebuked for not conforming to the standards of Bourbaki or Whitehead. We view the righteous insistence on logically based extensive formalization to be misconceived for a science like ours, which is nowhere near the state of development and conceptual stability reached after many centuries by mathematics and the physical sciences. We view premature formalizations of unsatisfactory analyses to be potentially regressive and harmful to the proper evolution of scientific understanding. We distinguish precision and explicitness, both highly desirable, from twentieth-century mathematical formalism, a desirable feature of certain types of research, but not a panacea. In this regard, the founder of mathematical linguistics, Noam Chomsky, remarks aptly that the natural sciences would rarely if ever take seriously the injunction to meet the criteria for formal theories set out in logic books. He writes:

At one time, there was some marginal interest in the project; Woodger's attempted formalization of biology is a well-known case, forgotten, because empirical consequences were lacking. Even in mathematics, the concept of formalization in our sense was not developed until a century ago, when it became important for advancing research and understanding. I know of no reason to suppose that linguistics is so much more advanced than 19th century mathematics or contemporary molecular biology that pursuit of [the injunction] would be helpful . . . [But] work should be clear enough so that it *could* be formalized further if there is some reason to do so (Chomsky (1990), p. 145).

The point, which would still hold if we replaced nineteenth by some earlier century, is well taken: There is nothing wrong with formalization if it is carried out at the right time and for the proper reasons; but it is never an end in itself and should not arbitrarily constrain the construction of theories. As mathematicians will tell you, the formal proofs are only the superficial manifestation of mathematical conceptual thought, and, in that sense, they are a socially convenient way of conveying and, of course, of keeping tabs on, that particular kind of thought.[4]

In the case of the present work on mental spaces, some aspects are easy in principle to formalize for a particular purpose, as shown, for example, by Dinsmore's SPACEPROBE implementations. Other aspects are not, simply because we don't know enough about them. For example, it is clear (see Chapter 2, section 2.5; Fujii (to appear); Fauconnier (to appear)) that mental spaces are set up not just by explicit space builders, but by other more indirect grammatical means, and also by nonlinguistic pragmatic, cultural, and contextual factors. It follows that there is no complete algorithm yielding a mental space configuration on the basis of available discourse only. This is not a weakness in the theory, it is one of its substantive claims, one for which there is considerable evidence. However, that claim results in the impossibility of a straightforward, context-independent pairing of linguistic form and meaning configurations, routinely assumed by standard formalizations. The point, again, is that formalizations necessarily carry implicit assumptions about what it is that they formalize, and that those assumptions, in the present case, are scientifically controversial in a crucial way. More often than not, insistence on formalization (admirable in itself) turns out to be insistence on a particular kind of formalization that carries with it important theoretical biases. Needless to say, whatever works works, and if those biases were to lead to successful analysis, that would be fine. Our position, however, is that they do not, that semantics is at best a fledgling science trying to find its conceptual and empirical bearings, and therefore is in no way on the same plane as centuries-old mathematics or physics.[5] And incidentally, even in physics, presumably on far more secure ground in its use of mathematical formalization, the issue of interpretation and modeling is one that remains undecided, mysterious, and contentious.

0.4 Development of Mental Space Research

The theory of mental spaces and its application to problems of reference and presupposition, some classical, some novel, was first presented in 1978 at the Accademia della Crusca, in Florence.[6] In later years, the approach was applied and extended to many areas that had not been foreseen, suggesting that mental spaces and mental space connections were far more pervasive than we had first imagined.

0.4.1 Mental Spaces: What They Are Not
For reasons outlined in the previous section, it doesn't make much sense to try to characterize mental spaces (or other theoretical constructs, for that matter) independently of the theory of which they are part. It is useful, however, to understand how they differ from other notions that may be felt to share some of their characteristics (and in fact, sometimes do). I will sketch some of these differences, using some broadly conceived shared characteristics; *partitioning, cross-domain functions, discourse processing, mental models.*

0.4.1.1 Partitioning: Worlds, Spaces, Domains. It has been commonplace for a long time to introduce some form of partitioning into semantic analysis, by distinguishing domains, in the widest sense. In realist approaches to the study of reference, such domains show up in the form of *possible worlds*. The possible worlds contain all referents and their properties. They are fully specified, nonlinguistic, and noncognitive. Frameworks employing the notion view semantics as being the study of links between linguistic forms and universes of possible worlds. Beyond the fact that this approach uses a form of partitioning, it has little in common with ours. The partitioning is metaphysical rather than cognitive. In contrast, mental space configurations are only very partially specified models of discourse understanding. They undergo continuous modification; some of their structure is specified as defeasible (obtained by defaults and optimization mechanisms, and revisable). The spaces do not in principle have to be logically consistent. The mental space constructions are cognitive; they are not something that is being referred to, but rather something that itself can be used to refer to real, and perhaps imaginary, worlds. And, importantly, they include elements (roles) that do not, and cannot, have direct reference in the world.

Independently (or perhaps not so independently) of their technical use in philosophy, possible and not-so-possible worlds are also an everyday, folk-theoretic construct, and as such they are certainly, like other domains, talked and thought about using mental spaces. And philosophical discourse itself, when talking about its possible worlds, is replete with corresponding mental space constructions.

The striking (and outrageous) feature of philosophical discussion about possible worlds is its use of *language* as evidence for or against hypotheses about such worlds.[7] This mistake is produced by confusing in effect the worlds with the mental spaces used to talk about them, by taking the grammatical structures (such as hypotheticals and counterfactuals) to reflect properties of worlds, rather than of cognitive constructions. This leads to paradox, as bravely acknowledged by Kripke (1980), and discussed (too briefly) in Chapter 5, section 5.2 of this book.

Another notion of world, more fruitful in my view, was introduced into linguistics by McCawley (1981), and Morgan (1973).

These authors talk about *world-creating* predicates. They recognize the dynamic aspect of such "worlds," and their importance for presupposition and reference phenomena. McCawley uses this notion somewhat informally in a manner very congenial to the mental space approach in discussing the famous Brigitte Bardot example:[8]

I dreamed that I was Brigitte Bardot and that I kissed me.

In our approach, "world creation" is seen as one particular type of mental space building, with a single-identity connector, plus the usual features of discourse construction; partial modeling, defeasibility, and dynamic transformation.

Jackendoff (1975, 1983) invokes another kind of partitioning, the distinction between reality and representations (pictures). This leads to the important insight that linguistically, sentences involving pictures share semantic properties with those involving beliefs (see Chapter 1, section 1.2 of the present book). This turns out to be another revealing case of mental space connection. The shared semantic properties follow from the more general Access Principle (also called here the Identification [ID] Principle).

0.4.1.2 Cross-domain Functions. The simple idea behind the approach explored in this book is that when we engage in any form of thought, typically mediated by language (for example, conversation, poetry, reading, storytelling), domains are set up, structured, and connected. The process is local: A multitude of such domains—mental spaces—are constructed for any stretch of thought, and language (grammar and lexicon) is a powerful means (but not the only one) of specifying or retrieving key aspects of this cognitive construction. Reference, inference, and, more generally, structure projection of various sorts operate by using the connections available to link the constructed mental spaces. Technically, such connections are *cross-domain functions* that specify counterparts and projected structure from one space to another. In simple cases, two spaces are connected by only one function, and intuitively this function seems to reflect some form of identity of the connected counterparts. For example, when talking about Dorian Gray and the portrait of Dorian Gray, we build two spaces, one for "reality" and one for the "picture";

there is a Dorian Gray in each one, and they are counterparts of each other. The connection is felt to be one of identity; it is "the same" Dorian Gray that appears in both domains. From an objective standpoint, there is of course no identity at all, just flesh and bones versus blobs of paint. And from a subjective standpoint, there is no identity either—the model and the man in the picture can differ as much as we like. That is the point of partitioning in the first place: keeping distinct properties, frames and structures in distinct domains, even when, in some sense, they apply to "the same thing." Interesting examples, some of which are discussed in Chapter 2, show that there can be several functions linking two given mental spaces in discourse, thereby providing several competing counterpart structures, and also that the connecting functions are not restricted to being one-to-one. McCawley and Lakoff's *Brigitte Bardot* sentence is one such example. The availability of multiple functions ("identity," representation, drama, analogy, instance, counterfactual, . . .) is a source of powerful semantic effects and accounts for several key puzzles of reference.

It is easy to see that cross-world identification in possible world approaches can be reinterpreted conceptually as the special case when only a single one-to-one identity (or similarity) function is considered.

0.4.1.3 Discourse Representation and Mental Models. Other approaches that employ partitioning and have some affinity to the present one are Kamp's theory of discourse representations (1984) and Seuren's discourse semantics (1984): Subdomains are distinguished in discourse for hypotheticals, beliefs, etcetera. Although these treatments differ sharply from possible worlds semantics, they share with it the simplified counterpart structure limited to identity. From the cognitive semantics perspective, identity is only one of many conceptual connections across spaces. Although perhaps the most obvious and the most typical, it is presumably only a special case of connections that do major conceptual and linguistic work, such as analogical and metaphorical projection, role to value functions, or pragmatic metonymy functions. Again, the important feature to bear in mind is the extraordinary underspecification of cognitive mental space configurations by language. There is no algorithm that would yield *the* space configuration corresponding to some linguistic form. Rather, the linguistic form will constrain the dynamic construction of the spaces, but that construction itself is highly dependent on previous constructions already effected at that point in discourse: available cross-space mappings; available frames and cognitive models; local features of the social framing in which the construction takes place; and, of course, real properties of the surrounding world.

Two notions easily overlooked in traditional accounts of reference and grammar seem crucial: *framing* and *point of view.* Work in cognitive and construction grammar (Langacker, Talmy, Fillmore, Lakoff, Brugman, Goldberg) suggests that syntactic configurations are a means of accessing very general (and generic) frames, which in turn map on to more specified frames, via lexical specification, and that those frames in turn map on to even more specific ones determined by the local context, local space connections, and relevant cultural and background knowledge. Space building, in this respect, is also frame building. The frames provide the abstract-induced schemas that drive mapping across mental spaces. The discourse construction process is highly fluid, dynamic, locally creative: Provisional categories are set up in appropriate spaces, temporary connections are established, new frames are created on line, meaning is negotiated. The power of grammar is to call up suitable generic frames that will serve in context to manipulate much more specific ones. The dynamics of this construction process implies that participants (speakers, hearers, thinkers, interlocutors) must keep track of the maze of spaces and connections being built, and one way in which this happens is through the use of *point of view* and *point of view shifts,* which are grammatically encoded by means of tenses, moods, space builders, anaphors, and other cognitive operators.

In this extended sense, mental space configurations are *mental models,* but of course they are mental models of discourse, not mental models of the world. Philip Johnson Laird has reminded me in this regard of the important difference between viewing a situation as impossible, because no model can be constructed for it, versus representing a situation as impossible in some mental space, for example, in a reductio ad absurdum. The counterfactual space corresponding to a reductio is not itself impossible, just logically contradictory, but the mental model of a logical contradiction is of course impossible. Interestingly, just as there are impossible mental models of reality, there are impossible models of discourse: cases where the grammatical instructions for building a mental space configuration cannot be carried out. The liar paradox and others like it are cases of impossible cognitive constructions, as opposed to simple contradictions, which lead to no impossibilities in the discourse model. A related antinomy, Curry's paradox, does not quite lead to impossibility, but to a type of looping in mental space "genealogy" that must be ruled out on the general grounds that a space cannot be the parent of one of its ancestors.

There are undoubtedly many other things that mental spaces are not, besides possible worlds, mental models of reality, pictorial representations, and model-theoretic discourse representations or files. In the years that followed the first publication of this book, research focused on their dynamic and conceptual properties: the nature of mappings that link them, the frames that structure them, the shifts in discourse from one space to another and the notions of base, focus, and point of view, the accessibility of one space with respect to another, and the resolution of pragmatic ambiguity. The following sections give a brief overview of this work.

0.4.2 Time, Tense, and Aspect
In several articles, and an important book published in 1991, *Partitioned Representations,* John Dinsmore showed how the reference point system for time reflected by language is a consequence of general principles of mental space tracking and organization. Grammatical tenses and aspects, and their combinations, serve to indicate relative relations between spaces and crucially, to keep track of the discourse "position" of the participants—which space is in *focus* (a dynamic notion), which one serves as *base* and what *shifts* are taking place. This elegant view of the dynamics of discourse applies quite generally to a variety of phenomena, such as reported belief, epistemic distance, and of course time, the prototypical relation linked to grammatical tense.

Recent work by Carey (1993) and Cutrer (1994) on tense, and Langacker (1993) on point of view and reference points in

grammatical phenomena, have led to an extension of Dinsmore's approach, in which the notion of abstract *viewpoint* is
added to that of focus and base. Like focus, viewpoint will shift
as discourse builds up, and grammatical tense, in addition to
space builders and other devices, will guide speakers (and hearers and readers) through the maze of connected mental spaces.[9]
It is especially interesting to observe how grammar provides
fine-grained tense and aspect combinations that reflect motion
through the space configuration during discourse, shifts of focus, abstract viewpoint, and sometimes base. Although space
tracking by means of grammatical devices appears to be linguistically universal, the indications provided are language specific,
and evolve diachronically: French and Spanish do not use the
imperfect in quite the same way; the present perfect in French
has evolved from the form of space tracking associated with the
English present perfect to the kind associated with the English
past tense.

0.4.3 Mood and Epistemic Stance
Chapters 3 (presuppositions) and 4 (counterfactuals) of the present work note the importance of assessing and marking various
types of mental space incompatibilities and the status of structure
in one space with respect to another ("real," "hypothetical,"
"counterfactual," shared presuppositions, shared belief, and so
on). Again, as shown in Sweetser's work (to appear a and b),
grammar, often in the form of tense and mood combinations, will
provide decisive clues as to such status, which we may call general-
ized relative epistemic stance. When understood in this way,
many surface features of grammatical distribution, such as presence or absence of tense concord, reveal elaborate and subtle
aspects of the hidden mental space configurations and the epistemic stances they entail. In remarkable work on the subjunctive
in Spanish, Errapel Mejias-Bikandi (1993) has shown that mood
can reflect the accessibility of one space from another. In the
special but typical case when the higher space corresponds to the
"speaker's reality," accessibility may correlate with the speaker's
commitment to the truth of some belief or subordinate presupposition, which explains why explanation of mood so often runs
along the line of epistemic stance, although strictly speaking, such

properties are only derivative. This is shown elegantly in Mejias-Bikandi's work.

0.4.4 Pragmatic Ambiguity

One significant consequence of the mental space approach has been to recast many scopal and logical phenomena: Ambiguities and multiple readings, which were previously thought to stem from underlying structural characteristics of sentences, follow more generally from the underspecified nature of the linguistic forms. Any such form is compatible with a potentially unlimited array of space configurations, sharply limited in practice by default principles (such as *Optimization,* see Chapters 3 and 4), the current state of a construction in a particular discourse, and contextual constraints as to the conceptual domains under consideration. The choice of particular spaces or available accessing strategies will yield interpretations perceived as sharply different, even though there will be no corresponding structural ambiguity for the linguistic form. As discussed in Chapter 2, the scope of indefinites is such a case: Linguistic forms (for example, *Susan wants to marry a Norwegian*) may set up a new discourse element (*a Norwegian*) without specifying which mental space it belongs to. The superficial effect is one of scope ambiguity.

Much more elaborate cases have been studied where pragmatic ambiguity is produced by the availability of different types of spaces and different accessing strategies. Claudia Brugman (1988; to appear) has analyzed the English *have* construction in great detail and shown that it includes depictive and predictive semantic interpretations that look superficially like a completely distinct construction, but in fact follow straightforwardly from the standard construction when an extra, invisible (linguistically unmarked) mental space is present. Relevant examples are: *The movie had him dying in the end; Jean Dixon has Dan Quayle winning the nomination in 1996.*

Fauconnier (1990a and b; to appear) offers a similar account of the multiple understandings of cognitive operators like *when, if, where:* The space-building instructions are the same for all uses, but the domain types for the mental spaces and the mappings linking the spaces can vary over a wide pragmatic range. This allows, among other things, a uniform treatment of multiple readings for the notorious donkey sentences (*If a man owns a donkey, he beats it*), which keeps the semantic interpretation of indefinites maximally simple and invariant ("set up a new element in space M"), but lets the space domain type vary.

0.4.5 Cognitive Mappings

Perhaps one of the most intriguing developments of the mental space work has been the discovery of elaborate space constructions and mappings in cases that do not seem to include explicit space builders or mapping operators. Mark Turner and I argue (1993) that a variety of constructions involving analogy, metaphor, and hedges set up multispace configurations with source, target, generic, and blended spaces that project onto each other in several directions. The XYZ metaphors studied in Turner (1991) are a good example of this type of process. The syntactic construction is deceptively simple

NP be NP of NP

X Y Z

as in *Vanity is the quicksand of reason.* This simple construction has a complex semantic/pragmatic interpretation: Construct a metaphorical mapping such that X in the target is the counterpart of Y in the source, and Z in the target is the counterpart of a fourth element, W, in the source, and use this construction to project appropriate inferences into the target. In the example, W is the traveler, who should reach a goal; as quicksand destroys the traveler, vanity destroys reason. The grammatical information is minimal and highly abstract: Find a mapping and a missing element; the rest is left to the cognitive competence of the user. An implicit generic space is also constructed. And interestingly, syntactic concatenation can activate a blended space, as in Turner's example *Language is fossil poetry.* With *language* as X, and *poetry* as Z, the modifier *fossil* identifies Y, a source counterpart for *language,* and a missing W ("living organism") completes the mapping. But this time a blended notion of something that is simultaneously language, poetry, and fossil has been constructed: In the blended space, poetry *is* a living organism that can evolve into a fossil (language). As in other examples, this is achieved through a local category extension in the blended space, where more things count as organisms and fossils than in the source. The simple syntactic construction '*NP* be *N NP*' exhibits complex features of meaning construction: It triggers a multispace configuration with source, target, generic, and blend, and it leads to the introduction of elements and structures (the living organism and its evolution) for which no explicit vocabulary appears. The emergent global view is that of language guiding the space construction process through space building, space blending, and projection of generic spaces.

Sweetser's work on metametaphors (to appear) is also quite interesting in this regard. She discusses examples like *If Notre Dame is the heart of Paris, then the Seine is its main artery,* to which we can add the "counterfactual" *If Paris were a human being, Notre Dame would be its heart.* It is apparent that the hypothetical construction (*if . . . then . . .*) that we find here is setting up cognitive mappings (in the protasis) and their natural extensions (in the apodosis). There is a fact of the matter as to whether and how the extensions follow from the core mapping (set up in the *if*-clause), even though, here, there can be no truth conditions linked to implication in the logical sense traditionally associated with such constructions.

Cognitive mappings and blendings are at the heart of meaning construction. Syntactic constructions, as studied by Langacker, Talmy, Fillmore, and their students, represent high-level generic spaces. Together with lexical items, which are themselves constructions, they can be mapped and blended into progressively more specific spaces. This general scheme allows multiple levels of organization to be simultaneously projected in one given mental space configuration. The role/value distinction, studied in Chapter 2, reflects such multiple projection. Fauconnier (1986) shows that the notion is relative: The same element can be a role with respect to a second element, and a value with respect to a third. So, we can say that *In the United States, the head of state is the president,* and *In the United States, the president is Clinton.* "The president" is a value for the role "the head of state," and a role for the value "Clinton." Three levels of genericness (and three corresponding spaces) have thus been introduced and connected. In this book, this aspect of linking between more or less generic spaces was not explored in detail. A more comprehensive account would take into account additional spaces and connectors.

0.4.6 Ramifications

Many more aspects of mental space organization have been explored, and this short introduction cannot do justice to all of them. Cognitive mappings, roles, and abstract change have been analyzed by Matsumoto (to appear), Sweetser (1989), and Sakahara (to appear). Takubo (1990), Takubo and Kinsui (1992) have discussed important aspects of discourse management linked to mental space organization. Lakoff (1987) provides a remarkable account of the complex English *there*-construction in terms of spaces. Rubba (to appear) and Encrevé (1988) have given insightful and original accounts of the sociological and cultural dimension of mental space phenomena. Lakoff (to appear) shows how folk-theoretical structure interacts with space-linking to produce "multiple selves" constructions. Dinsmore (1991), Magnini and Strapparava (1990), and Maida (1984) make the connection between areas studied in the present book and concerns of artificial intelligence. Michelle Cutrer (1994), and Sanders and Redeker (to appear) tackle the considerable intricacies of narrative structure and levels. And Karen Van Hoek (to appear) gives us fascinating evidence for mental space construction in American sign language. It is perhaps fitting to end this Preface by mentioning Van Hoek's work, since that work fulfills the prediction made in the last paragraph of the present book; that the visual and gestual modality of sign language will make it a rich area of study for understanding the cognitive underpinnings of meaning and reference.

Notes

1. In *Cognitive Mappings for Language and Thought,* the same point is made slightly differently: "When a sentence is examined in isolation, and its interpretations are studied, it is necessary to implicitly construct a discourse in which to interpret it. By default, a *minimum* discourse is usually chosen, with the implication that this will yield the 'real', 'core', context-independent meaning of the sentence. This implication is unwarranted; there is no reason why the *particular* configuration associated with a linguistic expression in a

minimum discourse should contain the defining characteristics for the meaning *potential* of that expression in *any* discourse" (Fauconnier (to appear)).

2. Compare Sweetser and Fauconnier (to appear); Mejias-Bikandi (1993).

3. Ross's work on squishes (1973) and L. and C. Fillmore's research on speech formulas had similar implications.

4. Edelman (1992) cites the useful article by mathematician G. C. Rota, criticizing "philosophers who ape the clarity of mathematics by adopting a symbolic mode of discussion" (compare Rota (1990)).

5. One review of the first edition of this book contains good examples of the frequent misunderstandings of such issues, and of the social biases that affect research. The reviewer (A. Cormack) writes at the beginning of her fourteen-page contribution to *Linguistics and Philosophy* (1987) that a theory "should at least be able to give distinct representations of the distinct readings a sentence can have" (p. 247), using a framing of the problems that is precisely the object of controversy behind the mental space approach in the first place. This is dogma, and there is circularity in evaluating theories that attack dogma on the basis of that very dogma. She also writes: "to discuss the book in its own terms would be to consign it to history; to use the currently fashionable terms is to make some distortions, but to treat it as a serious contribution to current concerns" (p. 248). Cormack's concern with being "currently fashionable" is misplaced, but does faithfully reflect the social pressures that can be brought to bear on academic research.

6. It caught the attention of attending semanticists, such as my friends Hans Kamp and Franz Guenthner.

7. Most notable in Kripke's jargon-free work.

8. Compare McCawley (1981); Lakoff (to appear).

9. Compare Fujii (1992).

Acknowledgments

A good part of the material in this book was presented and discussed from 1979 to 1983 in seminars at the Ecole des Hautes Etudes en Sciences Sociales, the University of Antwerp, the University of Paris VIII, and the University of California at San Diego. I am grateful to the participants who helped me with their comments, criticisms, and suggestions, in particular M. Borel, L. Tasmowski-De Ryck, M. Dominicy, M. Janta, P. Gochet, M. Goyssens, J. Dinsmore, F. Recanati, M. E. Ryder, and W. Van Langendonck, and also to others who commented on partial and/or preliminary versions, in particular J. Bien, A. Cicourel, S.-Y. Kuroda, G. Lakoff, J. McCawley, and C. Travis. Fauconnier (1984) is the French version of this work.

Introductory Note

In a short autobiographical piece published in the *New York Times Magazine,* an author writes about his childhood:[1]

My first friend was Slobo. I was still living in Yugoslavia at the time, and not far from my house there was an old German truck left abandoned after the war. It had no wheels. No windshield. No doors. But the steering wheel was intact. Slobo and I flew to America in that truck. It was our airplane. Even now, I remember the background moving as we took off down the street, across Europe, across the Atlantic.

He goes on (a few paragraphs later) to talk about an incident in his adult life:

A few years ago, we were swimming at a beach in East Hampton. The Atlantic! The very Atlantic I had flown over in my German truck with Slobo.

Now little of this is "true" in the sense that philosophers and linguists often cherish. So what is going on?

On one view, such uses of language are deviations, and like metaphor, metonymy, or other so-called rhetorical devices, they are parasitic on core semantics and literal meaning.

In this book, on the contrary, they are taken to be central, and much more widespread than is usually assumed. Understanding the linguistic organization involved leads to the study of domains that we set up as we talk or listen, and that we structure with elements, roles, strategies, and relations. These domains—or interconnected *mental spaces,* as I shall call them—are not part of the language itself, or of its grammars; they are not hidden levels of linguistic representation, but language does not come without them.

Many problems of natural language "logic" turn out to stem from features of mental space construction; examples given here include opacity, attributivity, intentional identity, presupposition projection, counterfactuals, and comparatives.

And yet this book is not about reference in the usual sense. I shall speak throughout of elements being *set up mentally, pointed to,* and *identified* by language forms; the language forms do not *refer* to such elements. If there is to be reference, it will go from the elements in mental spaces to the objects referred to.[2] Nevertheless, complete theories of truth and reference for natural language cannot bypass the space construction process (see section 5.3).

Another crucial feature of the analyses presented here must be emphasized at the outset. The standard way of trying to account for the multiple meanings of a given linguistic form consists in associating it systematically, at a more abstract level, with a set of representations (logical forms, semantic structures, etc.). The space format reveals a different organization: Relatively simple grammatical structures give instructions for space construction in context. But this construction process is often *underdetermined* by the grammatical instructions; thus, simple construction principles and simple linguistic structures may yield multiple space configurations. And this creates an illusion of structural complexity.[3]

To be sure, there is complexity somewhere, but the point here is that a good part of the load can (and should) be shifted from the intemporal language structures to the field of virtual and multiple mental constructions. What is complex for the linguist-observer may be much less so for the speaker-listener who is engaged in a single construction at a time, narrowly guided by context. This bears in turn on the fundamental problem of language acquisition.[4]

Language, then, is not merely interpreted with respect to worlds, models, contexts, situations, and so forth. Rather, it is involved in constructions of its own.[5] It builds up mental spaces, relations between them, and relations between elements within them. To the extent that two of us build up similar space configurations from the same linguistic and pragmatic data, we may "communicate"; communication is a possible corollary of the construction process.

Chapter 1
Pragmatic Functions and Images

1.1 Connectors

In the quest for a fully explicit and maximally integrated account of language organization, much attention has been focused on the multi-level structural intricacies of linguistic forms. Recently, however, some studies have shifted this focus of attention from the language forms themselves to other structures and networks on which they depend and to the correspondences that hold, or are established, between such structures and networks. Outstanding examples are the notions of frames and scenarios; literal metaphor as an elaborate structuring of conceptual networks via partial correspondences underlying semantic-pragmatic organization and its expression through language; the account of presupposition in terms of discourse worlds linked to each other; and the treatment of "scopal" phenomena like opacity and transparency as referential correspondence between concrete or mental images.[1]

In his excellent study of reference, G. Nunberg provides a key idea related to such correspondences: the notion of *pragmatic function*.[2] He shows that we establish links between objects of a different nature for psychological, cultural, or locally pragmatic reasons and that the links thus established allow reference to one object in terms of another appropriately linked to it. The general principle is this:

(1)
Identification (ID) Principle
If two objects (in the most general sense), a and b, are linked by a pragmatic function F $(b = F(a))$, a description of a, d_a, may be used to identify its counterpart b.

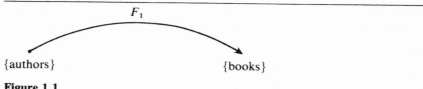

Figure 1.1

For instance, one function (call it F_1) links authors with the books containing their works, as shown in figure 1.1. Taking as an example a = "Plato," $b = F_1(a)$ = "books by Plato," the ID Principle allows (2) to mean (3):

(2)
Plato is on the top shelf.

(3)
The books by Plato are on the top shelf.

In (2), a description or name of a person, d_a (in this case the name *Plato,* but *Socrates' friend* or *the author of the Dialogues* would do just as well) identifies an object b, the collection of books.

Of course, other pragmatic functions are available to interpret (2)— for example, functions from persons to representations, from persons to information about them, from persons to bodies, from persons to names (= words), and so on. Using one of these instead of F_1, (2) could be interpreted to mean that a bust or portrait of Plato is on the top shelf, that the file containing information about Plato is on the top shelf, that Plato's body is on the top shelf, that the sign with the word *Plato* on it is on the top shelf, etc.

F may simply be the identity function, as in figure 1.2. In that case, b will be described in terms of its own properties—not a surprising possibility.

Pronominalization is one area where the possibility of "indirect" reference by means of pragmatic functions and the ID Principle has linguistic consequences.

Consider again the general situation in which b is linked to a by a pragmatic function F and may be referred to by means of a description of a, according to the ID Principle. Call a the reference *trigger,* b the reference *target,* and F the *connector,* as illustrated in figure 1.3.

The ID Principle states that in a connected situation, a description of the trigger may be used to identify the target. Clearly, this allows reference to the target *b:* in example (2), under the authors → books connector interpretation, there has been successful reference to certain books, and this reference target becomes a potential antecedent for pronouns and other anaphors:

(4)
Plato is on the top shelf. *It* is bound in leather.

However, the trigger *a* is also a potential antecedent in such situations:

(5)
Plato is on the top shelf. You'll find that *he* is a very interesting author.

Superficially, then, *Plato* in (2) can be an antecedent both for *it* and for *he*. More precisely, both the reference trigger (the author Plato) and the reference target (books by Plato) can be pronominal antecedents of discourse following (2). And this is not a matter of choosing one or the other as the antecedent for pronominalization, since both may simultaneously warrant anaphors in the same discourse:

(6)
Plato is on the top shelf. *It* is bound in leather. You'll find that *he* is a very interesting author.

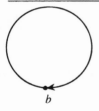

b

Figure 1.2

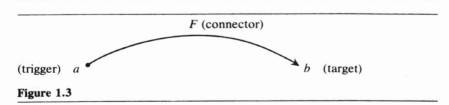

F (connector)

(trigger) *a*   *b*   (target)

Figure 1.3

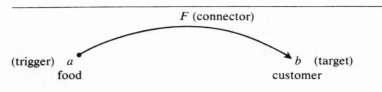

Figure 1.4

Nor is the choice of pronouns free:

(7)
*Plato is on the top shelf. *It* is a very interesting author.

Consider the connector linking food and customers induced by the restaurant "frame," illustrated in figure 1.4. In this context, statements like (8) are possible:

(8)
The mushroom omelet left without paying the bill.

(8) is understood with the interpretation that the customer who had ordered the mushroom omelet left without paying. The target may then serve as a pronominal antecedent:

(9)
The mushroom omelet left without paying *his* bill. *He* jumped into a taxi.

But in this case, pronominal reference to the trigger is more awkward:

(10)
The mushroom omelet left without paying. *?It* was inedible.

Reflexivization shows even stronger contrasts:

(11)
Norman Mailer likes to read *himself* before going to sleep.

(12)
*Norman Mailer likes to read *itself* before going to sleep.

(13)
The mushroom omelet was using chopsticks.

(14)
*The mushroom omelet was eating *itself* with chopsticks.

(15)
*The mushroom omelet was eating *himself* with chopsticks.

In (11), we find the masculine pronoun *himself* agreeing in gender with the trigger (Norman Mailer), but referring to the target (books by Mailer). A closer look shows that since the noun phrase *Norman Mailer* both describes and refers to the author, its interpretation does not involve the connector. The reflexive pronoun *himself*, on the other hand, although anaphoric to *Norman Mailer,* refers to the books: its interpretation *does* involve application of the connector, and this application must follow the reflexive "rule." This process can be schematized "interpretively" as follows:

(16)

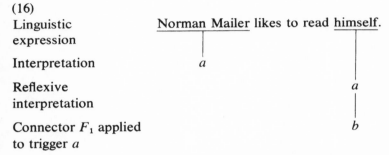

Linguistic expression: Norman Mailer likes to read himself.
Interpretation: *a*
Reflexive interpretation: *a*
Connector F_1 applied to trigger *a*: *b*

The impossibility of (12) also follows: *itself* would require the "inanimate" antecedent *b*, but only *a* is available. However, if the connector applies to the first instance of *a* (corresponding to the noun phrase *Norman Mailer*), yielding *b*, then *b* may serve as an antecedent for the reflexive *itself*:

(17)

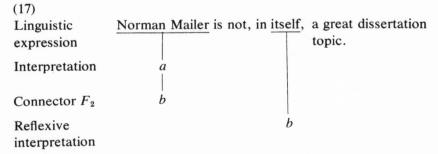

Linguistic expression: Norman Mailer is not, in itself, a great dissertation topic.
Interpretation: *a*
Connector F_2: *b*
Reflexive interpretation: *b*

Thus, examples like (11) and (17) show one anaphoric process, reflexive interpretation, applying either before or after the pragmatic connector. But in (14) the process schematized by (18) fails:

(18)

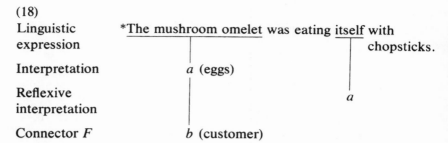

Linguistic   *The mushroom omelet was eating itself with
expression   chopsticks.

Interpretation   a (eggs)

Reflexive   a
interpretation

Connector F   b (customer)

The order of operations is the same as in (16), but in (18) the connector applies to the "antecedent," not the reflexive. Schema (16) applied to the mushroom omelet cases will not work either:

(19)
*The mushroom omelet appealed to itself.

 (Intended reading: the eggs appealed to the customer who ordered
 them)

The only order that works for such cases has the reflexive interpretation following the application of the connector:

(20)
The mushroom omelet paid only for himself.

Furthermore, this distribution of reflexives correlates with the contrast noted above between (5) and (10):

(5)
Plato is on the top shelf. You'll find that he is a very interesting author.

(10)
*?The mushroom omelet left without paying. It was inedible.[3]

In (5) the reference trigger Plato (author) is a suitable antecedent, but in (10) the reference trigger the mushroom omelet is not. Nor can a pronoun be a trigger in the omelet case; compare (21) and (22):

(21)
Plato is a great author. He is on the top shelf.

   a   a
                        |
                        b

(22)
*The mushroom omelet was too spicy. It left without paying.

Let us say that a connector is *open,* when it sets up both target and trigger as potential antecedents and may apply to the output of pronoun interpretation, and *closed,* when it sets up the target as foremost potential antecedent[4] and cannot apply to the output of pronoun interpretation. In the above examples, F_1 (authors → books) is open, and F (food → customers) is closed.

The behavior of relative and deictic pronouns is also consistent with this distinction:

(23)
Plato, *who* is on the top shelf, was a great man.

(24)
*The omelet, *which* left in a hurry, was too spicy.

(25)
Plato, *who* was a great man, is on the top shelf.

(26)
*The omelet, *which* was too spicy, left in a hurry.

Examples (23) through (26) contain *nonrestrictive* relatives. *Which* in (24) and (26) behaves like *it* in (22) and (10), respectively; *who* in (23) and (25) behaves like *he* in (21) and (5), respectively. The contrast follows from the open-closed distinction: In (24), the closed connector cannot apply to the pronoun *which.* In (26), the closed connector applies to "the omelet"; only the target (customer) is a potential antecedent—*which* has none.

With *restrictive* relatives we find a superficial difference because the connector will now apply to the interpretation of the full noun phrase, relative clause included:

(27)
*The omelet which left in a hurry was too spicy.

(28)
The omelet which was too spicy, left in a hurry.

(27) is (doubly) ruled out by the closed connector condition. But (28) is fine: the connector applies to the interpretation of the full noun phrase *the omelet which was too spicy,* yielding the customer who got that particular omelet.

In the case of deictics, one can point to the omelet and say "He/That one left in a hurry," but not "It/that left in a hurry," which would force the connector to apply to the interpretation of the inanimate pronoun *it* or *that*. In contrast, one *can* point to the person Norman Mailer and say "He's/that guy's on my top shelf."

What makes connectors available, and when are they open or closed? This is in itself a central and fascinating question involving psychological, cultural, and sociological conditions that bear directly on linguistic data. I cannot pursue it in detail here, but the following general point of view suggests itself: connectors are part of *idealized cognitive models* (ICMs), in the sense of Lakoff (1982), Fillmore (1982), and Sweetser (1981), which are set up locally, culturally, or on general experiential or psychological grounds. This implies possible variation from community to community, from context to context, and from individual to individual. Indeed, we find exactly such variation in informant judgments about openness of connectors: speakers are typically able to learn new connectors (by setting up new ICMs), and the more familiar, general, and useful a connector becomes, the more open it tends to be. Other related conditions come into play: for example, to what extent properties of the target are felt to reflect important characteristics of the trigger (to say "Norman Mailer is not selling at all right now" says something not only about the books but also perhaps about the author; for a nurse to say "The gastric ulcer in room 21 wants more coffee" may imply nothing about the illness itself) and to what extent the ICM fits the particular context (compare "Norman Mailer likes to bind himself" with (11)).

The connectors relevant to the rest of this study are those that link mental spaces and, as we shall see, they turn out to be invariably open. Central in the present context, then, will be the properties of *open* connectors, and in particular the ones already pointed out: the ID transfer principle, the capacity to set up target and trigger as potential antecedents, and applicability to anaphoric elements.

1.2 Images

As noted explicitly by Nunberg (1978, 1979), images, pictorial representations, photographs, etc., are clearly linked to their models by pragmatic connectors, as shown in figure 1.5, since for example *Lisa* in "Lisa is smiling" may point to Lisa *en chair et en os* or to Lisa in a picture.[5]

(trigger) *a*   *b*   (target)
     model   image

Figure 1.5

The following pronominalization data show that image connectors are open; that is, they set up both target and trigger as potential antecedents and may apply to the output of pronoun interpretation:

(29)
Lisa is smiling in the picture, but she has been depressed for months.
(Trigger antecedent of *she*)

(30)
Lisa has been depressed for months, but in the picture she is smiling.
(Connector applies to interpretation of pronoun *she*)

(31)
Lisa, who has been depressed for months, is smiling in the picture.
(Trigger antecedes *who*, target is smiling)

(32)
Lisa, who is smiling in the picture, has been depressed for months.
(Lisa (model) antecedes *who;* connector applies to *who*)

(33)
Lisa saw herself in Len's picture.
(Connector applies to the output of reflexive interpretation, so that *herself* = image; cf. (11))

(34)
In that drawing, *Lisa* appealed to *herself*.
(Connector applies to the interpretation of Lisa as a person, yielding the image (drawing); the reflexive interpretation is with respect to the trigger, *herself* referring to the person)

Jackendoff (1975; hereafter OBC) has also noted the possibility of giving a linguistic description of an image in terms of its model. He stresses that the phenomenon is not "imprecision" or "loose metaphor" but rather "the means the language has to refer to images in pictures,"[6] and he adds, "If one wants to study the semantics of natural

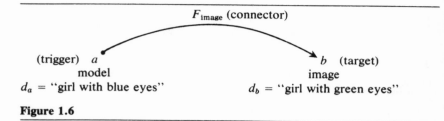

F_{image} (connector)

(trigger) *a*   *b* (target)
          model   image
d_a = "girl with blue eyes" d_b = "girl with green eyes"

Figure 1.6

language, the existence of this usage must be taken for granted and accepted" (p. 54).

This usage is indeed central to picture reference and follows from Nunberg's more general characterization of pragmatic reference. First, there is a pragmatic relation between a model and its representation. Something is a picture of something else by virtue of psychological perception, social convention, how it was actually produced, or any combination of those three: the artist's decision (especially in the case of the three-year-old child or the cubist painter), the viewer's perception with respect to various "likeness criteria," technical considerations (as in X-rays), and so on. This pragmatic relation meets the criteria for being a pragmatic reference function, a connector. Therefore, the ID Principle will apply, allowing a description of the trigger (in this case the model) to identify the target (in this case the image). In fact, as we have seen, image functions are open connectors.

This view puts Jackendoff's important observation in its proper perspective: the "means the language has to refer to images in pictures" follows from the very general ID Principle operating on trigger-target connections. Furthermore, the distribution of reflexives and anaphors for pictures is a general property of open connectors.

The characteristics of crucial examples in OBC, which have the form of (35),

(35)
In Len's painting, *the girl with blue eyes* has green eyes.

will then follow from this generalization. The adverbial phrase *in Len's painting* in (35) sets up an image situation. The model, *a* (say, Lisa, a girl who has blue eyes), triggers the image connector *F*, and the target, *b*, is the representation in the painting, with the property of having green eyes, as depicted in figure 1.6. The ID Principle very generally allows a description of the trigger to identify the target, so d_a (*the girl with blue eyes*) may identify *b*, the image. If so, sentence (35) is taken to mean that *b*, the image, has green eyes. We are in fact likely to interpret (35) in this way. However, the ID Principle also allows the description of the target, d_b, to identify the target *b* (the connector is then trivially the identity function). So nothing prevents *the girl with blue eyes* in (35) from being taken as a description of *b*, yielding a second (somewhat contradictory) reading to the effect that *b*'s eyes are both blue and green.

Now, Jackendoff makes the following essential point: the double possibility noticed in the case of pictures for expressions like (35) is quite parallel to the one found in so-called opacity-transparency phenomena linked to verbs of propositional attitude and, more generally, intensional contexts:

(36)
In Len's mind, the girl with blue eyes has green eyes.

(37)
Len believes that the girl with blue eyes has green eyes.

(38)
Len wants the girl with blue eyes to have green eyes.

All these expressions have a noncontradictory reading (for (37): Lisa has blue eyes, and Len believes she has green eyes) and a contradictory reading (Len believes that Lisa has blue eyes and has green eyes).

This parallel sets the stage for treating images, beliefs, stories, etc., in a similar way. If we assume that just as Lisa has a counterpart in Len's painting (her image), she has a counterpart in Len's mind, or (more precisely) if we assume that we talk *as if* she did,[7] then the world-mind function will operate as a connector and the ID Principle will work as before to yield potential interpretations for descriptions like *the girl with blue eyes* in (37): on the one hand, a description of the trigger *a* ("the real girl") identifying the target *b* ("the belief girl") (it is *b*, not *a*, who has green eyes) and, on the other hand, a direct description of *b*, identifying *b* (*b* has blue eyes and green eyes).

This unified analysis assumes an as yet ill-defined correspondence of the kind informally suggested by figure 1.7.[8]

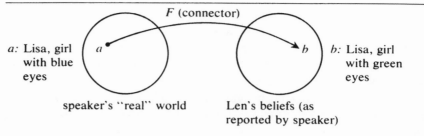

Figure 1.7

1.3 Reality

The pragmatic connectors in section 1.1 could be taken to represent links between real-world objects. In (36) through (38) and figure 1.7, on the other hand, the targets, whatever they may be, are not real-world objects, since they are part of beliefs, desires, and such. In OBC, a particular metaphysics is assumed, in order to allow the required extension: namely, there is a "reality" in which physical objects exist, and the normal situation is for linguistic descriptions to *refer* to these physical objects, but this reality may be connected to images (mental, verbal, concrete, etc.) by means of the relation "purports to refer" (the equivalent of the image connector). Something like the ID Principle will then create ambiguities of the opaque-transparent kind. In setting up his image operator, Jackendoff writes (p. 72), "Since the normal reading of *a girl* is as a physical object, we will choose the image reading as the modal reading. . . ." Thus, reality is sharply distinguished from images: there are real, essential referents on the one hand and various representations of these referents on the other. Under this view, the triggers will always be real referents, while the targets may be concrete or mental representations of them.

However, this asymmetrical view is not reflected by the linguistic data: the triggers may be in the pictures, beliefs, etc., and the targets in the so-called real world. Suppose we are in an artist's studio, looking at a painting that includes a girl with brown eyes. The artist might say:

(39)
In reality, the girl with brown eyes has blue eyes.

(39) is quite parallel to (35), but the scheme is reversed: instead of going from reality to the picture, we go from the picture to reality. The trigger

is the image ("girl with brown eyes in the picture"), and the target is the "real" girl. As usual, the ID Principle allows the target to be identified in terms of the trigger's description; in this case, the real girl is identified in terms of a description of the image (*the girl with brown eyes*), and it is predicated of her that she has blue eyes. So in this case the relevant connector is the inverse of the previous one. Instead of mapping reality onto the picture, it maps the picture onto reality. It is also an open connector. Notice that the direction of the mapping is indicated in such cases by the adverbial (e.g., *in Len's painting* or *in reality*). Similar connector inversions are possible in the case of "mental" images such as beliefs. If the context is such that Max believes he has inherited a castle with a park, the speaker might say:

(40)
In reality, *the castle* is a run-down shack and *the park* is a junkyard.

Again, descriptions valid in Max's belief system are used to identify "real" entities with different properties. This follows from the ID Principle operating on a connector from Max's beliefs to reality.

In presenting the fundamental symmetry of these reference phenomena, I have continued to use the terms *reality* and *real object*. But this cannot be right. The connectors are not linking real objects and representations, for the speaker who uses expressions like (36) through (40) need not be *right* about the properties he assigns to entities (including whether or not they exist). So what we have been calling "reality" must itself be a mental representation: the speaker's mental representation of reality.[9] In accounting for the *linguistic* phenomena under scrutiny, it is not our (immediate) concern to tell whether (or to what extent) such representations may be accurate; nor is it our concern to find the philosophical, psychological, or neurological nature of reality, beliefs, desires, and pictures. We are looking only at ways of talking about them, in principle a different issue.

We end up, then, with links between mental representations. And of course the same holds if we add more layers of mental "pictures": in (36) or (37), it cannot be that Len's beliefs in some absolute sense are involved; rather, we are dealing with the speaker's view of those beliefs—that is, a mental representation of a mental representation. This embedding is often reflected by corresponding syntactic embedding:

(41)
Max believes that Len wants to leave the country.

Here also, no absolute notion of what Len wants is involved, only what Len wants according to what Max believes, what Max believes being in turn according to the speaker's reality—that is, possibly different from another presumably mental object, namely, what Max actually believes.

But what about the picture cases? Aren't such things as paintings and photographs real objects? To be sure, the objects themselves are real, but their interpretation as images is mental.[10] The analysis in terms of only one connector is grossly oversimplified; at least three connectors are involved, linking the model to the paint on the canvas, the paint to the image perceived, and the model (in the speaker's mental reality) to the image perceived (also in the speaker's mental reality). This accounts for cases like (42):

(42)
In this painting, the house is acrylic, but the girl is oil.

1.4 Mental Spaces

1.4.1 Space-Builders

Having informally suggested that pragmatic connectors operate on mental objects and that such objects may fall within different domains, I shall now suggest a more precise model for the corresponding linguistic processes and mental constructs.

To this end, I introduce the notion of *mental spaces*, constructs distinct from linguistic structures but built up in any discourse according to guidelines provided by the linguistic expressions. In the model, mental spaces will be represented as structured, incrementable sets—that is, sets with elements $(a, b, c, ...)$ and relations holding between them $(R_1ab, R_2a, R_3cbf,...)$, such that new elements can be added to them and new relations established between their elements. (In a technical sense, an incrementable set is an ordered sequence of ordinary sets, but it will be convenient to speak of the mental space as being built up during ongoing discourse, rather than to refer to the corresponding sequence of sets.)[11] Expressions like "$Ra_1a_2...a_n$ holds in mental space M" will be taken to mean that $a_1, a_2, ..., a_n$ are elements of M and that the relation R holds of $(a_1, a_2, ..., a_n)$. A partial ordering relation is defined on spaces. I shall call it *inclusion* and use the usual notation $\subset$, but unlike set inclusion, it carries no entailments for the elements within the spaces: $a \in M$ and $M \subset N$ does not entail $a \in N$. In fact, I assume for the moment that all spaces are entirely distinct, that is, that they have no elements in common.

Linguistic expressions will typically establish new spaces, elements within them, and relations holding between the elements. I shall call *space-builders* expressions that may establish a new space or refer back to one already introduced in the discourse. Later sections will show that space-builders may be prepositional phrases (*in Len's picture, in John's mind, in 1929, at the factory, from her point of view*), adverbs (*really, probably, possibly, theoretically*), connectives (*if A then* _____, *either* _____ *or* _____), underlying subject-verb combinations (*Max believes* _____, *Mary hopes* _____, *Gertrude claims* _____). Space-builders come with linguistic clauses, which typically (but not always; see chapter 5) predicate relations holding between space elements.

Furthermore, the space-builder SB_M establishing space M will always establish M as included in some other space M' (its *parent space*). This inclusion may either be indicated explicitly by syntactic embedding of the space-builders for M' and M, as in (43),

(43)
Max believes that in Len's picture, the flowers are yellow.

$SB_{M'}$ SB_M

space M' $\supset$ space M

or be inferred pragmatically from previous discourse, as in (44), (45):

(44)
Discourse D starts relative to space R (origin (= "speaker's reality"))

a. Susan likes Harry.

    establishes relation
    between Susan and
        Harry in R

b. Max believes that Susan hates Harry.

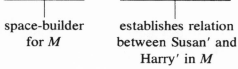

    space-builder   establishes relation
       for M between Susan' and
                            Harry' in M

In (44), no parent space is explicitly specified for M. R is inferred as the parent space: $M \subset R$.

(45)
Discourse D starts relative to R

a. In that play,   Othello is jealous.

    space-builder   establishes property
    for $M_1 \subset R$ of Othello in M_1

b. He believes that Desdemona is unfaithful.

    space-builder   property of
    for M_2 Desdemona in M_2

In (45), no parent space is explicitly specified for M_2. (45) is typically understood with M_1 as the parent space: $M_2 \subset M_1$ (that is, (45b) is taken to hold in the play, not in reality). But this interpretation is not imposed structurally; R is also a candidate for parenthood, as (46) shows:

(46)
a. In that movie, Clint Eastwood is a villain.

    M_1

b. But he thinks he's a hero.

    M_2

(46) has two likely interpretations: one in which, as in (45), M_1 is the parent space for M_2 (the character in the movie thinks he's a hero) and one in which R is the parent space (Clint Eastwood misunderstands the role). (There is an additional twist in this example, given that *he* (in *he's a hero*) may refer not to the target (the character in the movie), but to the trigger (Clint Eastwood himself); under this third interpretation, the "real" Clint Eastwood considers himself a hero.)

1.4.2 Connectors and Counterparts
When a space M is introduced in discourse by a space-builder SB_M, it must be pragmatically connected to its parent space: there must be a connector capable of connecting *triggers* and *targets* in the parent and daughter spaces. Typical cases are as follows:

(47)

	Parent Space	Space M	Connector
(in (46))	R (speaker's reality) or M_1 (movie reality)	SB_M = *he thinks*	mental image connector F_b: from "reality" to "beliefs"
	R	SB_M = *in Len's picture*	image connector F_i: from models to pictures
(in (46))	R	SB_M = *in that movie*	drama connector F_d: from actors to characters

Many other types of connectors are possible and will be exemplified below; it will also turn out that M and M' may be linked by more than one connector. Many linguistic reference phenomena do not depend on which particular connectors are involved but rather on general properties of open connectors and the trigger-target configurations they set up.

We have considered how spaces are built by space-builders, how they fit into other spaces by syntactically or pragmatically conditioned inclusion, and how the umbilical cord of pragmatic connectors keeps them in touch with their parents.

Having come this far, we are faced with another problem: How do spaces acquire elements? How are they "filled up" and internally structured? There are several strategies for introducing elements into spaces. As the following examples show, one device that does this explicitly is the indefinite article:

(48)
In Len's picture, *a witch* is riding *a unicorn*.

(49)
Len believes that *a witch* is riding *a unicorn*.

In (48), the space-builder *in Len's picture* sets up space M, the noun phrase *a witch* sets up element w in M with the property indicated by *witch* (I shall transcribe this as WITCH(w) for expository purposes).

Similarly, the noun phrase *a unicorn* sets up a new element u in M such that UNICORN(u). The verb form indicates among other things that a relation holds between u and w: RIDE(w,u). The same holds for (49) with the space-builder *Len believes*.[12]

Taking N to stand for a common noun, either simple or complex (*witch* or *wicked witch who came from the west*) and "N" the property it denotes,[13] the indefinite article can be partially characterized as follows:

(50)
Indefinite Interpretation
The noun phrase *a N* in a linguistic expression sets up a new element w in some space, such that "N"(w) holds in that space.

(I shall return to the question of determining what space w is introduced into.)

In contrast to indefinite descriptions that set up new elements, the *direct* function of *definite* descriptions is to point out elements already there (though, as we shall see, this may also result, albeit indirectly, in setting up elements).

(51)
Definite Interpretation
a. The noun phrase *the N* in a linguistic expression points to an element a already in some space M, such that "N"(a) holds in that space.
b. If N is a proper name, the noun phrase N points to an element a already in some space M, such that N is a name for a in M.

(Ultimately, (50) and (51) will only be partial characterizations, since, as shown in chapter 2, definites and indefinites can also set up "roles" rather than mere elements.)

Given (51), if the space M is pragmatically connected to another space M' by a connector F, then a in M may have a counterpart a' in M' such that $F(a) = a'$. a is a reference trigger with a' as its target, and, by the ID Principle, *the N* may be taken to identify the target a'. This is the typical situation that obtains in the paradigmatic examples of section 1.2 from OBC, such as (35):

(35)
In Len's painting, *the girl with blue eyes* has green eyes.

The space-builder *in Len's painting* sets up a space M'. The parent space M could be R (or some other origin: a story, a hypothetical situation, a movie with Len as one of its characters, etc., depending on previous discourse). By (51), the noun phrase *the girl with blue eyes* may point to a in M such that "a has blue eyes & a is a girl"; a (the model) has a counterpart a' (the image) in M'. By the ID Principle, the reference can shift from the trigger a to the target a', whereby (35) indicates that "a' has green eyes" holds in M'.

For the ID Principle to operate, linking the trigger-describing noun phrase to the target a', there must be some assumption that the trigger does in fact have a target counterpart. In the case of (35), this may be background information: the model and the image are already connected. But simple inspection is not enough to establish a connection. Consider (52):

(52)
a. Here is a picture of the European heads of state.
b. In the picture, Margaret Thatcher is completely hidden behind Helmut Kohl.

Margaret Thatcher has no physical counterpart in the picture, but given $SB_{M'}$ = *in the picture* and the corresponding space M', (52b) says that Margaret Thatcher's counterpart in M' is behind Helmut Kohl's counterpart. The assumption in (52) is that each head of state—that is, each "model," each potential trigger in M—has a counterpart in M'. The same phenomenon is apparent in (37):

(37)
Len believes that the girl with blue eyes has green eyes.

$SB_{M'}$ = *Len believes* sets up space M'. To interpret the sentence, we assume that a in M has a counterpart a' in M', but a' has actually never been set up independently of a.

The moral of these examples is that targets do not require explicit introduction. We might say that the system uses a shortcut here: instead of explicitly introducing targets in M', it lets the ID Principle apply freely to trigger elements in M with the implicit, "sensible" instruction, "If the ID Principle applies, assume there was a target for its application." Although ultimately such strategies follow from more general laws (see section 3.3), I shall, for the sake of explicitness, write down a temporary formulation:

(53)
ID Principle on Spaces
Given two spaces M, M', linked by a connector F and a noun phrase NP, introducing or pointing to an element x in M,
a. if x has a counterpart x' ($x = F(x')$) in M', NP may identify x';
b. if x has no established counterpart in M', NP may set up and identify a new element x' in M' such that $x' = F(x)$.

(This formulation is meant to cover both cases where NP is introducing x (50) and cases where NP is merely pointing back to x (51).)

From this perspective, consider (54):

(54)
Henry's girlfriend, Annette, is Swedish; but *Len believes* that *she*'s his wife, that *her* name is Lisa, and that *she*'s Spanish.

The space-builder *Len believes* sets up space M' with parent M. The noun phrase *Henry's girlfriend* points to a. a in M has several properties (girlfriend of h (Henry), name *Annette,* Swedish). The pronominal noun phrases *she* and *her* point to a. By (53), they set up a counterpart a' of a. *His* sets up a counterpart h' of h. a' has different properties from a (h''s wife, name *Lisa,* Spanish).

1.5 Scope of Indefinites

In virtue of Indefinite Interpretation (principle (50)), an indefinite noun phrase $a\ N$ will introduce a new element w into space M. Moreover, if M is connected to M' by F, then the ID Principle may apply to this noun phrase, so that $a\ N$ will identify a target of w, w'. If w has no target (typically the case, since w itself is a new element), then by (53) the noun phrase also sets up the target w'.

As noted in section 1.4.1, a space-builder comes with a companion clause specifying relations holding in the space (for example, *in Len's painting, S; Len believes that S*). Therefore, a noun phrase in that clause must[14] identify an element of the space, which it may do either by direct identification or by pointing to a trigger in a connected space.

Consider then the possible *interpretations* of a linguistic form consisting of a space-builder and a companion clause with an indefinite. Our example will be (55):

(55)
In that movie, *a former quarterback* adopts needy children.

In that movie is a space-builder for M', the parent space M may be R, the connector ($M \to M'$) is the actor-character pragmatic function F_d, "drama" of (47). The companion clause is $S = a$ *former quarterback adopts needy children*.

S must specify a relation holding in M'. Therefore, the noun phrase *a former quarterback* must identify an element in M'. It can do this in two ways:

(i) by directly setting up w in M' according to (50); then w in M' has the property $Q =$ "former quarterback." w, being in M', is a character in the movie. Property Q holds in the movie for this character; or

(ii) by setting up w in M by (50) and its target w' in M' by (53). Then w in M has the property Q. Since w is an actor, property Q holds in "reality" for this actor. That is, a former quarterback is playing the role of a character who adopts needy children.

What (55) shows is that if two spaces M and M' are relevant in the discourse and NP is an indefinite noun phrase in the companion clause, the characterization of indefinites (Indefinite Interpretation (50)) and the ID Principle on Spaces (principle (53)) allow NP to set up a new element either in M or in M'. This accounts for the so-called scope ambiguity of the indefinite in cases like (55). The same is true for the so-called specific-nonspecific contrast in (56):

(56)
John Paul hopes that *a former quarterback* will adopt needy children.

The only difference between (55) and (56) is the space-builders. In (56), the space-builder is *John Paul hopes*, there are two spaces M, M', and the connector F maps "reality" onto "hopes." If the noun phrase *a former quarterback* sets up w directly in M', then w has no counterpart in M; that is, no "real" quarterback is set up (the so-called nonspecific reading). If the noun phrase sets up a trigger w in M and a target w' in M', then a "real" quarterback, w, is set up, with a counterpart in M' (the specific reading). As figure 1.8 shows, in the first case, the property "quarterback" holds (for w) in M';[15] in the second, it holds in M. In this configuration (corresponding to the specific reading) "quarterback" is

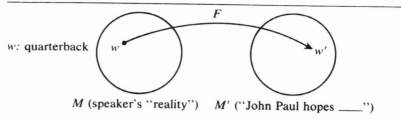

w: quarterback

M (speaker's "reality") M' ("John Paul hopes ____")

Figure 1.8

not necessarily a property of w': John Paul may know the speaker's former quarterback only in his capacity as a missionary.

Note one important general type of justification for setting up space elements in both the specific and the nonspecific situations: further discourse reference is possible in all cases. That is, (56) can be continued by utterances like (57), regardless of the interpretation:

(57)

John Paul prays that $\left\{ \begin{array}{l} \text{he} \\ \text{this quarterback} \\ \text{this former football player} \end{array} \right\}$ will be an example to all.

Also, returning to the concrete model-image correspondence, we find the parallel between pictures and spaces still in force. The following sentence has two readings relevant to the issue:[16]

(58)
Ari painted a tanker.

A tanker may be a "model" (i.e., a real boat) for whatever is in the picture, or it may point solely to the boat in the picture (in which case there may have been no model). Since *Ari painted* is a space-builder,[17] this double possibility follows straightforwardly as before from the indeterminacy of Indefinite Interpretation (principle (50)): the new element set up by *a tanker* may be in either of the two discourse spaces R or M ("Ari painted ____"). In the former case, as in figure 1.8, a target is available via (53).

Incidentally, example (58) underscores two major flaws in the traditional and still popular scopal treatment of specificity. First, (58) has only one possible scope position for an "existential" quantifier and yet has two interpretations, in accord with a space-connector approach.[18] Second, existence is not at issue: model and image are both quite real.

(56) followed by (57) illustrates another flaw: the possibility of discourse reference on the nonspecific reading runs counter to a representation in terms of narrow-scope quantifiers (e.g., John Paul hopes $(\exists x(x$ adopt needy children))) or for that matter in terms of intensions.

If current discourse involves more than two spaces (say, n), the possibility arises that the element corresponding to the indefinite will be introduced in any one of the n spaces, giving rise, in a sense, to n contextual readings for the utterance of the sentence. For example, consider (59):

(59)
Margaret is looking for a mouse.

(59) is of course true (for the speaker) if Margaret is looking for Minnie, Minnie being a mouse (so-called specific reading). It is also true if any mouse will do, for instance, one from the next-door pet shop (so-called nonspecific reading). But it is true as well in other cases, for instance, if Margaret's son Jack claims to have seen a mouse in the bedroom and this is the one Margaret is looking for. This third situation not only does not entail the existence of any mouse for the speaker but also does not imply any belief in the mouse on Margaret's part—she may be looking for it essentially to make sure that Jack told a fib. Still, the mouse here is not nonspecific in the usual sense: it is very precisely the one Jack claimed he saw, and no other will do. Given the pragmatically present spaces M_1 ("Jack claims ____") and M_2 ("Margaret is looking for ____"), we have three configurations according to (50) and (53) (see figures 1.9, 1.10, 1.11). The introduction into M_1 can be made explicit by an appropriate relative clause:

(60)
Margaret is looking for a mouse *that Jack claims he saw*.

Figure 1.11 corresponds to the third situation: not any old mouse, but no existence entailments.

The possibility of such situations has not been entirely overlooked. Following Fodor (1970), Ioup (1977, 235) comments:

The following sentence is ambiguous with respect to specificity, even though no referent of the indefinite exists ontologically; and the sentence could be true on either reading.
(6)
Alberta believes that a dragon ate her petunias.

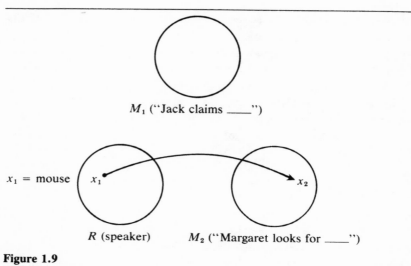

Figure 1.9

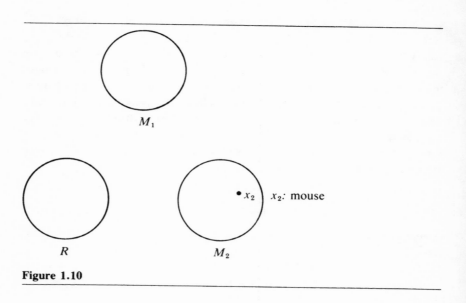

Figure 1.10

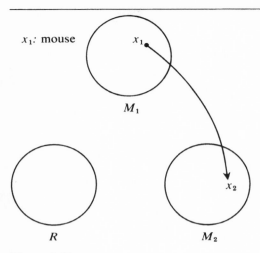

x_1: mouse

M_1

R M_2

Figure 1.11

Whether or not dragons exist, Alberta may believe they do and (6) is ambiguous as to whether Alberta maintains a belief about a particular dragon or about some unspecified dragon. We could paraphrase the specific reading by:

(7)
There is a particular dragon that Alberta believes ate her petunias.

which could be true without the ontological reality of dragons; for example, she could intend Puff, the Magic Dragon. The ambiguities concerning specificity appear to be independent of ontological existence entailments. The distinguishing factor which separates the two readings is that of individuation.

(59) shows that ontological reality is not the issue, nor is "existence" (imaginary or "real"). The possibility of introducing the "indefinite" element into various spaces gives rise to this type of pseudoproblem when a linear, "scopal" representation is attempted. From the present point of view, the interpretations can just as well be regarded as instances of vagueness with respect to which space the trigger belongs to and which connector is involved. Individuation is related to role-value contrasts (see chapter 2).

1.6 Simple Ambiguities

We have seen in section 1.2 that the simple opaque-transparent ambiguities associated with verbs of propositional attitude follow directly

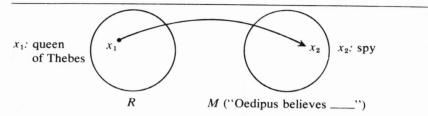

Figure 1.12

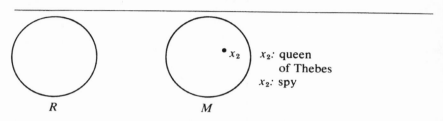

Figure 1.13

from natural language trigger-target identification, that is, from the operation of the ID Principle across spaces. For example, consider (61):

(61)
Oedipus believes that the queen of Thebes is a spy.

If R is the origin space (e.g., speaker's reality or story containing (61)) and *Oedipus believes* is a space-builder that sets up space M within R, which is linked to R by a connector F, then by principles (51) and (53), the noun phrase *the queen of Thebes* may point to an element in R or to an element in M. In the former case, the element in R, x_1, will be a trigger for identification of x_2 in M (see figures 1.12, 1.13). Figure 1.12 corresponds to the classical transparent reading: it allows the possibility that x_2 does not have the property "queen of Thebes" (hence the possible, noncontradictory reading of "Oedipus believes that the queen of Thebes is not the queen of Thebes"). Figure 1.13 corresponds to the classical opaque reading: "queen of Thebes" is a property of x_2 (i.e., informally, part of Oedipus's belief); x_2 may turn out to have no counterpart in R (discourse: ". . . Actually, there is no queen of Thebes") or a counterpart with different properties (e.g., someone Oedipus mistakenly takes for the queen).

Notice that the availability of two "interpretations" for a sentence like (61) is purely a consequence of the discourse processing involved

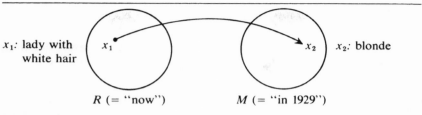

x_1: lady with white hair

x_2: blonde

R (= "now") M (= "in 1929")

Figure 1.14

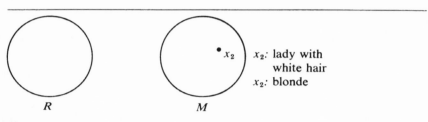

x_2: lady with white hair
x_2: blonde

R M

Figure 1.15

(construction of spaces, connectors, etc.); it is not linked to any structural ambiguity of the linguistic form at deep, semantic, or logical levels.[19]

Typically, then, the double processing possibility will appear if there is more than one space—in particular, if the relevant sentence contains a space-builder.[20] Therefore, we expect to find similar ambiguities with space-builders other than image creators or propositional attitudes. This is indeed the case, as a brief survey of various kinds of spaces will show.

1.6.1 Time Space

As mentioned in section 1.4.1, time adverbials such as *in 1929, last year, next time you're here* are space-builders. Informally, the counterpart of an element in some space corresponding to time t is "that element at time t." Let us consider some examples:

(62)
In 1929, *the lady with white hair* was blonde.

In 1929 sets up space M. Assume the parent space R corresponds to "now."[21] The noun phrase *the lady with white hair* may set up x_1 in R and identify its counterpart x_2 in M (x_1 "is" the old lady today, x_2 the "same" person when she was young, in 1929) (see figure 1.14). But, as in all our previous examples, the noun phrase *the lady with white hair* could also be a direct description of the target x_2, yielding the somewhat contradictory reading depicted in figure 1.15 that the lady was a blonde with white hair. (Compare "In 1929, the aging president resigned," "Forty years from now, my middle-aged daughter will get married.")

Consider another context. We are talking about the young woman I fell in love with when I lived in Spain in 1929, and I say:

(63)
Today, *that young woman* is an old lady with white hair.

This time, the origin space happens to be "1929." The space-builder *today* sets up a space corresponding to the present. The noncontradictory reading of (63) is obtained as for (62), by letting *that young woman* point to an element in R_{1929} and identify its target counterpart in M_{today}.

Other well-known ambiguities are accounted for in the same way:

(64)
In 1929, the president was a baby.[22]

(65)
At that time, my husband was a traveling salesman.
(The husband changed professions *or* the speaker changed husbands)

(66)
When Jimmy was born, we had *the table* in the bedroom.
(Followed in discourse by, for example, "It was a bed at the time, which we later converted into a table" or "We don't have a table anymore")

1.6.2 Space Space
Not surprisingly, geographical spaces are also linguistic spaces:

(67)
In Moldavia, the president is a tyrant.

In Moldavia sets up a new space M different from the origin R (say, "here"). The noun phrase *the president* may point directly to an element in M (reading: the president of Moldavia is a tyrant), or it may point to a trigger in R (the president here), identifying a target in M (the president when in Moldavia) (reading: when in Moldavia, the president (from here) is a tyrant).

Again, any noun will do:

(68)
In the other apartment, the chandelier looks fine.
(The chandelier, when in the other apartment, looks fine, *or* the chandelier of the other apartment looks fine)

1.6.3 Domain Spaces
A domain of activity (game, field of science, sport, type of literature, etc.) can be processed linguistically as a mental space, and we observe the usual ambiguities. Consider in particular the transparent noncontradictory readings of the following examples:

(69)
In Canadian football, the 50-yard line is 55 yards away.

(70)
In Martian chess, the bishops are castles.

(71)
In Rubik's new theory, transformations are phrase structure rules and phrase structure rules are transformations.

(72)
In this new Californian religion, the devil is an angel.

1.6.4 Hypothetical Spaces
Linguistic forms such as *if p, then q* set up a new space H in which p and q hold.[23] *If p* is the space-builder. Again we find noncontradictory "transparent" readings and somewhat contradictory opaque ones, as in (73) through (75). Figure 1.16 depicts the mental spaces set up in (73).

(73)
If I were a millionaire, my VW would be a Rolls.

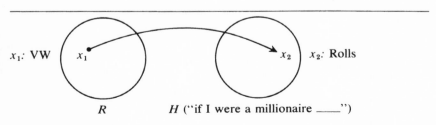

Figure 1.16

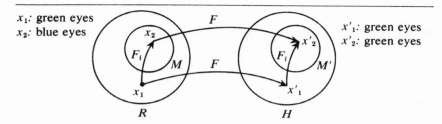

Figure 1.17

(74)
If he had listened to his mother, this criminal would be a saint.

(75)
If you were a good painter, the girl with blue eyes would have green eyes.

Notice also:

(76)
If you were a good painter, the girl with green eyes would have green eyes.

As depicted in figure 1.17, four spaces are involved: R ("reality"), M (the painting), H (the counterfactual hypothetical space), and M' (the counterpart of M within H). *The girl with green eyes* points to a trigger in R ("the model") and identifies a target in M' after successive applications of the ID Principle.

The properties of hypothetical spaces will be examined more carefully in chapters 3 and 4 in connection with presuppositions and indefinites. Similar counterfactual spaces can be set up by *otherwise* or sometimes directly, after a negative utterance:

(77)
Too bad you were never baptized. (Otherwise), *your godfather* could take care of you.

(78)
I don't have a car. Otherwise, I would drive *it* to work.

Your godfather and *it* set up elements in the hypothetical space ("otherwise _____") with no counterpart in R.

1.6.5 Tenses and Moods

Tenses and moods do not by themselves explicitly set up spaces, but they give important grammatical clues concerning the spaces relevant for the sentence being processed. For instance, (62) followed by a past tense means that we stay in M (1929); followed by a present tense, it signals a shift back to R; the "conditionals" (*could, would*) in (77), (78) signal the counterfactual space M. When they appear within a description (inside a relative clause), tenses and moods can signal explicitly what kind of space the description is relative to, thereby removing some or all of the indeterminacy of the ID Principle on Spaces (principle (53)). For instance, in examples like the following, from French, the subjunctive marks propositions in the "want" space W and the present indicative marks propositions in the origin space R:

(79)
Marie veut que Gudule *mette* une robe qui *soit* jolie.
                 subj.   subj.

(Lit.: Marie wants that Gudule *wear* a dress that *be* pretty)

(80)
Marie veut que Gudule *mette* une robe qui *est* jolie.
                 subj.   ind.

Potentially, the indefinite noun phrase *une robe qui . . .* is either a description in R (d_R) or a description in W (d_W). The subjunctive in (79) indicates that the description is in W and forces the d_W interpretation (that is, the "nonspecific" reading) for that sentence. The indicative in (80) signals that the description is in R and forces the d_R interpretation ("specific"). The readings and ambiguities linked to such sentences are unrelated to the indefinite article, which preserves the same semantic function (introduction of new element in discourse) in all cases. Rather, the multiple interpretations stem from the ID Principle and may be resolved if grammatical mood indicates explicitly which space the descriptions are made in. We shall see that the same is true of definite noun phrases.

Sequence-of-tense constraints are an example of the same process for time spaces.

(81)
Freud *believed* that Jung *was* a psychotic.
       past   past

A "past space of Freud's beliefs" is introduced by the space-builder *Freud believed,* and propositions holding in that space are accordingly marked grammatically as *past.* Not surprisingly, then, tense can indicate which space a description belongs to, as in (82) and (83):

(82)
In 1929, she married someone who *was* a friend of mine.

(83)
In 1929, she married someone who *is* a friend of mine.

(84)
In 1929, she married a friend of mine.

It may be appropriate at this point to emphasize an important methodological difference between the approach followed here and classical generative grammar: the space format and the ID Principle account directly for the interpretations of (82) through (84) and explain as a consequence why the linguistic form (84) may have the same reading as (82) or the same reading as (83). It does not follow from this semantic relationship that (84) is structurally related to (82) and (83) (e.g., through underlying forms). The relationship is a consequence of the discourse-processing possibilities and is not a property of the syntax; reflecting the relationship directly in the syntax by means of underlying forms amounts to arbitrary reduplication, since the posited underlying forms will be different in every case. For time, tensed clauses will be reconstructed; for propositional attitudes (*want, believe,* etc.), logical forms will have to be reconstructed, since no linguistic paraphrase happens to exist; for concrete images, (*paint, draw,* etc.), a third kind of form would have to be devised; and so on. This is really a badly disguised form of paraphrase that masks the generalization that all the ambiguities in cases like (85) follow directly from the ID Principle:

(85)

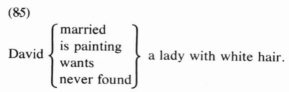

Chapter 2
Roles and Multiple Connectors

Archie: "My sister's father is a rich sewer tycoon."

Barrow: "Your father? Where?"

Archie: "I said my sister's father. My family connections are none of your business, and besides, they're too complicated for you to understand. He is also occasionally my mother's father, on account of the fact that on the telephone last night my sister was my mother. But he isn't my father because I've never met him."

Rex Stout, *Some Buried Caesar*

2.1 Pronouns across Spaces

Because the connectors that link elements in different spaces are *open*, in the sense of section 1.1, a pronoun with an antecedent in one space can freely identify its counterpart in another, connected space.

(1)
Vivien saw herself in *Gone with the Wind*.

(2)
Harry believed himself to be a woman.

(3)
Julian thought of himself back in 1929.

This would come as no surprise if one viewed all the counterparts as being in some sense "the same" element. However, there are some interesting facts that seem to rule out this possibility even in its weakest form (e.g., equivalence class of counterparts or cross-world identification function).[1]

The relevant cases can be subdivided into three main categories: multiple connectors, multiple counterparts, and multiple descriptions.

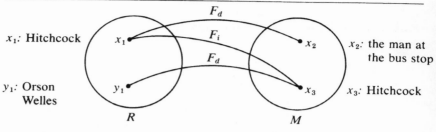

x_1: Hitchcock

x_2: the man at the bus stop

y_1: Orson Welles

x_3: Hitchcock

Figure 2.1

2.1.1 Multiple Connectors

Suppose a movie is made about Alfred Hitchcock's life; the main role (Hitchcock) is played by Orson Welles, but Hitchcock himself plays a minor role (the man at the bus stop).[2] R (the speaker's reality) and M (the movie) are linked by two connectors (see section 1.4.2): the drama connector F_d from actors to characters and an image connector F_i from real-life people to their movie counterparts. This is shown schematically in figure 2.1. Hitchcock (x_1) happens to be linked to two elements of M, by two different connectors, which is confirmed by the ambiguity of (4) and (5):

(4)
Hitchcock saw himself in that movie.

(5)
Hitchcock liked himself in that movie.
(He liked the man at the bus stop *or* he liked the character played by Welles)

Any form of identity between counterparts would have to be at least an equivalence relation, $=$. This would spell disaster in all situations of the form shown in figure 2.1:

(6)
$$x_1 = x_3 \quad \text{(by connector } F_i\text{)}$$
$$y_1 = x_3 \quad \text{(by connector } F_d\text{)}$$
hence $y_1 = x_1$

Hitchcock would be Orson Welles in reality; furthermore, since $x_1 = x_2$, Orson Welles would also be the man at the bus stop. This would entail $x_2 = x_3$. But x_2 and x_3 are not connected: in particular, if, in the movie, the man at the bus stop shot Hitchcock (i.e., "x_2 shot x_3"), it could not be reported by either (7) or (8):

(7)

In the movie, the man at the bus stop shoots himself.

(8)

In the movie, Orson Welles shoots himself.

The only, marginally possible, reflexive form would be "Hitchcock shoots himself," obtained via the connectors in the following way:[3]

(9)

$$\text{Hitchcock shoots himself.}$$

Definite Inter-pretation (51)	x_1	
Reflexive		x_1
F_d	x_2	
F_i		x_3

Such cases clearly show that counterparts cannot be lumped into a single equivalence class, that no single function can identify counterparts across worlds, and that an approach allowing one individual to be in many spaces at once will not work. The next two ranges of cases confirm this finding.

2.1.2 Multiple Counterparts

A single connector can also produce more than one counterpart per element: if Luke doesn't know that his new neighbor is Dracula, one element in R (a = Dracula = Luke's new neighbor) has two counterparts in M (SB_M = *Luke thinks*), as depicted in figure 2.2. Assume that the following hold:

a'_1 lives in Transylvania ("Luke thinks Dracula lives in Transylvania")

a'_2 makes too much noise ("Luke thinks his new neighbor makes too much noise")

Then the following utterances can be true under the interpretation in which the ID Principle applies to the single trigger a and to either one of the two targets a'_1, a'_2:

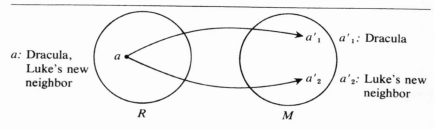

Figure 2.2

(10)
a. Luke thinks Dracula makes too much noise.
b. Luke thinks his new neighbor lives in Transylvania.

Other examples are easy to come by. A striking one pointed out in lectures by G. Lakoff has the following form:

(11)
If X had been born twins, they would have hated each other.

X in space R has two counterparts in the counterfactual space M ("if ____").

Again, as in the previous section, no treatment of such cases is possible in terms of counterpart equivalence or "sameness": the two counterparts of Dracula and the two counterparts of X must count as different.

2.1.3 Multiple Descriptions
Consider a dancing contest situation (assume women are competing) and the following speaker utterance:

(12)
The winner will get a new toaster, but George thinks she will go to Hong Kong.

It might seem natural in light of section 2.1 to take *the winner* as identifying someone in R and *she* as identifying its counterpart in the space "George thinks." However, suppose that the winner has just been announced and that the speaker and George disagree about who won: for the speaker it's Rose, for George it's Olive. Suppose further that Olive has red hair and Rose is blonde, and George and the speaker agree on these points. The speaker can now truthfully say (13) or (14):

(13)
George thinks *the winner* has red hair.

(14)
The winner is blonde, but George thinks *she*'s a redhead.

((14) has a number of other interpretations that we shall ignore for the moment.) But *the winner* and *Rose* are both correct descriptions of the same individual in *R*. Thus, (14) should be equivalent to (15):

(15)
Rose is blonde, but George thinks *she*'s a redhead.

This is patently false, since (14) is quite compatible with George's belief that Rose in blonde, but not (15). Superficially, here, as in figure 2.1, there is an overabundance of counterparts but apparently only one connector linking *R* to *M* ("George thinks").

With phenomena of this type in mind, let us turn to a more general account of descriptions than the one given in section 1.4.2.

2.2 Roles

In chapter 1, noun phrases were taken to point to elements (or objects, individuals, etc.). This classical view was implicit in the ID Principle and explicit in principles (50), Indefinite Interpretation, and (51), Definite Interpretation. However, as I have stressed in previous work related to quantification (Fauconnier (1978a)), this classical view cannot be right in general; definite descriptions have many features suggesting a treatment in terms of functions ("roles") rather than in terms of direct reference.

Consider some straightforward examples:

(16)
The president changes every seven years.

(17)
Your car is always different.

(18)
Your apartment keeps getting bigger and bigger.

(19)
She likes to tie her hat with a string.

(20)
The leaves of that tree are greener every year.

(21)
The food here is worse and worse.

All these examples have readings in which the noun phrase refers to a single element: for example, for (16), the individual who happens to be president (say, Mitterrand) changes every seven years (becomes arrogant, or bald, or insane); for (17), the "same" car takes on different appearances (new colors, smashed fenders, whitewall tires); for (18), the same apartment is apt to shrink or expand, as in Boris Vian's "Ecume des Jours"; for (19), she owns a single hat; for (20), the tree is an evergreen with the same leaves for years on end; for (21), some particular food in the cupboard is rotting away; and so on.

But equally acceptable, and perhaps pragmatically more salient, readings involve a variable denotation for the noun phrase: for (16), there is a new president every seven years; for (17), you always show up with a different car; for (18), you keep moving into bigger apartments; for (19), she likes to tie whatever hat she's wearing with a string; for (20), this year's leaves are greener than last year's; for (21), the food served this week is worse than the food served last week.

Also, except for (19), such examples on that reading cannot be perceived as somehow generic or universal. They have no universally quantified equivalent:

(16) $\neq \forall x$ (x = president) (x changes every seven years)

(17) $\neq \forall x$ (x = car, yours) (x is always different)

(18) $\neq \forall x$ (x = apartment, yours) (x gets bigger)

(Compare "The president lives in the White House," $\forall x$ (x = president) (x lives in the White House).)

This range of data confirms an approach with ample justification of other sorts, by which definite descriptions are primarily role functions and secondarily the values taken by such roles. The domain of the role may include times, places, situations, contexts, and much more; its range will consist of elements having the particular property "N" indicated by *the N*, in the corresponding setting.

In many ways, this is not a controversial or novel conception: *the president*, for instance, will be a role taking different values in different countries at different times, in different organizations, and so on, the values being the individuals who happen to be president of *that* organization, or *that* country, at *that* time.

Quantificational contexts highlight the functional value of a definite description and the multiple values at hand:

(22)
Every man built himself a house. In John's case, *the house* was a two-story brick structure; in Harry's case, *the house* was a huge glass frame design; in most cases, *the house* was conceived for four or five people; etc.

In (22), the role *the house* takes the men as its domain and the houses built as its range. By specifying subdomains, expressions like *in John's case* assign the corresponding role value to the definite description (i.e., "the house built by John").

Return to examples like (16): given that *the president* corresponds to a role, the first reading (= Mitterrand) gives us a property of the value of that role in some particular context, and the second reading yields a property of the role itself.

I shall use the following notation: let P represent the predication involved (e.g., "____ changes every seven years" or "____ keeps getting bigger"), r the definite description role function (e.g., the president, your apartment), and m the relevant contextual parameters in the domain of r (e.g., time, place, organization). Linguistic forms like (16) through (21) will correspond to two fundamental readings:

(23)
$P(r)$ property of a role
$P(r(m))$ property of a value of that role

($r(m)$ is the value of role r for the contextual parameters m.) At this point, the notation $P(r)$ should not be taken to prejudge the actual semantics of these readings: the predications on functions and particular values are of course different in nature "mathematically," although conveyed by the same linguistic forms. Nonetheless, a unified view suggests itself: The elements we have talked about until now have a fixed identity, but their other properties can change. *Roles* are also elements, but such that identity (i.e., role value) can change, while one particular property (e.g., president, house) is fixed; for such elements, as opposed to others, identity is a variable property. This view has the advantage of yielding a unified analysis of verbs like *change:* if "*X* changes" entails that some property of *X* is added, lost, or replaced, then that property can be identity in the case of roles (as in "The president changes at each election"), but will be a property other than identity for values ("Reagan has changed during the last two months"). There may also be "magical" situations (Dr. Jekyll/Mr. Hyde) in which identities of value elements can change.

The fact that a linguistic description may identify a role or its value may itself be considered a case of transferred trigger reference, since the link between a role and its value for some setting of parameters *m* is itself a pragmatic function, *F:*

(24)
$F(m,r) = r(m)$

Consider now a point of special relevance to the present study: mental spaces, as presented in chapter 1, belong to the domains of role functions. That is, a role (e.g., in the form of a definite description such as *the president*) will take different values in different spaces, and these values need not be images of one another:

(25)
The president is Reagan. Irving *believes* the president is Kissinger. He *would like* Brown to be the president. *In the movie,* Goofy is the president.

A discourse like (25) sets up four spaces in which *the president* takes different, unconnected values. Leaving aside other contextual parameters, I shall write $r(M)$ for the value taken by r in space M.

With this in mind, let us turn back to the dancing contest situation of (12):

(26)
George thinks the winner will go to Hong Kong.

Space-builder	*George thinks*	(space M)
Predication P	"____ will go to Hong Kong"	
Role r	*the winner*	

(26) can be interpreted in several ways, among which are (27) and (28) (other interpretations will be given later in this section):

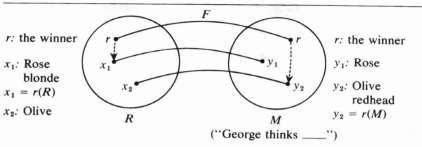

r: the winner

x₁: Rose
   blonde
$x_1 = r(R)$

x₂: Olive

r: the winner

y₁: Rose

y₂: Olive
   redhead
$y_2 = r(M)$

("George thinks ____")

Figure 2.3

(27)
$P(r)$ holds in M

(28)
$P(r(M))$ holds in M

(Recall that roles are themselves elements of spaces.)

The first reading corresponds to a property of role r (the winner); it can be paraphrased clumsily by saying that role r takes as its values individuals who will go to Hong Kong. It does *not* require that $r(M)$ be defined (that is, that r have a value in M or in other words that George should hold a particular individual to be the winner); nor does it require George to think that there is a winner.

On the other hand, the second reading, (28), corresponds to a property of the value of r in M, $r(M)$. George must have established some individual as being "the winner"; this individual has property P.

Consider then the space configuration corresponding to example (14) ("The winner is blonde, but George thinks she's a redhead"), depicted in figure 2.3. The interpretation proceeds in several steps: *the winner* is first interpreted as role r, and *she* has the same interpretation by ordinary pronominalization. Then value interpretation applies (optionally of course), relative to the appropriate space:

(29)

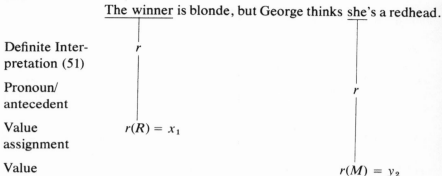

The winner is blonde, but George thinks she's a redhead.

Definite Inter- r
pretation (51)

Pronoun/ r
antecedent

Value $r(R) = x_1$
assignment

Value $r(M) = y_2$
assignment

If we take P and Q to represent the properties "blonde" and "red-head," the interpretation is something like (30):

(30)
$P(r(R))$ but $Q(r(M))$

Contrast this interpretation with the one for (15):

(31)

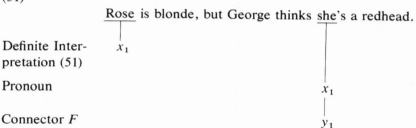

Rose is blonde, but George thinks she's a redhead.

Definite Inter- x_1
pretation (51)

Pronoun x_1

Connector F y_1

There is no way that *she* in (15) (with antecedent *Rose*) could identify either r or y_2. (31) makes the simplifying assumption that proper names are interpreted directly as values, not functions (roles). This is probably wrong, since names can behave like other properties (see section 2.5): (15) could be used in a context where we are not sure which person is (called) *Rose*, to express that George is mistaken about the identity of that person. The relevant role would be r' (having the name *Rose*). The interpretation, quite parallel to (29), would be (32):

(32)

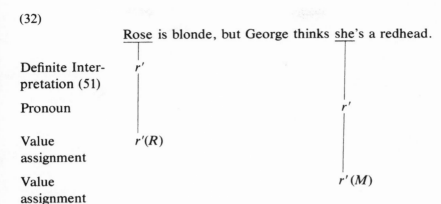

Rose is blonde, but George thinks she's a redhead.

Definite Interpretation (51)	r'	
Pronoun		r'
Value assignment	$r'(R)$	
Value assignment		$r'(M)$

(That is, George might know that the winner's name is *Rose* and yet still believe erroneously that Olive, whose name he *doesn't* know, or takes to be *Rose,* is the winner!)

Furthermore, there is also a transparent reading of (14) that is essentially equivalent to (31). The interpretation proceeds as follows:

(33)

The winner is blonde, but George thinks she's a redhead.

Definite Interpretation (51)	r	
Value assignment	$r(R) = x_1$	
Pronoun		x_1
Connector F		y_1

In fact, given the optionality of value assignment and the unordered position of pronoun interpretation with respect to value assignment, we already have five readings (in principle) for a sentence like (14):

(34)

the winner	she
r	r
$r(R)$	r
r	$r(M)$
$r(R)$	$r(M)$
$r(R)$	$F(r(R))$

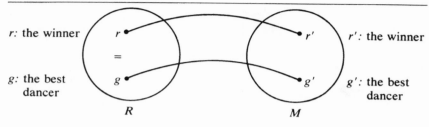

r: the winner

g: the best
dancer

r': the winner

g': the best
dancer

Figure 2.4

But this is not the end of the story, because the role itself, and not just its values, can be a trigger or a target for the ID Principle. Suppose the speaker, but not George, assumes that the winner is necessarily the best dancer. The speaker can then report George's belief that the winner will go to Hong Kong, as follows:

(35)
George thinks the best dancer will go to Hong Kong.

This is a straightforward application of the ID Principle: describing the element in M in terms of its counterpart in R. But notice that element and counterpart in this instance are both roles. Schematically, (35) could correspond to the space configuration shown in figure 2.4.

The roles themselves are now viewed as elements in the spaces with counterparts that may differ not just in the value they take, but in their definitional properties. I shall continue to use expressions like $r(R)$ or $r'(M)$ for the particular values that such a role may take within its space. Furthermore, I shall introduce an equality relation between roles: for example, in figure 2.4 *the winner* and *the best dancer* remain two distinct elements in space R, but they are *equal* insofar as any setting of other contextual parameters in R is presumed to induce the same values for r and g.

Consider another example, related to (16). The scene is set in France, presently a republic with a president. George is a staunch monarchist and believes that the head of state is a king (the appropriate member of the royal family—currently the Comte de Paris). He is also aware of the presidential system (but does not regard the president as a head of state). If George believes that the president changes every five years, this can be reported by a more republican speaker as in (36):

(36)
George thinks the head of state changes every five years.

And of course, if George believes there is a new king every thirty years, this can be reported as in (37):

(37)
George thinks the head of state changes every thirty years.

(36) and (37) are classically transparent and opaque in the relevant context, but the descriptions do not refer to individuals. Six roles could be involved:

(38)
$$\left.\begin{cases} f \text{ (head of state)} \\ g \text{ (president)} \\ k \text{ (king)} \end{cases}\right\} \text{ in } R \text{ and its counterpart } \left.\begin{cases} f' \\ g' \\ k' \end{cases}\right\} \text{ in } M$$

Different equalities hold in R and M:

(39)
$f = g$ (in R)
$f' = k'$ (in M)

And presumably there is no value for $k(R)$. Taking $P(\underline{\quad}) = $ "$\underline{\quad}$ changes every five years" and $Q(\underline{\quad}) = $ "$\underline{\quad}$ changes every thirty years," (34) expresses (40):

(40)
$P(g')$ holds in M

This is possible via the ID Principle, because g' can be identified by a description of its counterpart g and because, given $f = g$, a description of f (head of state) is a description of g. (37) expresses (41):

(41)
$Q(f')$ holds in M

Again, a description of f (head of state) identifies its counterpart f'. And because $f' = k'$, $Q(f')$ is equivalent to $Q(k')$ ("the king changes every thirty years").

   Notice that it would be a mistake to take f and g or f' and k' as being *the same* role (i.e., the same space element) rather than merely equal, because a description of g could then identify k', leading to the impossible reading (43) for (42):

(42)

George thinks the president changes every five years.

(43)

"George thinks the king changes every five years."

(Incidentally, a different context could allow reading (43) for (42): if George mistakenly takes the president to be a king, then either g' itself happens to have the description "king" or else $g' = k'$: a description of g ("president") may then identify a function in M with the property "king" (g' or k').)

The possibility that descriptions not only of referential elements but also of roles may be opaque multiplies the possible combinations for examples like (14) (i.e., readings in the traditional view):

(44)

the winner	she
r	r'
r	g'
$r(R)$	r'
$r(R)$	g'
r	$r'(M)$
r	$g'(M)$
$r(R)$	$r'(M)$
$r(R)$	$g'(M)$
$r(R)$	$F(r(R))$

By and large, interpretations of the form $P(r)$ correspond in simple cases to what have been called attributive readings and interpretations $P(r(H))$ to referential ones. The relatively great number of available combinations tends to cloud some of the relevant issues and the standard philosophical discussions implicitly focus only on some of the parameters involved. Before taking up a specific example in some detail, I should like to comment briefly on some general aspects of the analysis. I have stressed before that the multiple interpretations associated with a particular sentence are *not* linked to corresponding *structural* complexities of that sentence. They stem from the underdetermined nature of mental construction processes such as the ID Principle, role value assignment, or pronoun interpretation and are therefore a matter of strategy. The variety of possible strategies shows up when connected spaces are strongly dissimilar, as in the examples I made up, but such extreme cases are "in practice" unusual: connected

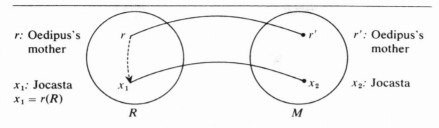

r: Oedipus's mother

x_1: Jocasta
$x_1 = r(R)$

r': Oedipus's mother

x_2: Jocasta

Figure 2.5

spaces often differ minimally (in fact, assuming maximum similarity is itself an interpretation strategy; see chapter 3). Suppose by way of illustration, then, that (14) is uttered in a context of similar spaces (i.e., $r' = g'$, $r'(M) = g'(M) = F(r(R))$): the possible strategies reduce to two at most (and likewise the corresponding interpretations). In that context, the nine interpretations uncovered before could not, *even in principle,* be distinguished. This points to a crucial difference between what goes on in linguistic mental construction and what a structural (e.g., logically based) approach would suggest, namely, that a sentence always comes with the full range of its semantic interpretations (specified by the grammar) and that speakers and hearers cancel out the inappropriate ones.

As an illustration, consider a familiar example:

(45)
Oedipus believes he will marry his mother.

Oedipus believes sets up space M (in R); *his mother* corresponds to role r in R with counterpart r' in M. We assume first a situation with no "role opacity" (i.e., no roles g and g' as in (36), (37)). Assume further that Oedipus is taken to have no idea of who his mother is—that is, there is no value for $r'(M)$ in M at that point in the discourse. The speaker takes Oedipus's mother to be Jocasta, so $r(R) = $ Jocasta. The situation is given schematically in figure 2.5. We are interested only in the interpretations of (45) where *he* and *his* are coreferential with *Oedipus.* Let $P(\underline{\hspace{1cm}})$ stand for the predication "he will marry $\underline{\hspace{1cm}}$." With respect to figure 2.5, *his mother* is a linguistic description of r, of r', and of $r(R)$. Furthermore, it must identify an element in M, either directly or by the ID Principle. We have the following three possibilities:

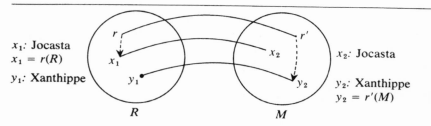

x_1: Jocasta
$x_1 = r(R)$
y_1: Xanthippe

x_2: Jocasta

y_2: Xanthippe
$y_2 = r'(M)$

R   M

Figure 2.6

(46)
his mother

	describes	identifies	
a.	r	r'	(counterpart of r in M)
b.	r'	r'	(direct description)
c.	$r(R)$	x_2	(counterpart of x_1)

In this particular case, the first two possibilities collapse. (45) expresses either proposition (47) or proposition (48), relative to space M:

(47)
$P(r')$ (Attributive and opaque reading: Oedipus believes that whoever turns out to be his mother will also be his wife)

(48)
$P(x_2)$ (Referential and transparent reading: Oedipus believes he will marry Jocasta; speaker provides description "his mother," inappropriate in M)

Suppose now that $r'(M)$ does have a value in M, distinct from x_2. That is (according to the speaker), Oedipus takes another woman (say, Xanthippe) to be his mother, as depicted in figure 2.6. A fourth interpretation of *his mother* is now available, namely, $r'(M)$:

(49)
his mother

	describes	identifies	
	((a–c) as in (46))		
d.	$r'(M)$	y_2	$(= r'(M))$

Thus, we have a third reading:

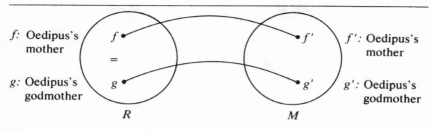

f: Oedipus's mother

g: Oedipus's godmother

f': Oedipus's mother

g': Oedipus's godmother

Figure 2.7

(50)

$P(y_2)$ (Referential and opaque reading: Oedipus believes he will marry Xanthippe (whom he takes to be his mother))

Other interpretations will appear if role opacity is added to the situation. For example, as shown in figure 2.7, it may be true for the speaker, but not for Oedipus viewed by the speaker, that Oedipus's godmother (g) is necessarily his mother (f). Then "his mother" is a valid description of g in R and may identify g' in M. The corresponding fourth reading is then as follows:

(51)

$P(g')$ (Attributive and transparent reading: Oedipus believes he will marry whoever happens to be his godmother)

2.3 First-Order Equivalences

In many cases, the interpretations characterized above as properties of roles and noted $P(r)$ seem to admit a first-order equivalent universal reading $\forall mP(r(m))$ (where m represents the relevant parameters).[4] For instance, granting the role HER HAT(m) = "the hat she wears in 'situation' m," (19) corresponds to something like (52):

(19)
She likes to tie her hat with a string.

(52)
$\forall m$(she likes to tie HER HAT(m) with a string)

Should one, then, regard some of the ambiguities in section 2.2 as stemming not from a contrast between role and value interpretations but rather from contrasts between particular (one value) interpretations and general (all values) interpretations?

This move is certainly not generally possible since examples like (16), (17), (18), etc., do not have the straightforward first-order equivalent. Still, it might cover a substantial subset of cases of simple predication (e.g., not involving comparatives or verbs like *change, rise*). Closer examination of the data, however, suggests that the first-order readings are at best derivative, not fundamental. Consider (53):

(53)
The president lives in the White House.

(53) appears truth-conditionally equivalent to (54), a universally quantified first-order formula:

(54)
$\forall x$(president(x) → x lives in the White House)

(Or, in the notation of (52), $\forall m$(PRESIDENT(m) lives in the White House).)
   Now consider (55):

(55)
Every year, the president gives civil servants \$2 billion.

Suppose there is a change of presidents in August—for example, Nixon resigns, Ford takes over. A natural interpretation of (55) is that if Nixon has already paid \$1 billion, then Ford should pay another \$1 billion, bringing the total to the required \$2 billion. Clearly, neither president will have paid \$2 billion, and so the first-order reading of (55) is false:

(56)
$\forall y \ \forall x$ (president(x,y) → x give civil servants \$2 billion in y)

What such examples show is that non-first-order interpretations will be necessary independently of particular lexical properties of the verbs or nouns involved. However, nothing seems to rule out another, universal first-order, interpretation for cases structurally like (55). For instance, consider (57):

(57)
Every year, the president undergoes a medical checkup.

Here, presumably for pragmatic reasons, the universal interpretation seems quite acceptable: that is, in the previous context, both Nixon and Ford might undergo medical checkups.

These remarks can also serve to highlight previously unmentioned interpretations for examples like (16):

(16)
The president changes every seven years.

Suppose that every seven years, changes in astrological configurations have corresponding effects on the president's mood—that is, on the mood of *whoever* happens to be president at the time. Then (16) is true without a change of persons and on a universal reading. This reading in effect involves values of role *r* at the end of seven-year periods.

Another universal interpretation of (16) seems available, with wider scope for *the president:* "whoever is president has the property of changing every seven years" (regardless of whether that person is yet/ still president).

Also, as F. Recanati (personal communication) points out, universal interpretations appear in addition to the functional ones in constructions involving space-builders:

(58)
In 1929, the president was a baby.
("Whoever is president these days was a baby in 1929")

Taking *m* to range over current situations ("these days"), *r* to be the role THE PRESIDENT, *B* to be the property "baby," and *F* to be the connector between spaces *M* ("in 1929") and *R*, this translates as (59):

(59)
$\forall m\ B(F(r(m)))$

(59) is distinct from the interpretations mentioned in previous sections. Leaving aside the possibility of role opacity, recall that there are three main interpretations:

(60)

<u>In 1929,</u> <u>the president</u> <u>was a baby</u>.

a. space M	$r(M)$	P
b. space M	$F(r(R))$	P
c. space M	r	P

a′. in 1929, a baby was president $P(r(M))$
b′. the current president was a baby in 1929 $P(F(r(R)))$
c′. in 1929, presidents were chosen among babies $P(r)$

To explain the nature and the origin of "additional" readings like (59), it is appropriate to comment further on the notion of "property" involved in these phenomena. As described so far, typical space-building (or space-bound) utterances have the structure (61),

(61)
$\mathcal{M}[P(a)]$

where P is a property, $\mathcal{M}$ (corresponding to the linguistic space-builder SB_M) indicates that the property holds in space M, and a is an element: if a is in R, then P holds of the counterpart of a in M, $F(a)$; if a is in M, then P holds of a. Thus, if a is in R, then (61) expresses that a's counterpart in M has property P. But this itself is of course a property of a, namely, to have a counterpart in M with property P (= property $\mathcal{M}^\circ P$). To say "In that picture, Mary has blue eyes" is not only to give a property of Mary's image ("having blue eyes") but also to give a property of Mary, namely, "having a counterpart in the picture with blue eyes." This equivalence follows trivially as a theorem from the ID Principle and may be expressed as follows:

(62)
Property Equivalence Theorem
If F is the relevant connector linking space M and its parent space R, and a is an element of R, then

$$\mathcal{M}[P(a)] \leftrightarrow P[F(a)]$$
  or equivalently
$$\mathcal{M}^\circ P(a) \leftrightarrow P[F(a)]$$

where "$\mathcal{M}^\circ P$" is the property of having a counterpart in space M with property P.

Now, the universal readings studied in this section correspond generally (and independently of spaces) to the *special* interpretation of $Q(r)$ (Q being some first-order property) as $\forall m\ Q(r(m))$:

(63)
First-Order Universal Interpretation
$$Q(r) \leftrightarrow \forall m\ Q(r(m))$$

(*m* ranging over situations)

(For example, "The president governs the country" $\leftrightarrow$ "Whoever is president governs the country.")

If interpretation (63) applies to space-bound structures like (61), there is an obvious ambiguity: given $\mathcal{M}°P(r)$, we can apply (63) to $P(r)$, yielding (64):

(64)
$\mathcal{M}°P(r) \leftrightarrow \mathcal{M}[\forall m\ P(r(m))]$

In this case, the universal holds in $M;$ or, to paraphrase, for every situation m in M, $P(r(m))$ holds. This is the possibility exemplified by the universal interpretation of reading (c) for (60): all 1929 presidents were babies.

But since $\mathcal{M}°P$ is also a property (for elements of R), interpretation (63) could apply to $\mathcal{M}°P$, yielding (65):

(65)
$\mathcal{M}°P(r) \leftrightarrow \forall m\ \mathcal{M}°P(r(m))$

The universal holds in parent space $R:$ for every situation m in R, $r(m)$ has a counterpart in M with property P. (65) is further reducible by the Property Equivalence Theorem (62):

(66)
By (62): $\mathcal{M}°P(r(m)) \leftrightarrow P[F(r(m))]$
By (65): $\mathcal{M}°P(r) \leftrightarrow \forall m\ P(F(r(m)))$

The second half of this equivalence is precisely (59).

The general problem concerns the interpretation of $Q(r)$, and it may have no general solution in traditional semantic terms if, as suggested (e.g., (55), (57)), pragmatic considerations play a crucial role. There are special cases for which (63) applies, however, accounting (together with theorems like (62)) for the superficial observation of ambiguous universal interpretations.

2.4 Indefinites

In section 1.4 (Indefinite Interpretation (50)), the indefinite article was taken to be simply an explicit means of introducing new elements in spaces; combined with the standard properties of trigger-target config-urations, (50) accounted directly for basic scope properties of indefi-nites. The data examined in section 2.2 have made it apparent that the space elements include not only individuals but also roles, and further-more that a linguistic description may identify a function or its value.

Indefinite descriptions are similar in this respect to definite ones: they can set up roles as new elements and identify the role itself or its value in some space. Consider the following examples:

(67)
On the Supreme Court, *one judge* is under twenty.

(68)
In 1936, $\begin{Bmatrix} he \\ that\ judge \end{Bmatrix}$ was from California.

(69)
Now, *he*'s from Brooklyn.

(70)
He's generally Irish.

A favored interpretation of this mini-discourse is that the Supreme Court invariably includes a teenager among its members. On this kind of reading, (67) sets up a role r from Supreme Court instances to individuals under twenty.

A valid definite description of r in discourse following (67) would be "the Supreme Court judge who is under twenty." (68) and (69) involve spaces M_1 ("in 1936") and M_2 ("now"). The pronouns (*he*) or descriptions (*that judge*) identify the values of r in spaces M_1 and M_2, $r(M_1)$ and $r(M_2)$. This is a straightforward application of the principles in section 2.2. The pronoun *he* in (70) identifies role r.

Of course, another reading of (67) by itself involves no such role: it simply picks a member of the court who happens to have the property "under twenty." This is the "simple" interpretation provided by Indefinite Interpretation: a new object element is set up with the relevant properties.

Consider another example:

(71)
Oedipus believes he will marry one of his aunts.

Assume that (71) involves space R and space M ("Oedipus believes ____"). According to Indefinite Interpretation, *one of his aunts* may set up a new element in R, with the property "aunt of Oedipus" or a similar element in M. The first configuration would be compatible for example with Oedipus believing he will marry Xanthippe, but not knowing that Xanthippe is an aunt of his. The second would be compatible with

Oedipus believing he will marry Xanthippe and that she is an aunt of his, although in fact she may not be (or may not exist, etc.). Both readings are, in a sense, "specific"; but only the first entails existence for the speaker.

One of his aunts can also set up a role, in which case no actual values are specified by (71). (Other chunks of discourse may assign particular values in particular spaces, as in (68), (69).) If the role r is set up in M, Q standing for the property "he will marry . . . ," $Q(r)$ holds in M. This results in a nonspecific and "attributive" reading: Oedipus believes that whomever he marries will also have the property of being his aunt. Discourse reference to r is possible as usual, in effect specifying further properties of r: for example, after (71) ". . . ; he hopes *she* will keep him out of mischief; he would like *the aunt he marries* to be kind and understanding; etc." Furthermore, values of r can be specified: ". . . ; *last week* he thought it would be Xanthippe, but *now,* he's afraid it might be Antiope."

The combinations available to interpretation strategies for indefinites (which space hosts the new element, how the ID Principle applies, role vs. value interpretation) lead to various apparent and sometimes neglected or misinterpreted ambiguities. Consider (72):

(72)
Ursula wants to marry a millionaire.

Space-builder	*Ursula wants*	(space M, origin space R)
Property P	"Ursula marry ____"	
Role r		
or	*a millionaire*	(property Q)
element x		

Particular interpretations are favored by what follows. For example:

(73)
. . . , but she thinks he's a pauper.
(Likely interpretation for (72): x is set up in R such that $Q(x)$; counterpart x' is set up in M such that $P(x')$)

(74)
. . . , but he's really a con man.
(x is set up in M such that $P(x)$, $Q(x)$; x has a counterpart x_0 in R such that $\sim Q(x_0)$)

(75)
. . . ; she heard of this guy, but he doesn't exist.
(x in M, $P(x)$, $Q(x)$; no counterpart in R)

(76)
. . . , but she won't find one.
(Role r in M such that $P(r)$, $Q(r)$)

Now consider a discourse containing (72) followed by (77):

(72)
Ursula wants to marry a millionaire.

(77)
Sometimes $\begin{cases}\text{this millionaire}\\ \text{he}\end{cases}$ is a Brazilian yachtsman, and
sometimes he's a Russian polo-player.

First, assume a role interpretation for (72) (as in (76)); then in (77) *this millionaire* corresponds to the role r just set up. It may therefore identify that role itself or its value in space S_1 ("sometimes$_1$ ____") or space S_2 ("sometimes$_2$ ____"). In the first case, we understand (77) as specifying the role, that is, Ursula's desire. In other words, further conditions are imposed on the role—Ursula wants to find a husband who is a millionaire and a Brazilian yachtsman. In the second case, $r(S_1)$ and $r(S_2)$ are selected, that is, particular values of role r in certain spaces. To paraphrase crudely: "Sometimes she has a particular Brazilian yachtsman in mind, sometimes a particular Russian polo-player." In other words, r is instantiated.

Of course, this instantiation can itself be in R rather than M, giving "transparent" interpretations from M to R, as in (78):

(78)
Last week, the millionaire was (actually) an American gigolo; this week, *he*'s a clever megalomaniac.

Finally, (77) could encompass several nonrole readings: if, as in (73), x is set up in R, (77) would indicate that the man in question is indeed a millionaire for the speaker and undergoes various transformations (e.g., acquiring Russian nationality, taking up polo). If, as in (73), x is set up in M, (77) could indicate varying opinions about him (the millionaire) on Ursula's part. Of course, other interpretations could arise if other spaces are explicitly or implicitly brought in, such as the millionaire's pretenses or claims.

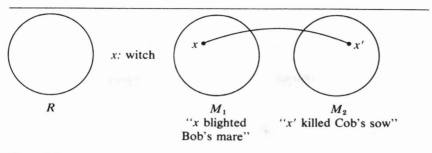

Figure 2.8

As a straightforward application of the properties of indefinites just considered, we can turn to cases of so-called intentional identity discussed by Geach (1972) and Ioup (1977). Geach's example is (79):

(79)
Hob thinks *a witch* has blighted Bob's mare, and Nob believes that *she* killed Cob's sow.

This sentence explicitly sets up two spaces: M_1 ("Hob thinks ____"), M_2 ("Nob believes ____"). *A witch* may set up an element in R with counterparts in M_1 and M_2 (in traditional terms: a specific, wide-scope, transparent interpretation). But it may also set up an element directly in M_1 with a counterpart in M_2, a situation depicted in figure 2.8. This interpretation would be appropriate, for example, if Hob believed in the existence of a person (say, Hilda), thought she had blighted the mare, and, perhaps incidentally, believed her to be a witch. (Compare: "Hob believes Bellerophon caught Pegasus" → "Hob believes Bellerophon caught a winged horse.")

Finally, *a witch* may set up role r in M_1 with a counterpart r' in M_2, such that "witch(r)" and "r blighted Bob's mare" and "r' killed Cob's sow" or "$r'(M_2)$ killed Cob's sow." This is the role describable as "the witch who blighted Bob's mare," and it can take particular values in some spaces. (Hob thinks the witch who blighted his mare *could* have been Hilda. According to Nob, it was Brunehilde or Hildegarde. And so on.) And, as usual, the descriptions need not carry from space to space: Hob's witch may be a nymph for Nob, a sylphid for Dob.

From the same perspective, consider Ioup's more complex example:

(80)
Everybody believes that a witch blighted the mare.

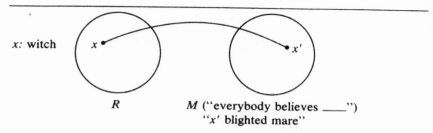

Figure 2.9

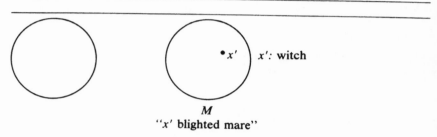

Figure 2.10

As Ioup notes, there is a reading of (80) on which *a witch,* in traditional terms, has wide scope over *every* (same witch for all) but narrow scope under *believe* (a "nonspecific" witch). This reading would elude representation in the familiar linear (or, for that matter, branching) transcription of predicate calculus.

In space terms, a number of basic configurations are available (see figures 2.9 through 2.13), depending on the interpretation strategy for indefinites and also on whether *every* is taken collectively or distributively (as in "Everybody carried a couch upstairs").

Figures 2.9 and 2.13 correspond to the traditional strongly specific (existential) readings with wide or narrow scope, often transcribed as follows:

(81)
For figure 2.9: $\exists x$ (x = witch) $\forall y$ (y believes x blighted mare)
For figure 2.13: $\forall y$ $\exists x$ (x = witch) (y believes x blighted mare)

The so-called nonspecific narrow-scope interpretation ($\approx \forall y$ (y believes ($\exists x$ (x = witch) (x blighted mare)))) would fit either figure 2.11 or figure 2.12. For figure 2.11, everyone has a culprit of his own in mind,

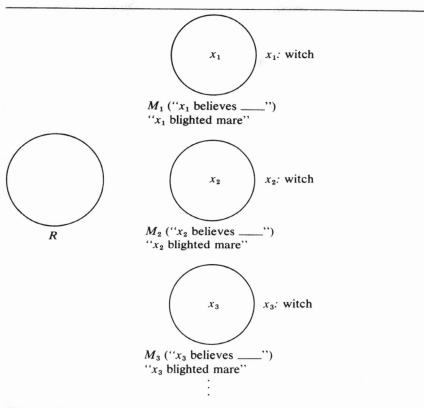

x_1: witch

M_1 ("x_1 believes ____")
"x_1 blighted mare"

x_2: witch

M_2 ("x_2 believes ____")
"x_2 blighted mare"

R

x_3: witch

M_3 ("x_3 believes ____")
"x_3 blighted mare"

Figure 2.11

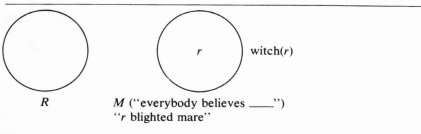

witch(r)

R M ("everybody believes ____")
                "r blighted mare"

Figure 2.12

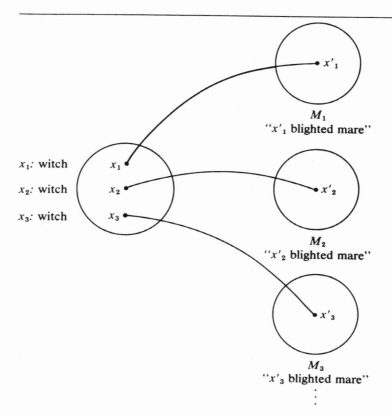

x_1: witch

x_2: witch

x_3: witch

M_1
"x'_1 blighted mare"

M_2
"x'_2 blighted mare"

M_3
"x'_3 blighted mare"

Figure 2.13

and they all happen to be believed to be witches. (In the case of figure 2.11, each person's real or imaginary witch is possibly different from all the others'.) For figure 2.12, there is only a common belief that there is a culprit, and whoever that is is a witch (an "attributive" reading, if you will). Figure 2.10 shows the very "simple" configuration corresponding to a unique witch in people's minds. In the case of figure 2.12, role r may take particular values in the individual belief spaces: Hob thinks it was Hilda; Nob is sure it was Brunehilde; the others have no idea who it was; etc. But notice that figure 2.12 is also compatible with a uniqueness interpretation in the sense that if r takes no particular values in the individual belief spaces, it is the "same" (i.e., undifferentiated) in all.

From the present perspective, then, standard logical transcription is inadequate not only in failing to reflect the reading corresponding to figure 2.10, but also in making no distinction between the fundamentally different readings depicted in figures 2.11 and 2.12. Perhaps even more importantly, it.sheds no light on the possibility in all these cases of subsequent reference in discourse, since the bound variables are locked into their scopal positions.

Technically, in the treatment of quantification suggested in section 5.3, only figures 2.9, 2.10, and 2.12 are set up as mental space configurations corresponding to (80). Figures 2.11 and 2.13 are expansion schemata that can fit figures 2.10 and 2.9, respectively.

2.5 Names and Roles

"You can call me Javitt," he said, "but only because it's not my real name. You don't believe I'd give you that, do you? And Maria's not Maria—it's just a sound she answers to, you understand me, like Jupiter."
"No."
"If you had a dog called Jupiter, you wouldn't believe he was really Jupiter, would you?"
"I've got a dog called Joe."
"The same applies," he said and drank his soup.

Graham Greene, *Under the Garden*

In the discussion of example (15), interpretation (31), I mentioned that proper names were being interpreted directly as values: *Rose* identifies an element x_1 in some space M. But I noted that (15) can also have a "nonrigid" interpretation, as in (32):

(15)
Rose is blonde, but George thinks *she*'s a redhead.
(George has Rose and Olive mixed up, and he is simply attributing the name *Rose* to the wrong person.)

The meaning of a definite description explicitly indicates a corresponding role (president, butcher, man at the bus stop, etc.). A proper name does not, unless specific pragmatic conventions apply (e.g., naming one's fifth son *Quintus,* calling all of one's successive watchdogs *Fido,* or calling the place where the president lives *the White House,* perhaps regardless of its color or location).

If there happen to be such conventions in force, then the corresponding proper names will behave like other roles. Suppose it is agreed to name the first child born in the twenty-first century *Amadeus,* and suppose the following sentence is uttered by a speaker in the year 2014:

(82)

I would have liked *Amadeus* to be *my brother*.

Call r the role "first child born in the twenty-first century," which *Amadeus* can stand for, and r' the role "my brother." (82) could mean that I wish my parents had had a child before anyone else in the twenty-first century, that is, that I wish the two roles r and r' had taken the same value. This wish is formulated without regard for the individuals who in reality occupy these roles: I may have no idea who Amadeus actually turned out to be; in fact, I may have no brother and there may have been no children born at all after 1999, and so no Amadeus.

Sentence (82) could also refer to the real person Amadeus, also known to his friends as *Max*. I wish Max had been my brother, that is, that he occupied role r'. In this case too, it does not matter whether I actually have a brother or not; nor does it matter that Max (Amadeus) was born first in the twenty-first century (although of course this *could* be one of the things I like about him).

Now suppose I have a brother, say, Luke; (82) could indicate that I wish Luke had been the twenty-first century's first-born. Under this interpretation, I need not know the real Amadeus. In fact, again there need not be one: perhaps Luke was the last human being ever born and his birthdate was December 31, 1999. In this case, I wish that the real value of r' had been the value of r. This does not entail the first interpretation, by the way, since I may wish that Luke had been Amadeus-the-first-born *instead* of being my brother.

Suppose next that I know both people, Max (alias Amadeus) and Luke (my brother); I can use (82) to say that I wish they had been *one and the same*. This reading does not entail that this unique individual would have been my brother or the twenty-first century's first-born (although it may implicate one or the other or both by counterfactual inheritance principles (see chapter 4)); I might for instance wish them to be one and the same and also my father (instead of my present father). The convention on Amadeus's name is irrelevant under this reading, but I must have a brother.

Finally, I may know both people, as before, and wish that Max had been Luke, but that Luke had been somebody else (other than Max and Luke). I leave it to the reader's imagination to decide what sense, if any, can be made of the last two interpretations.

The five interpretations just mentioned follow directly from the principles of role-value assignment in section 2.2. The corresponding space configurations are given in figures 2.14 through 2.18.

Consider another case that works in the same way: Suppose the neighbors always call their watchdog *Fido;* that is, *Fido* is the name they give to every dog they employ in the capacity of watchdog, one at a time. Given this particular convention, *Fido* corresponds not only to the dog who happens to be guarding the neighbors' house at the moment, but also to the role "neighbors' watchdog," role *r*. Accordingly, two interpretations are possible for (83):

(83)
I wish Fido would be more quiet.

Under the value interpretation, (83) is about the particular dog currently mounting guard. Under the role interpretation, (83) is about the successive watchdogs (and so presumably includes the present Fido as well). Depending on which interpretation is relevant, (83) can be followed by (84) or (85):

(84)
They should replace him as soon as possible.

(85)
Next time, they should buy him from a better breeder.

Examples like (82), (83) show that proper names can have role interpretations under suitable pragmatic conditions. In (15), under interpretation (32), the role is simply "being called *Rose.*" But even this simple role is only relevant in association with the name *Rose* under special, or at least unusual, pragmatic conditions of relevance. Notice, incidentally, that more complex roles, as for Amadeus or Fido, become prominent when the "simple" one, "being called *X,*" is explicitly linked to the complex one ("being the twenty-first century's first-born" or "being the neighbors' watchdog").

A very different question is the following: given some individual, the name of that individual, and a role the individual happens to fill, can the name stand for the role? A positive answer is practically taken for

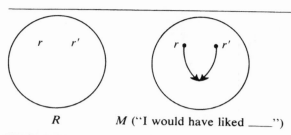

Figure 2.14

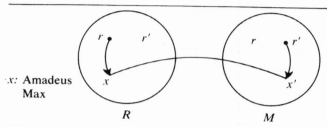

Figure 2.15

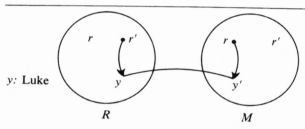

Figure 2.16

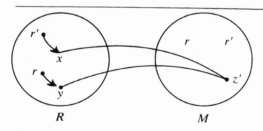

Figure 2.17

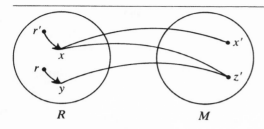

Figure 2.18

granted by Hofstadter, Clossman, and Meredith (HCM) (1982), on the basis of (86):

(86)
Ben thought Henry was George.
(Context: Ben rang up George's apartment. Henry happened to answer the phone, but Ben mistakenly thought it was George.)

HCM's reasoning is essentially as follows: (i) Ben did not think that Henry and George were (or had become) identical; (ii) What Ben did think was that "the person who answered the phone" was George— that is, that George, rather than Henry, was occupying the role "person who answered the phone." But since "the person who answered the phone" is *in fact* Henry, HCM take (86) to be essentially equivalent to "Ben thought that *the person who answered the phone* was George"; that is, they take *Henry* in (86) to stand for Henry's actual role, "the person who answered the phone." In fact, they explicitly say that "the name Henry is used as a shorthand" in such cases.

This view, however, raises a host of difficulties. First, it certainly cannot be that a role is *in general* identifiable by the name of the individual (or object, etc.) that happens to fill it. For instance, in 1983 "The president changes every four years" is not equivalent to "Reagan changes every four years." The same applies to all the similar examples reviewed in sections 2.2 and 2.3. In (82) the substitution of *Luke* for *my brother,* assuming of course that we know Luke is my brother, removes the first two (and most probable) interpretations (cf. "I would have liked Amadeus to be Luke"), since neither depends on my actually having a brother. Probably even worse for the "shorthand" thesis is the failure it suffers in context (86) itself. Suppose that Ben is calling up people to hand out free trips to Florida. Then (87) is true:

(87)

Ben thought that *the person who answered the phone* would go to Florida.

(I assume for convenience that Ben also thinks all answerers will accept his offer.) In this context, given that Ben mistakenly takes George to have answered, (88) is also true:

(88)

Ben thought that *George* would go to Florida.

Now, is (89) also true?

(89)

Ben thought that *Henry* would go to Florida.

Probably yes, under a "transparent" interpretation that could be emphasized as in (90):

(90)

Ben thought that Henry would go to Florida, except he didn't know it was Henry. (. . . In fact, he thought it was George.)

(89) and (90) support the "name-for-role" shorthand thesis. Now suppose that at the time Ben made his phone call he also believed that George was a student of Sanskrit. Then (91) and (92) are also true:

(91)

Ben thought that *George* studied Sanskrit.

(92)

Ben thought that *the person who answered the phone* studied Sanskrit.

Given that (92) is true and that, actually, the person who answered the phone was Henry, if we took role-name substitution literally, (93) would also be true, which it is not:

(93)

Ben thought that *Henry* studied Sanskrit.

Readers at this point might find the criticism unfair or misconceived. Surely there is a crucial difference between (87) and (92): in (87), the role "phone answerer" is prominent (in traditional terms, the reading is "attributive": Ben thinks that "whoever answers the phone" will go to Florida); but in (92), the role is incidental and has no bearing on being a Sanskrit student (in traditional terms, the reading is "referential," al-

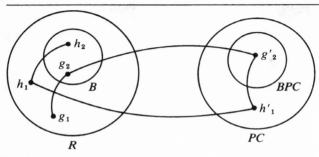

PC ("during the phone call _____")
B, BPC ("Ben thinks _____")
name *George:* g_1, g_2, g'_2
name *Henry:* h_1, h_2, h'_1

Figure 2.19

beit opaquely since the description does not actually refer to George). In fact, suppose the topic "study of Sanskrit" had actually come up during the phone conversation instead of Florida and that Ben had said something like, "Since you know Sanskrit, . . ."; then Henry could report, "Ben thought I studied Sanskrit," and one could say (93) truthfully. Compare (94):

(94)
Ben thought Henry studied Sanskrit, because he thought Henry was George.

The upshot of these observations is straightforward: confusion of identities and properties takes place *during the phone call.* All the relevant examples (86), (89), (94) could be prefaced grammatically with an adverbial like *during the phone call,* which is a space-builder. They are relative to this particular space, which we may call *PC.* The situation is diagrammed in figure 2.19. Henry and George are not linked in *R* and *B,* but their counterparts in *PC* are linked and occupy corresponding roles (*r:* "phone answerer"). *BPC* is itself the counterpart space of *B,* in *PC:* optimization (see chapters 3 and 5) operates to make such counterpart spaces as structurally similar as possible (i.e., without contradiction; see section 3.2), so that "George" in *B* will have the same properties as "George" in *BPC.*

 What the speaker "says" in using (86) is that "h'_1 in *PC* has the counterpart g'_2 in *BPC,* where h'_1 is the counterpart in *PC* of h_1 in *R,* and g'_2 is the counterpart in *BPC* of g_2 in *B,* and g_1 in *R.*" The ID

Principle allows h'_1 and g'_2 to be identified by the names of their counterparts h_1 and g_1. The relevant spaces are indicated by space-builders; schematically, the linguistic form will be as follows:

(95)

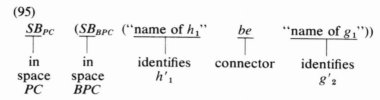

Given SB_{PC} = *during the phone call*, SB_{BPC} = *Ben thought*, "name of h_1" = *Henry*, and "name of g_1" = *George*, (95) comes out as (96):

(96)
During the phone call, Ben thought that Henry was George.

If previous discourse is already about the phone call (i.e., "within *PC*"), then SB_{PC} need not appear (or reappear) and the result is the simple (86).

In the same way, given the property F = "go to Florida," (89) expresses "$F(g'_2)$" (in *BPC*). Linguistically:

(97)

$$\underline{SB_{PC}} \quad (\underline{SB_{BPC}} \quad (\text{``\underline{name of $h_1$}''} \quad \text{``\underline{have property F}''}))$$

in	in	identifies	property F
space	space	g'_2 by way of	
PC	*BPC*	its counter-	
		part h'_1 in *PC*	

This yields (98):

(98)
During the phone call, Ben thought Henry would go to Florida.

Or, if *PC* is already set up, (89) without the explicit SB_{PC}.

In (97), the ID Principle operates recursively: identification goes from h_1 to h'_1 and then to g'_2. Notice that g'_2 is *not* a counterpart in *BPC* of h_2 in *B*: there is no confusion in Ben's mind about Henry and George, only error about which is which *during* the phone call.

Figure 2.19 highlights another feature of space constructions and correspondences: spaces themselves count as "elements" of parent spaces and accordingly may have counterparts and be referred to. The ID Principle applies as usual to such configurations, so that corresponding spaces such as *B* and *BPC* have the same linguistic space-builder *Ben thinks*.

Also, mini-spaces like "the phone call" will typically be associated with frames that fit them, with roles like "caller," "answerer," etc. If the roles are identifying properties for the elements, elements occupying the same role will tend to be linked, *within* the mini-space (e.g., h'_1 and g'_2). This is not a necessity, however, as a little stretching of the imagination can show:

(99)
During the phone call, Sue thought Henry was George although she didn't realize he was answering.

(Context: The phone has a loudspeaker; Sue heard Henry's voice, thought it was George, and thought that George was actually in the room.)

Consider a slightly different example involving neighbors and Dracula, as in section 2.1.2: Luke's neighbor is actually Dracula, but Luke mistakenly thinks it's Frank Sinatra. Luke also thinks, correctly this time, that this neighbor is noisy. Furthermore, Luke has read somewhere that Sinatra was married to Ava Gardner. The following could be said:

(100)
Luke thinks Sinatra is noisy.

(101)
Luke thinks Dracula is noisy.

(102)
Luke thinks Sinatra is married to Ava Gardner.

(103)
Luke is bothered by all that noise next door, but he doesn't complain because he thinks Dracula is Sinatra.

But (104) and (105) sound inappropriate:

(104)
Luke thinks Dracula is married to Ava Gardner.

(105)
Luke thinks that Dracula lives in Transylvania and that he is Frank Sinatra.

This case is much like the phone call example: the link between Dracula and Sinatra-in-Luke's-beliefs holds only with respect to a particular space—essentially "what goes on in, or what has to do with, the apartment next door"—and (104), (105) apparently hold outside of that space, so that substitution of Sinatra for Dracula is inapplicable. However, as in the Sanskrit example (93), (104) can be relativized to the mini-space, which makes it acceptable. For instance, one could say to Dracula in regard to his neighbor Luke:

(106)
Luke thinks that you're Frank Sinatra, and that you're married to Ava Gardner.

Or again, if Dracula asked, "Why is Luke so eager to meet my wife?", I might answer:

(107)
Because he thinks you're married to Ava Gardner.

One could also say:

(108)
Luke is bothered by all that noise next door, but he doesn't complain because he thinks Dracula is married to Ava Gardner.

The space configuration for this, given in figure 2.20, is formally parallel to the one in figure 2.19.

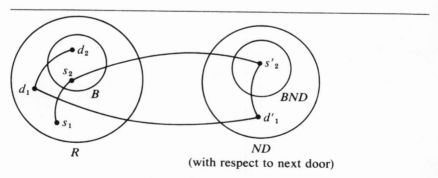

R

ND
(with respect to next door)

B, BND ("Luke thinks _____")
name *Dracula*: d_1, d_2, d'_1
name *Sinatra*: s_1, s_2, s'_1

Figure 2.20

There is a striking analogy between the way we talk about the preceding situations (phone call, Dracula)—that is, the way we set up subspaces—and the way we talk about "theatrical" situations (plays, movies, make-believe, masked balls, etc.). Such situations have already been mentioned several times in this chapter and in chapter 1, but the analysis has been simplified in one respect: we have assumed only two spaces, "the speaker's reality" (origin R) and "the play" (target or image space). A complete theatrical situation is liable to involve at least four spaces:[5]

(109)
a. The origin R, which includes the actors in their "real," everyday life and also, if the play is nonfictional, some of the real people that the play is meant to represent.
b. The "play," for example as written by the author (that is, with characters, events, dialogues, etc., unspecified as to which actors will play the parts); call this space Pl.
c. The "performance," Pe, as viewed by the audience, with real people on stage who "are" the characters of Pl and say and do what those characters say and do (in Pl).
d. The "real" situation on stage (that is, what the actors as persons (of R) are doing): this is a subspace of R, T.

Suppose, by way of illustration, that Golda Meir and Ingrid Bergman are still alive and that Ingrid Bergman is playing the part of Golda Meir in a biographical play. The corresponding space configuration appears in figure 2.21.

All the connectors are image ("identity") connectors except for F_d, which links Pe to T and which I call a *drama connector*.

Call P the property "to hug a baby" and S the property "to forget three lines," and consider the following utterances, with their associated interpretations:

(110)
In the play, Golda Meir hugs a baby.
$P(b)/Pl$

(111)
In tonight's performance, Golda Meir hugged a baby.
$P(c)/Pe$
or
$P(d)/T$ by application of the ID Principle from Pe to T

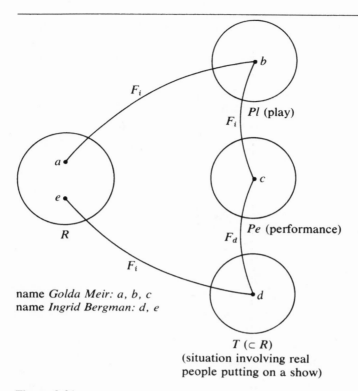

name *Golda Meir: a, b, c*
name *Ingrid Bergman: d, e*

Figure 2.21

(112)
In tonight's performance, Ingrid Bergman hugged a baby.
P(d)/T
or
P(c)/Pe   by application of the ID Principle from *T* to *Pe*

(113)
In tonight's performance, Golda Meir forgot three lines.
S(d)/T   by application of the ID Principle from *Pe* to *T*

These examples show that the ID Principle operates bidirectionally on *Pe* and *T*.

Assume further, for the moment, that a different actress plays the part of Golda Meir every night. Such a context highlights the lack of connection from *T* to *Pl: b* in *Pl* cannot be identified by a description of *d* in *T;* (114) is not equivalent to (115):

(114)
In Richard Attenborough's play, Golda Meir is very emotional.
$E(b)/Pl$ (E = "very emotional")

(115)
In Richard Attenborough's play, Ingrid Bergman is very emotional.
$E(d)/T$
or
$E(c)/Pe$

This would suggest that the link between Pl and Pe is unidirectional, but in fact one can say, when watching the performance:

(116)
In the play, the high-strung, clumsy woman is (really) peaceful and comfortable.

where "the high-strung, clumsy woman" is a description of c, valid in Pe, and identifies b in Pl. So we must conclude that although F_d ($T \rightarrow Pe$) and F_i ($Pe \rightarrow Pl$) are both independently bidirectional, there is no composite connector $F_i{}^\circ F_d$ from T to Pl.

Call L the relation "look like":

(117)
In the play, Ingrid Bergman looks like Golda Meir.
(Interpretation: $L(d, a)$)

Because d and c are linked, the ID Principle can apply, and (118) can have the same interpretation as (117):

(118)
In the play, Golda Meir looks like Golda Meir.
(Interpretation: $L(d, a)$)

But because there is no link between b (in Pl) and d (in T) or e (in R), there is no link between a on the one hand and e or d on the other: a description of e will not identify a, and so (119) does not have the same interpretation as (117) or (118):

(119)
In the play, Ingrid Bergman looks like Ingrid Bergman.

In such cases, linguistic reflexivization works on identical triggers (rather than targets), so that, for the interpretation $L(d, a)$ above, we get (120) (cf. (118)) but not (121) (cf. the impossibility of (119)):

(120)

In the play, Golda Meir looks like herself.

(121)

%In the play, Ingrid Bergman looks like herself.[6]

The lack of connection between a and e is also the reason why we cannot report (122) as (123),

(122)

Golda Meir went to Peru last week.

(123)

Ingrid Bergman went to Peru last week.

but we can report (124) as (125),

(124)

Ingrid Bergman went to Peru last week.

(125)

Golda Meir went to Peru last week.

because *Golda Meir* is the name of c, e's counterpart in *Pe*. Of course, (125) is then understood as "the actress who plays the part of Golda Meir"; compare "Golda Meir is in Peru this week, so we'll have to postpone rehearsals."

All this is very much like the phone call in which Henry and George get mixed up: Ingrid Bergman is not Golda Meir in general, but only with respect to the subspace *Pe,* just as Henry was not George in general, but only with respect to the subspace *PC* (*to be* meaning here "to have as a counterpart").

Suppose now that in "real life," the prime minister Golda Meir once met the actress Ingrid Bergman, and that the play reflects this real-life event, with perhaps some third person playing the part of Ingrid Bergman. The configuration becomes the one shown in figure 2.22. We wish to express the following situation:

(126)

c meets v

e (Ingrid Bergman in R) is linked to c via d and can be a trigger for its identification. e is also linked to v via w, so e can be a trigger for the identification of both c and v. Identity of triggers will allow reflexivization to yield (127):

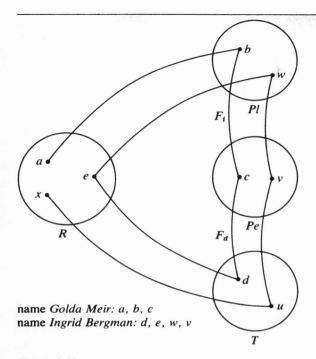

name *Golda Meir: a, b, c*
name *Ingrid Bergman: d, e, w, v*

Figure 2.22

(127)
In the play, Ingrid Bergman meets herself.

But *c* is also linked to *a* via *b*, so that (126) can surface as (128):

(128)
In the play, Golda Meir meets Ingrid Bergman.

Furthermore, *c* itself can be the trigger, because it is linked to *v* via *d*, *e*, *w*. Taking *c* (description in *Pe:* "Golda Meir") as a common trigger will again induce reflexivization:

(129)
?In the play, Golda Meir meets herself.
(Interpretation: In the part of Golda Meir, the actress playing that part meets the person playing the part of that actress as she is in reality(!).)

Notice that the link here between c and v does not involve $F_i°F_d$. Still, it is a very long link (four spaces), a probable reason for the relatively poor acceptability of (129) (under the circumstances).

If different triggers with the same name, d and w, are chosen for c and v, respectively, in (126), the result is a nonreflexivized version of (127):

(130)
In the play, Ingrid Bergman meets Ingrid Bergman.

Not so good is (131), with c itself as a trigger for v, via d, e, w:

(131)
*?In the play, Golda Meir meets Golda Meir.

This is presumably because of the length of the path from c to v, plus the fact that reflexivization should then apply to the identical triggers.

Finally, suppose that one actress, Mia Farrow, plays the part of Golda as a young girl, and another, Ingrid Bergman, plays the part of Golda as a woman. It would seem that a single element in Pl and Pe (Golda) has two counterparts in T (Mia and Ingrid). But again, as in the phone call and Dracula examples, Pe subdivides into two spaces ("Golda's youth," "Golda's womanhood"), with the resulting configuration shown in figure 2.23. So if $P(c')$ is the case (young Golda hugged a baby), either b or d' can be a target, yielding (132) or (133):

(132)
In the play, Golda Meir hugged a baby.

(133)
In the play, Mia Farrow hugged a baby.

But there is no path from d to c' (no composite function $F_d°F_i$); d cannot be a target, and (134) is inappropriate:

(134)
In the play, Ingrid Bergman hugged a baby.

J. McCawley (personal communication) points out another nice contrast in this context (Mia Farrow plays Golda Meir in act 1, Ingrid Bergman plays her in act 2):

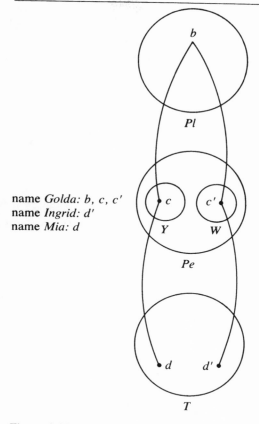

name *Golda: b, c, c'*
name *Ingrid: d'*
name *Mia: d*

Figure 2.23

(135)

In act 2, $\begin{Bmatrix} \text{Meir} \\ \text{?*Bergman} \end{Bmatrix}$ argues with the same politician she argued with in act 1.

d' is not a good antecedent for *b* or *c*. (See McCawley (1978) for similar examples.)

Before I conclude this chapter, it is appropriate and useful to mention the connection between spaces in the linguistic sense and the notion of frame in the sociological sense of Erving Goffman's frame analysis (Goffman (1974)).[7] Actions and situations are framed in various "realms of being," such as make-believe, dreams, ritual, contests, rehearsals, dramas, and of course "everyday life." The same objective events could take on different meanings depending on frame, which allows for fabrications, deceptions, jokes, theater, and much more. One may differentiate frames in speech by constructing corresponding spaces: "They are *pretending* to fight," "They are not *really* fighting," "We made *him believe* that Joe was a banker and Mary a duchess" (con game). And of course, by choosing descriptions of an object or event that are good in one frame but not in another, one may select a certain frame, or switch frames, or even mix them. A frequent technique of reporting, or political speech, consists in using the ID Principle to give in one frame for some event or action a description satisfied in another frame. For example, the French Communist party newspaper, *l'Humanité*, writes of a political opponent, "He strongly criticized the Communist party for *helping Vietnam in its reconstruction efforts and fight for progress,*" (*l'Humanité*, November 16, 1979, cited in Darde (1984)). What the opponent had said was that the party was "supporting executioners and invaders."

Goffman (1974) provides a superb and very detailed study of framing, being "out-of-frame," breaking frame, etc. Among other things, Goffman focuses on the particular case of the theatrical frame. As mentioned before (note 5), this leads to distinctions analogous to those made in terms of mental spaces. For example, Goffman illustrates role and frame ambiguities with respect to the theatrical audience:

The difference between theatergoer and onlooker is nicely illustrated in regard to laughter, demonstrating again the need to be very clear about the syntax of response. Laughter by members of the audience in sympathetic response to an effective bit of buffoonery by a staged character is clearly distinguished on both sides of the stage line from audience laughter that can greet an actor who flubs, trips, or breaks up in some unscripted way. In the first case the individual laughs as onlooker, in the second as theatergoer. . . . And, of course, both kinds of laughter are radically different from the kind enacted by a character; *that* kind of laughter *is* heard officially by the other characters. (1974, sec. 5.2)

Some of the examples combine several levels of frame, showing the looping and symmetry possibilities outlined here for corresponding spaces (sections 1.2, 2.1). In the following situation, cited in Goffman (1974, sec. 4.5), reality becomes a fabrication for a movie:

London—Actress Vanessa Redgrave, 30, stunned a packed theatre here by ripping away the top of her stage costume and dancing around half naked.

Movie cameras rolled, recording Miss Redgrave's dance and the embarrassed reactions of the richly dressed audience—all paid film extras who had no previous hint of what would happen.

It happened Wednesday as one scene of her new picture "Isadora."

As Goffman adds, "The movie *Isadora* is a 'real' movie, not a faked one, except for one bit in it which is not genuine cinema, having been produced by a real set producing not scripted response but the real thing." Notice, with regard to this example, that although the stripping and dancing will ultimately be in the movie (that is, they will be actions of Isadora's), it would be quite awkward in the above description, if not unintelligible, to use the name *Isadora* instead of *Vanessa* (or *Miss Redgrave*). The reason is of course frame-mixing: it is not Isadora but Miss Redgrave who stuns the audience, and the item is newsworthy in one frame but not in the other.

All of which suggests that, among other things, mental spaces provide a linguistic and cognitive means for setting up and distinguishing frames.

Chapter 3
Presuppositions: Floating, Transfer, and Projection Strategies

3.1 Preliminaries

The vast literature on presuppositional phenomena periodically raises the following general questions: Is there a unified theoretical notion of presupposition? Can it be given a semantic or a pragmatic characterization? What grammatical constructions are associated with (or give rise to) presupposition? What is the effect of negation on presuppositions? How can one determine the presuppositions of complex sentences given the presuppositions of simple ones? Are "virtual" presuppositions cancellable by "stronger" implicatures and implications? What is the communicative purpose of presuppositions?

In the present chapter I will by no means deal with all these questions, but I will recast some of them and suggest somewhat straightforward answers within a "mental space" framework. As in many linguistically oriented studies, the focus will be on the so-called projection problem, but I will suggest that the very formulation of this problem is essentially misconceived.

Before coming to grips with the actual phenomena, I will try to avoid possible misunderstandings by circumscribing explicitly the range of facts dealt with in the present context.

There is no agreement among presuppositionists about any precise definitional characterization of presupposition, and indeed such characterizations, when proposed, have so far proven inadequate (see the examples below). Surprisingly, however, there is a widespread consensus about which grammatical constructions are relevant in regard to the projection problem: namely, definite descriptions, factives, clefts, aspectuals, adverbial iteratives, and perhaps quantifiers such as *only* (in other words, essentially the list provided by Keenan (1971)).

In spite of its tenuous theoretical motivation, I will follow this particular tradition, which assumes, for example, that "the person who won," "It was Mary who won," "We regret that somebody won," "Somebody won again," "Somebody stopped winning," etc., all presuppose "somebody won." This is a grammatical characterization of presupposition; of course, these grammatical presuppositions do tend to be preserved under negation (the semantic characterization) and will often in practice correspond to given (vs. new) information (the pragmatic characterization). Yet a nongrammatical definition eludes us: the difficulties with the negation test are notorious, and pragmatic characterizations in the usual sense seem out of reach.[1]

Given the pragmatic orientation of this study, the last point possibly requires some justification. Consider first the following recent valiant attempt to define utterance presupposition (Soames (1982, 486)):

An utterance U presupposes P (at t) iff one can reasonably infer from U that the speaker S accepts P and regards it as uncontroversial, either because
a. S thinks that it is already part of the conversational context at t, or because
b. S thinks that the audience is prepared to add it, without objection, to the context against which U is evaluated.

(The conversational context at t = the set of propositions P such that at t speakers and hearers
a. believe or assume P; and
b. recognize this about each other.)

The problem with such definitions is that they make no real distinction between presuppositions and uncontroversial assertions. Consider the following dialogues:

(1)
A: Why is that fellow (C) looking so glum?
   (A has never seen or heard of C before)
B: a. Oh, *his wife* just left him.
   b. Oh, *he's married* and his wife just left him.
   a'. He just *quit smoking*.
   b'. He *used to smoke* and he just quit.
   a''. *It's somebody else that* got the job he wanted.
   b''. *Somebody got the job he wanted* and it wasn't him.
   a'''. He just realized *he had no money left*.
   b'''. *He has no money left* (and he just realized it).

The (a) utterances in B's answer contain grammatically paradigmatic cases of presupposition (definite description, aspectual, cleft, factive), but in each case the equivalent (b) answer presents the same information in asserted rather than presupposed form. In every case this information is new and relevant, and there is no reason to think that A would take it for granted. One would therefore have to say that in giving the (a) answers, the speaker "thinks the audience is prepared to add [P] without objection to the context against which U is being evaluated," but not in giving the (b) answers. However, since there is no independent characterization of "without objection," and since assertions are themselves usually added "without objection" to the conversational context, the definition is quite circular.

The proposed condition does not work in the other direction either, since assertions may well be part of the overt, established conversational context:

(2)
A: Bill's very strong, as you know.
B: Yes, you're right, *Bill's very strong.*
   (Agreeing)

A: *Two and two are four.*
   Hence, an even number can be the sum of two even numbers.
   (Recalling a premise)

A: I love you, I love you, I love you, . . .
   (Repetition for emphasis)

A: *You're my friend* and you betrayed me!
   (Drawing attention to old information for implicature)

The above examples do not just show the inadequacy of Soames's particular definition: they are major obstacles for any distinction between assertion and presupposition in standard pragmatic terms.

The treatment of presuppositions I consider here will actually give rise to a theory-internal semantic characterization of presupposition, and I will make some attempt to explain where the popular, but mistaken, view of presupposition as old or uncontroversial information comes from and what is in some ways not so wrong about it.

There are three main approaches to the projection problem, that is, the problem of determining the presuppositions of complex sentences on the basis of the presuppositions of simple ones:

The *combinatorial approach* seeks to provide explicit algorithms for computing presuppositions of complex constructions on the basis of the simple clause presuppositions and projection properties of the higher verbs, connectives, adverbs, etc., of the complex construction. Well-known instances are found in Langendoen and Savin (1971), Karttunen (1973), and Karttunen and Peters (1979).

The *cancellation approach,* best known through Gazdar's work (1979), defines potential presuppositions grammatically and allows them to emerge as actual presuppositions if they are not superseded by an incompatible implicature or implication.

Procedural approaches, as in Morgan (1973), Schiebe (1975), and Dinsmore (1979), view discourse as "creating" worlds to which presuppositions attach. Here the projection problem amounts to determining which presuppositions are transferred to the "actual" world.

The mental space approach outlined here is essentially procedural; from this perspective, the combinatorial or cancellation methods, although sometimes descriptively adequate, are at best artifacts of a misconceived conceptualization of presuppositional phenomena. The main feature to be emphasized about the analysis is that it sets up hardly any principles meant to deal specifically with presupposition: the strategic principles invoked are quite general.

In the sections to follow, I will discuss presuppositions in the space format, give an account of a wide array of "difficult" and controversial presupposition cases, compare the mental space approach with the usual approaches, and consider further presupposition phenomena.

3.2 Presuppositions and Spaces

3.2.1 Rules and Strategies

Consider the prototype case often mentioned in previous chapters, in which an utterance consists of a space-builder, SB_M, and a "propositional" part, *Prop,* establishing relations between elements in the space:

(3)

$$SB_M \qquad\qquad\qquad Prop$$

$$
\left\{
\begin{array}{l}
\text{In the picture} \\
\text{Luke believes} \\
\text{If Boris comes} \\
\text{Maybe}
\end{array}
\right\}
\left\{
\begin{array}{l}
\text{Maxine has blue eyes} \\
\text{Olga will come} \\
\text{Max stopped smoking}
\end{array}
\right\}
$$

We divide *Prop* into an asserted part *A* and a presupposed one *P* in the customary way, and on *grammatical* grounds (recall section 3.1): for example, {Max doesn't smoke now} = *A*, {Max smoked before} = *P*.[2] *A* and *P* express that certain relations hold between certain elements in spaces. We say that *Q* (= *Q'*(*a*, *b*, *c*, ...)) is satisfied in space *H* if the (possibly complex) relation *Q'* holds of the counterparts of *a*, *b*, *c*, ..., in space *H*.

Notation

Q/H   *Q* is satisfied in space *H*

~Q/H   *Q* is not satisfied in space *H*

We say that *Q* is *determined* in space *H* if it is either satisfied or not satisfied, even though the actual value may not be accessible at that point in the discourse, as in "Max knows whether Olga came": *Olga came* is determined with respect to Max's beliefs but not established as satisfied or not satisfied.

Notation

Q!H   *Q* is determined in *H*

Q is *undetermined* in *H* if it is not determined in *H*, that is, if *Q* and ~*Q* are both possible with respect to *H*.

Notation

Q?H   *Q* is undetermined in *H*

Given an utterance structure like (3), and calling *R* the parent space for *M*, the following rules operate:

Rules

R_1:   *A/M*   ("asserted part *A* is satisfied in space *M*")

R_2:   *P/M*   ("presupposed part *P* is satisfied in space *M*")

R_3:   *P/R*   ("presupposed part *P* is satisfied in parent space *R*)

(optional)   (R_3 applies *only* as part of strategy SP_2)

Definition

D_1:   If *Q/M* is established at discourse time *t*, then the accessible consequences of *Q* are *explicit presuppositions in M* after *t*.[3]

Strategic Principles

SP_1:   Avoid contradiction within a space (e.g., avoid ~*Q/H* and *Q/H*).

SP_2:   Structure space M and its parent space R as closely as
          possible with respect to background assumptions and *implicit*
          presuppositions.[4]
(SP_1 has precedence over SP_2)

Obvious Corollaries
C_1:   If P/R, then $P/R,M$.   (by R_2)
C_2:   If $\sim P/R$, then do not apply R_3.   (by SP_1)
C_3:   If $P!R$, then apply R_3.   (by SP_2)
          (i.e., assume P satisfied in R to maximize *implicit*
          presupposition correlation)
C_4:   If $P?R$, then do not apply R_3.   (by SP_1)
          (because $P?R$ implies the possibility of $\sim P$ in R and
          so is incompatible with P)

Informally, D_1 defines an *explicit* presupposition in M at discourse
time t as background information established *before t*. An *implicit* presupposition (at t in M) is a presupposition set up in M at t by virtue of
some grammatical construction, and not established in M independently before t. For example, in a discourse that starts at t with *Harry*
believes my car is red (SB_M = *Harry believes* ____), "I have a car" is an
implicit presupposition in M at t; in a discourse that starts at t_0 with
Harry believes I have a car, "I have a car" is an explicit presupposition
in M at t later than t_0.

Notice that implicit presuppositions established in M at t_i are explicit
presuppositions in M at any time after t_i.

The corollaries are included only to abbreviate later discussion of
examples. C_1 is notational: $P/R,M$ means P/R and P/M. P/M holds in
virtue of R_2. C_2 follows from SP_1 (noncontradiction): applying R_3 would
yield P/R (by definition), contradicting $\sim P/R$. C_3 follows from the optimization strategy SP_2: $P!R$ means that either P or $\sim P$ holds in R;
since P holds in M (as an implicit presupposition), we assume that P,
rather than $\sim P$, holds in R. Conversely (corollary C_4), if $P?R$, then
what holds in R is $\diamond \sim P$ (the possibility that $\sim P$) which would be
contradicted by assuming P/R.

The functioning of this set of rules is illustrated in the next section
(3.2.2).

Notice the general character of these principles: R_1 and R_2 simply
follow from the general definition of space-builders, namely, "*Prop*
holds in space M"; and D_1 corresponds to the "intuition" that new
information once expressed becomes old information. SP_1 (noncontra-

diction) is demoted from its usual lawlike status to a discourse strategy, since contradictory spaces cannot be ruled out (contradictory beliefs, desires, etc., may be reported). SP_2 is an important general strategy for "filling in" spaces: in fiction, fantasy, reporting desires, beliefs, and so on, we typically take the world to be as we know it unless explicitly specified otherwise. SP_2 plays an important role in the analysis of counterfactuals, which requires the loose expression "as closely as possible" to be given precise and explicit content (see chapter 4).

The only rule, then, that specifically and technically applies to presuppositions is the optional rule R_3, allowing grammatical presuppositions (as opposed to assertions) to be attached to more than one space by a single utterance.[5] R_3 is furthermore taken to apply recursively: that is, if R itself has a parent space R', then P/R' *optionally,* subject to D_1, SP_1, SP_2.

The standard projection problem—whether a complex sentence inherits the presuppositions of its simple parts—amounts in procedural terms to whether a presupposition satisfied in M can or must be satisfied in parent space R. As we shall see, other complex presuppositions of complex sentences superficially reflect the satisfaction of the presuppositions with respect to various spaces.

3.2.2 Test Cases

3.2.2.1 Maybe.   *Maybe* is a space-builder that sets up a possibility space M within R.

First context: The speaker A knows Max and is assumed to know whether he has any sons or whether he has been a smoker. A says:

(4)

a. Maybe *Max's son* is giving him trouble.
   (Presupposition P: "Max has a son")

   or

b. Maybe Max just *stopped* smoking.
   (P: "Max smoked before")

Interpretation: A knows whether P, hence $P!R$. By C_3, R_3 applies, hence P/R. By C_1, $P/R,M$. P holds in R and M: the presupposition is "inherited."

Second context: A and B see a man on the street looking glum. A says:

(5)

a. Maybe *that guy's son* is giving him trouble.
   (*P:* "that guy has a son")

   or

b. Maybe that guy just *stopped* smoking.
   (*P:* "that guy used to smoke")

Interpretation: This time, it is assumed that A has no prior information about "that guy," so $P?R$. By C_4, R_3 does not apply, hence $P?R$, P/M. P holds in M, but not in R: the presupposition is not "inherited." Indeed, (5a,b) do not imply that "that guy" has a son or used to smoke.

   Third context: Speaker A says to hearer B:

(6)

Maybe *Beethoven's son* gave him a lot of trouble.

This time, B happens to have no clue about whether A has prior information about Beethoven, in particular with respect to Beethoven having children or not. That is, B can assume neither $P!R$ nor $P?R$. B is free in principle to apply R_3 or not, choosing either the inherited or noninherited interpretation. However, all other things being equal, B will tend to apply SP_2 (optimization), which nothing blocks, deriving P/R (inherited presupposition).

3.2.2.2 If S then _____. *If S* is a space-builder that sets up a space M in which S is satisfied.

   First context: As for (4) (the speaker A knows Max and is assumed to know whether he has any children). A says:

(7)

If *Max's children* are away, he's all alone.
(*P:* "Max has children")

Interpretation: As in (4): $P!R$ gives $P/R,M$ by C_1 and C_3. P is "inherited."

   Second context: As for (5) (speaker A has no prior information about "that guy"; that is, $P?R$). A says:

(8)

If *that guy's children* are away, he's all alone.
(*P:* "that guy has children")

Interpretation: As for (5), P/M by R_2 and $P?R$ by C_4. P is not inherited; speaker A may know nothing about "that guy" and only set up P as part of the hypothesis.

Finally, as for *maybe*, if neither $P!R$ nor $P?R$ can be presumed, there is a choice of two interpretations, with a "preference" for inherited presupposition by SP_2.

Needless to say, the choice of *Max* and *that guy* in such examples only serves to facilitate the relevant pragmatic strategy, and different assumptions could be made about the speaker's knowledge in each case. Incidentally, combinatorial and cancellation approaches to projection both wrongly predict inheritance for all the above *maybe* and *if* cases.

Now consider a classical example:

(9)
If <u>Max has children</u>, <u>Max's children</u> are American.

       | |

     S P: "Max has children"

Since S is satisfied in space M, by D_1, P is an explicit presupposition in M (P is an obvious consequence of S ($P = S$), and S is established in M before P). Therefore, SP_2 does not apply to P, and so R_3 (which is part of SP_2) does not apply: we have only P/M, and the presupposition is not "inherited."

In fact, typically (but not always), *if* + $S_{present\ tense}$ is used if S is undetermined in R: $S?R$. The application of R_3 is then also independently prevented by C_4. However, the fact that the optional rule cannot apply does not in itself prevent the presupposition P from being satisfied in both spaces; that is, there are circumstances in which (9) can be uttered and P presupposed. Suppose for example that (9) fits into a discourse like (10):

(10)
Parents of American children get financial aid. Max, as you know, has children. And if Max has children, Max's children are American, because he himself is from California. Therefore, he is entitled to financial aid.

In this case, by D_1, "Max has children" happens to be an explicit presupposition in R at the time when (9) is uttered. Thus, we have P/R

and also *P/M: P*, the presupposition, is satisfied both in the parent space and in the daughter space "if *S*, _____."

There is a very general strategy for filling in spaces, to which we shall return in some detail in chapter 4 and of which SP_2 is only a subpart. Expressed informally and somewhat approximately, it is as follows:

(11)
Space Optimization
When a daughter space *M* is set up within a parent space *R*,
structure *M* implicitly so as to maximize similarity with *R*. In
particular, in the absence of *explicit* contrary stipulation, assume that
a. elements in *R* have counterparts in *M*,
b. the relations holding in *R* hold for the counterparts in *M*, and
c. background assumptions in *R* hold in *M*.

There are many practical difficulties, both in the actual application of the strategy and in its precise formulation; we shall return to some of them in later chapters.

For now, the effect of Space Optimization is that when an "if" space "if S, _____" is set up within a parent space *R*, the background assumptions and explicit relations satisfied in *R* (call them *E* globally) can be assumed to hold in the "if" space *M*, insofar as they are compatible with *S* (see chapter 4). The accessible consequences of *S* in space *M* are then the accessible consequences of $S + E$. Consider (12):

(12)
If <u>Max has gone to the meeting,</u> <u>Max's children</u> are alone.

             | |

       S   *P*: "Max has children"

In most contexts, *P* is not a consequence of *S;* nothing blocks SP_2: $R_{3'}$ applies to maximize space similarity, yielding *P/R,M*. The presupposition is "inherited" (satisfied in both spaces). If, however, we happen to know that this is a school meeting for parents only, then *P* (Max having children) becomes a consequence of *S* (his being at the meeting) and therefore an explicit presupposition in *M* (by D_1). Accordingly, SP_2 no longer applies; only R_2 can apply, to give *P/M; P* is not "inherited."

Finally, consider examples like (13), which, as Soames (1982) correctly observes, undermine cancellation theories of projection:

(13)

If <u>Oakland beats Montreal,</u>
              |
              S

Chicago will beat Montreal <u>too.</u>
                            |
                    P: "some team other than Chicago
                         beats Montreal"

P is a direct consequence of *S* and therefore (by D_1) an explicit presupposition in *M:* SP_2 and R_3 do not apply; R_2 yields *P/M,* and the presupposition is not "inherited." This corresponds faithfully to the intuition that (13) does not imply that anybody has beaten or will beat Montreal. But, as in the case of (10), *P* could well be satisfied in *R* independently: (13) could be part of a discourse having already established that San Diego, Atlanta, New York, and Los Angeles have beaten Montreal.

3.2.2.3 Either ____ or ____. *Either* S_1 *or* S_2 is a "double" space-builder: it sets up two possibility spaces at once, M_1 and M_2. In M_1, S_1 is satisfied; in M_2, S_2 is satisfied. Furthermore, both spaces, M_1 and M_2, are *compatible* with parent space *R*.

The following kind of example is notoriously difficult for combinatorial approaches to presupposition projection to handle:

(14)

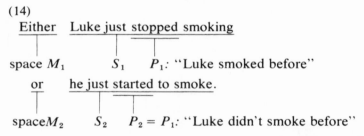

Either   Luke just stopped smoking
  | | |
space M_1 S_1 P_1: "Luke smoked before"

  or   he just started to smoke.
  | | |
space M_2 S_2 $P_2 = P_1$: "Luke didn't smoke before"

It is clear that P_1 cannot be satisfied in *R* (this would make *R* incompatible with M_2); nor can P_2 be satisfied in *R* (this would make *R* incompatible with M_1). Thus, any application of R_3 (i.e., SP_2) is blocked by the *compatibility* requirement: no presupposition is inherited.

In (15), on the other hand, nothing (except further context specifications) prevents SP_2 from applying:

(15)
Either Luke just <u>stopped</u> smoking or <u>his children</u> have left.

$P_1:$ "Luke smoked $P_2:$ "Luke has children"
before"

3.2.2.4 Believe, Hope.   Some spaces are linked in special ways. For instance, one's hopes depend on one's beliefs: one can hope that Smith will resign insofar as one believes that Smith is in office; one can hope that Max's children are in New York insofar as one believes that Max has children, that there is such a place as New York, etc. Call the space upon which another depends its *mentor*. M_1 ("Luke believes ____") is the mentor space of M_2 ("Luke hopes ____"). Space Optimization (principle (11)) applies to spaces and their mentors. This is true in particular of the maximization strategy SP_2.

The classical example (16) (Karttunen (1973)) involves a mentor space:

(16)
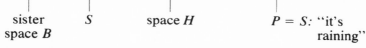
Luke <u>believes</u> <u>it's raining</u> and <u>hopes</u> that it will <u>stop</u> raining.

sister S space H $P = S:$ "it's
space B raining"

As shown in figure 3.1, optimization goes from H to its mentor space B and then from B to parent space R. In such configurations there is no *direct* optimization between H and R. In (16), we find (explicitly) P/B and (by R_2) P/H. Since S is not a presupposition in B, R_3 is inapplicable: $P(= S)$ will not be "transferred" to parent space R.

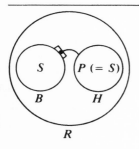

Figure 3.1

Compare this with (17):

(17)
Luke hopes that it will stop raining.

Assume that at the point in discourse when (17) is uttered, P ("it's raining") does not follow from anything explicit in B: it can then be transferred to B from H by R_3 (SP_2, maximization) as an implicit presupposition and then again to R by the same strategy, provided of course that no contradiction ensues in R (SP_1). Superficially, the presupposition is "inherited."

Another controversial example is (18):

(18)
Oedipus believes that he killed his father
      | |

    space B S

and he regrets killing his father.
        |

        P: "Oedipus killed his father"

In principle, *regret* could be treated exactly like *hope*, but in fact there is no reason to think that it sets up spaces distinct from beliefs. It is presumably only a relation holding between its grammatical subject and the fact, proposition, event, etc., expressed by its direct object complement clause and valid in the appropriate belief space B. In (18), the presupposition P ($= S$) "Oedipus killed his father" is explicit in B; SP_2 does not apply, and P is not transferred to the parent space R, although again it could be valid in R independently.

In (19), on the other hand, P is only implicit in B:

(19)
Oedipus regrets killing his father.

Space Optimization will apply, validating the presupposition P in R, in the absence of any prior contrary assumption in R. This is why factives like *regret* are most often viewed as strong presupposition triggers, on the basis of isolated minimum examples like (19). Notice that (19) still implies (presupposes in fact) that Oedipus believes he killed his father.

3.2.2.5 Factives. Consider the following example involving a factive expression:

(20)

If   Lucy realizes that she was mistaken, she will be ashamed.

space H P: "Lucy was mistaken"

(20) can of course be understood with the presupposition that Lucy was indeed mistaken and the implicature that she may or may not realize it. It can also be used and understood under the different assumption that P is undetermined—we do not know whether Lucy made a mistake or not. It is then roughly equivalent to "If Lucy was mistaken and if she should realize it, she will be ashamed." In the first interpretation, SP_2 (R_3) is applying to optimize H and R: the presupposition is satisfied in the "if" space and in its parent space. In the second interpretation, the assumption $P?R$ blocks SP_2 (by C_4). The presupposition is not transferred.

Incidentally, attention is usually focused on a first-person version of (20):

(21)

If   I realize that I was mistaken, I will be ashamed.

space H S P

As noted earlier, the *if* construction typically implies $S?R$: the protasis is undetermined (in R). But in (21) P/R and $S?R$ are incompatible because the speaker cannot imply both that he knows that P and that he does not realize it (except perhaps if he utters (21) under hypnosis, revealing unconscious knowledge). Therefore, by SP_1 (noncontradiction) we derive $P?R$, which corresponds to the second case in (20) and blocks inheritance by C_4.

3.2.2.6 Possible. Another counterexample to combinatorial accounts is cited by Gazdar (1979):

(22)

It is possible that John has children, and it is possible that his children are away'.

Possible (or rather, *it is possible that* ____) is a space-builder. In discourse, a second occurrence of *possible* can refer back to the first possibility space introduced (as in (22)), or it may set up a second possibility space different from the first, as in (23):

(23)
It is possible that John has children, and it is possible that John has no children.

The analysis of (22) is straightforward:

(24)
It is possible that John has children,
_____   _____
       | |
   space *M*   *S*

and it is possible that his children are away.
   _____   _____
          | |
      space *M*   *P = S:* "John has children"

S is stipulated explicitly in space *M*, so that *P* (= *S*) is an explicit presupposition in *M* and SP$_2$ (optimization) does not apply. We have *P?R* and *P/M* (no inheritance).

3.2.2.7 Negation. It was pointed out in section 1.6.4 that negatives set up corresponding counterfactual spaces in which the positive version of the sentence is satisfied:

(25)
Too bad you were *never* baptized. *Your godfather* could take care of you. (cf. (77) from chapter 1)

(26)
I did*n't* buy a car. There was no room for *it* in the garage.

(27)
Alexander did*n't* read your book. *It* would have made him mad.

The usual optimization strategies will apply to this kind of counterfactual space and the corresponding parent space:

(28)
The king of France is   not   bald.
_____   _____
         | |
     P: "there is   space *N*
     a king of
     France"

By R$_2$, we have *P/N*. SP$_2$ seeks to optimize the similarity between space *N* and parent space *R*, so that by R$_3$, we have *P/R: P* is satisfied both in *N* and in *R*. Of course, SP$_2$ applies only to implicit material (see

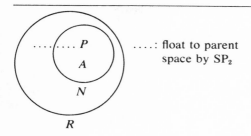

.....: float to parent
space by SP_2

Figure 3.2

D_1); as depicted in figure 3.2, the explicit proposition "the king of France is bald" holds in N and not in R. We notice that independent space properties of negatives combined with the standard rules and strategies for presuppositions explain why in simple cases negation maintains presuppositions. As usual, SP_1 will override SP_2: if P is contradicted in R, R_3 is blocked and the presupposition does not carry over:

(29)
The king of France did not visit the exhibition, because there is no king of France.

P ("there is a king of France") holds in the negative space; it cannot float to R without contradiction.

Consider finally a case involving three spaces:

(30)
   If   the exhibition was not visited by the king of France,

space H: parent R space N: parent H

then France is a republic.

"France is a republic" holds in H, contradicts P ("there is a king of France"), and therefore blocks optimization of N and H. P does not transfer to H, and, a fortiori, not being in H, does not transfer from H to R: there is no inheritance at any level. Related examples are (31) and (32):

(31)
If the exhibition was not visited by the king of France, then the king of France is in New York.

(32)
If the exhibition was not visited by the king of France, it won't get any financial support.

In (31), P is independently (from the protasis) a presupposition in H; SP_2 extends it to H's parent space R. In (32), nothing blocks extension from N to H (by SP_2) and again from H to R: there is inheritance all the way.

3.2.2.8 Other Related Cases. Gazdar and Soames discuss (33):

(33)
If all countries are now republics, then it is unlikely that the

P_1: "there is a president of France"

president of France still feels lonely.

P_2: "the president of France felt lonely before"

Many spaces are involved here: R, the origin, its daughter H ("if ____ then ____"), N ("now"), and U ("it is unlikely ____") within H. "The president of France" may be a description in any, or all, of these spaces (chapter 1) and it identifies an element x in U. It is also of course a role r (chapter 2). Let us single out two of the relevant readings. First, on the "value" interpretation, if P_2 is "x felt lonely before," it can extend to H and then to R by SP_2. *Before* will then set up another space B in R (with counterparts in H and U). Optimization would tend to assign the same role to x and its counterparts in the various spaces; this yields an interpretation where the same individual was president before and lonely, and is president now and perhaps no longer lonely. In this case, the *description* "the president of France" and the corresponding presupposition P_1 originate in R, and the fact that it also happens to follow *in H* from "all countries are now republics" is irrelevant, since H is in R.

The same can be said, mutatis mutandis, for the "role" interpretation: if P_2 is taken to hold for whoever happened to be president before (i.e., loneliness was a characteristic of filling the role "president of France"), then again the description of the role originates in R (or in B), together with P_1. The property "(still) lonely" holds of the counterpart of that role in U (via a third counterpart in H).

Evidently, depending on background assumptions and on the various combinations of the ID Principle and role-value assignment, other interpretations are possible in which the description and P_1 would originate in a lower space and the explicit protasis "all countries are now republics" would block extension of P_1 to R. For instance, suppose France was a monarchy just before (33) was uttered, and suppose further that when a country becomes a republic, the head of state (former king, dictator, emperor, etc.) automatically becomes president. Then P_1 can only be satisfied in H and U but not in R and B; as a consequence of the protasis, it is an explicit presupposition in H. The description "the president of France" does not hold in B, but $P_2 =$ "the president of France felt lonely" does. Therefore, the ID Principle is at work in P_2: *the president of France* points to the appropriate element in U and identifies its counterpart in B, in this case "the king of France." So the king of France was lonely, but if all countries are now republics, he has become a president and is probably no longer lonely.

Another reading with no presupposition "inheritance" could rest on the following assumptions: although France has been a monarchy up to now, we know that were it to become a republic, Lamartine would inevitably become president, and further that Lamartine has been lonely and isolated for the last ten years. Then "the president of France" is a correct description of Lamartine in H and U but not in B and R. Nevertheless, according to the ID Principle, it identifies Lamartine in all the spaces.

A final example involving kings and presidents is a variant of (14):

(34)
Either the president of France is a royalist or the king of France is a socialist.
(Assumption: France has either a king or a president but not both)

Then the two presuppositions "there is a king of France" and "there is a president of France" are incompatible and respectively satisfied (via R_2) in the two spaces set up by *either* ____ *or* ____. Extending either one to R would make R incompatible with the space in which the other is satisfied, in violation of the semantics of *either* ____ *or* ____. The "logic" of *either* ____ *or* ____ can be viewed as a constraint on further incrementation of R: R must fit one of the spaces set up by *either* ____ *or* ____.

If the assumption that France cannot have both a king and a president is dropped, then nothing blocks SP_2 and R_3. The presuppositions will be extended to the parent space R; that is, it will be assumed that France indeed has a president and a king.

3.3 Remarks about Combinatorial, Cancellation, and Previous Procedural Approaches

The unifying semantic property of presuppositions as presented in section 3.2 would be this: they are able to *float* from space to space under optimization strategies. Section 3.2 presents a general account of how this floating takes place and of the strategies that guide it. From that perspective, the standard "projection" problem is just one special case of floating—namely, under what circumstances do presuppositions introduced into "lower" spaces float all the way up to the parent space R for the entire utterance?

One part of the strategies amounts to this: implicit presuppositions float up until, or unless, they are blocked by incompatibility in a higher space (SP_2 followed by SP_1). In some respects, this view is close in spirit to the principle of cancellation theories (cf. Gazdar (1979)) that "potential" presuppositions are canceled out by stronger implicatures or entailments. Indeed, it seems to me that cancellation accounts are most successful precisely in those cases when cancellation (or suspension) can be directly reinterpreted as blockage of SP_2 by SP_1. There are, however, major theoretical differences with nontrivial empirical consequences.

Under a cancellation view, the hierarchy of entailments, implicatures, and presuppositions is *stipulated:* it is a law of the theory that (virtual) presuppositions occupy the lowest position on a scale. The "space-floating" account does not include this kind of stipulation: floating a presupposition up is a matter of choice (by R_3) and when the choice is precluded (typically by SP_1), no particular "weakness" of the presupposition is invoked, only the fact that this particular choice, and not the other, would lead to contradiction. This feature correlates with another, perhaps equally crucial difference: under a cancellation view, virtual presuppositions (pre-suppositions in Gazdar's notation) that do not surface (i.e., canceled ones) simply die. They are formal presuppositions of the *sentence,* but not semantic presuppositions of the utterance. In contrast, floating presuppositions from space to space does not change their status: it only changes the number of spaces in which (or "with respect to which") they are satisfied. In fact, it is important for presuppositions that do not float all the way up to remain presuppositions in the space in which they originated and in the intermediate spaces to which they may have floated.

For example, once presupposition P has been introduced into space B ("Luke believes ____"), either explicitly or by SP_2, it will continue to be presupposed in following discourse that "Luke believes that P." In space terms this simply amounts to having P satisfied in B. To take an example:

(35)
Luke believes that it is probable that the king of France is bald, even though in fact there is no king of France.

Presupposition P ("there is a king of France") will float up from space K ("it is probable that ____") to space B ("Luke believes ____") by SP_2 and will be blocked from floating into R by SP_1 (contradiction in R with the explicit "there is no king of France"). Standard cancellation would simply kill the presupposition, or rather "virtual" presupposition, of the lowest clause ("it is probable that ____") because of the "stronger" entailment "in fact there is no king of France," and this would not account for the implication, and subsequent presupposition, linked to (35) that Luke believes there is a king.

Notice incidentally that there can be conflicts in optimization. Consider (36):

(36)

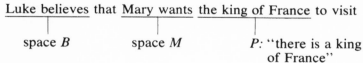

the exhibition.

Context (in R): there is no king of France
Mentor space: "Mary believes ____" (M')

Neglecting various possible "transparent" readings of *the king of France*, we obtain P/M by R_2, *and* P/M' by mentor space transfer. If we now choose to optimize R and B, we obtain P/B: "Luke believes there is no king of France." This blocks floating from M' to B: Luke thinks that Mary believes P, but does not himself believe P. If, instead, we optimize B and M', then P floats up to B (by SP_2) but is blocked by SP_1 from going all the way up to R: Luke then believes P and also that Mary shares this belief. As far as I can tell, both interpretations are equally possible for (36). In terms of actual decoding in conversation, a hearer can of course postpone choosing a strategy until further information is available.

Empirically, and focusing now only on the descriptive adequacy of cancellation accounts, they will typically make erroneous predictions when canceling implicatures are not available or when they fail to distinguish explicit from implicit presuppositions. Both defects are apparent in the case of the earlier example (13):

(13)
If Oakland beats Montreal, Chicago will beat Montreal too.

There is no implicature that Montreal has not already beaten, and no way (for the cancellation account) to say that "somebody else has beaten Montreal" is already an explicit presupposition in the hypothetical space H when the apodosis ("Chicago will beat Montreal too") is produced. Likewise, the absence of obvious canceling implicatures has led to wrong predictions (obligatory inheritance) in the case of *maybe* (cf. (5)). Consider finally the earlier examples (20) and (21):

(20)
If Lucy realizes that she was mistaken, she will be ashamed.

(21)
If I realize that I was mistaken, I will be ashamed.

Cancellation excludes inheritance in (21) by implicature: the speaker cannot both presuppose that he is mistaken and not realize it. But that implicature is not available for (20), so the account wrongly predicts that the presupposition is necessarily inherited in that example, which is factually not the case.

As Dinsmore (1981a) notes, cancellation will not account for presupposition plugs either. In (37),

(37)
Mary said she saw the sea-serpent.

there is no actual implicature to override "there is a sea-serpent" (unless of course the speaker has previously ruled out sea-serpents explicitly). SP_2 can be more flexible, blocking the floating insofar as $P?R$—that is, insofar as the existence of the sea-serpent is deemed controversial (in R) or insofar as no link is assumed between what Mary says, what she believes, and what she has evidence for. Idealized cognitive models (ICMs) (Fillmore (1982), Lakoff (1982)) presumably guide optimization strategies in various ways: in prototypical cases, Mary says what she believes, and background assumptions for her beliefs are in harmony with the speaker's, so presuppositions can float up freely; but if Mary's reliability is itself in question, then P/M corresponds to $P?R$ and floating is (at least temporarily) halted. Notice, by the way, that in terms of processing, presuppositions may float up long after the sentence was uttered, for example in this case when the reliability of Mary's background assumptions is established.

As noted by Soames (1982), combinatorial accounts of presupposition (see Karttunen and Peters (1979)) typically do not stumble on the same obstacles as cancellation: for examples like (13),

(13)
If Oakland beats Montreal, Chicago will beat Montreal too.

the projection algorithm explicitly precludes consequences of the protasis from being inherited. The algorithm faces serious problems, however, when SP_2 is actually at work, as in examples (14), (16), (20), and (22):

(14)
Either Luke just stopped smoking or he just started to smoke.

(16)
Luke believes it's raining, and hopes that it will stop raining.

(20)
If Lucy realizes that she was mistaken, she will be ashamed.

(22)
It is possible that John has children, and it is possible that his children are away.

Given this often complementary success of cancellation and combinatorial accounts, Soames bravely suggests combining them. This brute force (and ecumenical) solution is more powerful descriptively, which comes as no surprise. But it still accounts incorrectly or not at all for adverbials like *maybe* (5), conditionals (8), factives (20), and plugs. More importantly, as Soames immediately acknowledges, it is strikingly unexplanatory. From the present perspective, I would say that cancellation is descriptively successful insofar as it simulates part of SP_2 in the special case of floating to R, and that combinatorial projection is descriptively successful insofar as it stipulates some of the observed surface properties lexically and explicitly in the algorithms, such as the noninheritance of explicit presuppositions in the apodosis of conditionals. However, such lexical stipulation remains quite ad hoc, redundant, and, it turns out, insufficient.

As mentioned before, the understanding of presuppositions in terms of spaces is procedural, and I find it kindred in spirit to Dinsmore's approach (Dinsmore (1979, 1981b)). Technically, the presentation is different, given Dinsmore's emphasis on "world-binding" functions that link propositions true in one world to propositions true in another (in particular the actual one). These notions are absent in the present framework. There are also more interesting, substantial differences. Dinsmore retains the notion of presupposition as given information (but with respect to particular discourse worlds); as noted in section 3.1 and exemplified in (5), (8), (14), etc., this requirement is too strong. Presumably, being "given information" is closer to a prototype property of presupposition use than to a general pragmatic characterization of presuppositions.

In Dinsmore's approach, verbs like *wish* and *hope* do not set up spaces (or worlds) because wish(p) does not entail wish(q) when $p \rightarrow q$. For example, "Mary hopes John has stopped smoking" does not entail "Mary hopes John used to smoke." In the present format, Dinsmore's condition would correspond to (38):

(38)
If $p \rightarrow q/R$, then p/M entails q/M.

There is no reason, however, to think that such a condition should hold for spaces in general: for example, if "being a cow" (p) entails "having no feathers" (q) in reality, it does not follow that cows in pictures cannot have feathers, or that no one can believe cows to have feathers, or that one cannot write a story about cows with feathers. Even purely logical consequences do not obey the condition: believing all the axioms does not entail believing all the theorems.

Wish, hope, and so on, set up spaces in the sense of chapters 1 and 2, if only because they are associated with all the usual opacity, specificity, and referentiality phenomena. In fact, they introduce counterfactual or hypothetical spaces much like *if* ___, *then* ___ (see chapter 4), but because there can be different (grammatical) subjects for such verbs, they also bring along mentor spaces (corresponding to the beliefs of the subject).

It is important to stress that the validity of P in a hope or wish space (e.g., "Luke hopes ___") does *not* imply that P is hoped or wished for (i.e., "Luke hopes that P"). Intuitively, a wish space resembles a (possibly counterfactual) situation in which the wish is realized; this hypothetical situation will have a lot in common with "reality" (except for the wish, its accessible consequences, etc.), and the common features in question need not (indeed most often will not) themselves be wished for. Wishing that you wouldn't step on my sore feet doesn't mean I wish to have sore feet, although the desired state of affairs alluded to is one in which I have sore feet and you manage not to step on them.

I now turn to further presupposition phenomena that have previously gone unnoticed in spite of somewhat bizarre features.

3.4 Presupposition Transfer

Presupposition transfer, distinct from *floating*, refers to the rather remarkable cases in which a presupposition, apparently relative to space M, is valid not in M but in its parent R. Some examples follow:

(39)
(Hey), in that picture, Luke has *stopped* smoking.

(Context: In reality, Luke chain-smokes, looks nervous and unhealthy, etc.; in the picture, he is represented without a cigarette and with rosy cheeks.)

The presupposition "Luke smoked before" is valid in R, but seems invalid in M, the picture in which Luke never smoked.

(40)
In this painting, Gudule is beautiful *again*.

(Context: Gudule is no longer beautiful in reality.)

The presupposition (linked to *again*) "Gudule was once beautiful, and later not beautiful" is valid in R but seems invalid in M, the picture, in which Gudule has always been beautiful. (I do not envisage Dorian Gray–like situations.)

(Readers can check that in (39) and (40), if picture and painting are replaced by movies, an ambiguity arises concerning whether the presupposition holds only in reality (Luke and Gudule being actors) or only in the "imaginary" world of the movie.)

(41)

Lucy claims that Jack called *again* at six.

P: "Jack called before six"

(Context: The speaker and hearer know that Jack called before six, but Lucy doesn't; all she actually claimed was that Jack called at six, without the presupposition that he called before.)

P holds in R but not in M ("Lucy claims ____")

(42)

Your mother would like you to *stop* smoking.

(Context: Mother wants me not to smoke, but she doesn't know that I have been smoking; the speaker does.)

(43)

Mary thinks that Max *regrets* having gone to England.

(Context: In fact, Mary doesn't know where Max went; she only knows he took a trip, and thinks he's sorry.)

(44)

According to George, Lucy is *no longer* beautiful.

(*P:* "Lucy used to be beautiful")

(Context: All George said was that Lucy was not beautiful; he didn't know her in the past and has no idea what she looked like.)

All these examples are prima facie violations of R_2: the presupposition apparently does not hold in space M, although it is directly in the scope of the space-builder. Worse yet, since it does not hold in M, it cannot float up to R by R_3 and SP_2; but it *is* satisfied in R.

On the other hand, there is something familiar about the situation: holding in R and not in M is precisely the property of definite descriptions to which the ID Principle applies. And the ID Principle does not violate R_2, because the definite description originates in the parent space (R), not in the daughter space (M).

This suggests that in cases of "transfer," the presuppositions also originate directly in R. How do they show up grammatically in the scope of the space-builder for M?

In the case of pictures (see (39), (40)), I suggest the following: As explained in chapter 1, the mental space corresponding to a concrete picture involves more than what the picture concretely represents (for example, Margaret Thatcher completely hidden behind Helmut Kohl and therefore without any concrete counterpart in the photograph).

That is, optimization from R to M works in the picture cases. In that sense, (39) and (40) are like counterfactuals; the situation explicitly described is different from reality, but background assumptions and implicit presuppositions are the same. Thus, Luke who doesn't smoke in (39) is assumed to have smoked before, just like his counterpart, the real Luke. Contrary to appearances, then, the presupposition linked to *stop* (or *again* in (40)) is satisfied in the appropriate "counterfactual" picture space. It is transferred from R to M by optimization.

The case of (41) through (44) is different. Here the context explicitly prevents the presupposition from being valid in M. These examples work by a natural extension of the ID Principle to facts and events; instead of describing an event in terms of its properties in M, the speaker uses a description of the counterpart event in R. For instance, "Max's taking a trip" for Mary in (43) corresponds to "Max's having gone to England" for the speaker, so a description of the latter (trigger) can identify the former (target). The description of the event originates in the parent space, but note that the presupposition that the event *took place* is linked to *regret* and originates in the daughter space M. It will float up to R insofar as SP_2 is possible; the speaker may add, after (43), that *in fact* Max never went. This leads to the superficially bizarre possibility that (43) might be true without Max's having gone to England and without Mary's believing that he did.

The tricky part of this extension of the ID Principle is that events in R need not have taken place (in R); "taking place" is just a property that events may or may not have. In the case of (41), the event "Jack called at six" for Lucy would be correctly described in R (i.,e., for the speaker) as "Jack called again at six," but (41) does not imply that this event actually took place. In (42), the event "your not smoking" for the mother corresponds to "your having stopped smoking" for the speaker (event in R), and this is assumed not to have taken place.

For (44), the "fact" for George that "Lucy is not beautiful" would be correctly described in R as "Lucy is no longer beautiful," given the background assumptions in R. This fact, although "represented" in R, may well be false in R: the speaker can continue (44) with ". . . ; this is false."

This phenomenon, by the way, should probably be related to cases where consequences in one space are transferred to another. Consider the following example (from Darde (1982)):

(45)

Borg thinks that Judith can learn to play tennis in two weeks.

(Context: Judith is my ten-year-old daughter. Borg doesn't know her. What Borg has actually said in magazine interviews is that "All ten-year-olds can learn to play tennis in two weeks.")

Calling M the space "Borg thinks ____" and R the origin space (speaker = me), the "fact" that Judith can learn in two weeks follows in R from the "fact" (F) that all ten-year-olds can learn in two weeks. F is not established true in R, and strictly speaking, its consequence (C) cannot hold in M, where Judith has no counterpart. Attributing C to Borg is a transfer of virtual consequences from R to M: this is another instance of space optimization.

One last remark about the pragmatics of presupposition. I noted in section 3.1 that presuppositions cannot be equated with given (or potentially given) information in general. I characterized presuppositions as being the "propositional" parts of sentences that can float from space to space. Evidently, floating from M to R is simplest if P is already established in R: optimization works in both directions. In that sense, then, we might perhaps view the use of presuppositions for given information as prototypical. From a space viewpoint, presuppositions are linguistically efficient (mentally and communicationally) because through SP_2 they allow a quick (implicit) filling in of spaces; they are also, as often noted, communicationally devious in making the hearer feel they are already somehow given and therefore difficult to question or refute. This is a combined effect of the prototype property and the fact explained in section 3.2.2 that negation lets them float up.

Chapter 4
Counterfactuals and Comparatives

4.1 Counterfactuals

Traditionally, counterfactuals like "If men had wings, they would fly" are viewed as cases of possibly valid reasoning from premises that are false in actuality. Attempts to evaluate the truth conditions of counterfactuals involve, among others, two general kinds of questions: the problem of determining which true statements are combined with the false premises to carry out the reasoning (Goodman's puzzle; see Goodman (1947)) and the problem of determining when (and which) logical laws apply to counterfactuals. For example, (1) does not straightforwardly contrapose to produce (2) (Lewis (1973)):

(1)
If Boris had gone to the party, Olga would still have gone.

(2)
If Olga had not gone, Boris would still not have gone.

Linguistically, we do not directly tackle the logical problem of truth conditions for counterfactuals, but rather the cognitive-semantic question of how counterfactual spaces are set up and structured. This can be viewed, however, as another version of Goodman's puzzle.

Counterfactuality is a case of forced incompatibility between spaces; a space M_1 is incompatible with another space M_2 if some relation explicitly specified in M_1 is not satisfied for the corresponding elements in M_2. We focus on the case where a space is set up and is incompatible with its parent.

In all the following examples, the first sentence can be understood to set up a counterfactual space (incompatible with the origin), and the second one expresses some relation satisfied in that counterfactual space:

(3)

If Lucky had won, I would be rich. I would have moved to Tahiti.

(4)

I *wish* Lucky had won. I would be rich.

(5)

Fortunately, the fire did *not* cross the highway. My house would have been destroyed.

(6)

Luckily, the fire was *prevented* from crossing the highway. My house would have been destroyed.

Many spaces can be incompatible with their parents, in particular beliefs, pictures, desires, times, etc.:

(7)

The race was canceled; (but) *George believes* that Lucky won.

(8)

In that movie, Brigitte Bardot is an ugly witch.

In (7) and (8), incompatibility follows from pragmatic properties of the discourse, including background knowledge: space-builders like *George believes* and *in that movie* of course do not impose or in any way require that the relation expressed in their scope not be satisfied in the parent space. In fact, the guiding folk-theory for space construction and interpretation is that "normally" people share beliefs, which are furthermore correct. *But* in (7) signals that this implicature is suspended. More generally, as noted in chapter 3, spaces are subject to optimization strategies, which assume similar structure ceteris paribus. *But, although, however* are explicit linguistic warnings against likely implicatures, in this case against optimization:

(9)

Brigitte Bardot is strikingly beautiful, *but*

$$\left\{ \begin{array}{l} \text{in that movie, she's an ugly witch} \\ \text{Max believes she's an ugly witch} \\ \text{I wish she were an ugly witch} \\ \text{if she were an ugly witch, I would still love her} \end{array} \right\} .$$

Clearly, counterfactuality may be lexically imposed, as it is by strong "negatives" such as *not* and *prevent* in (5) and (6). The strong (lexical) entailment automatically cancels the optimization implicature, without *but*'s or *although*'s. Looking only at the forms of the utterances, we find two dimensions of counterfactuality. The first is a lexical dimension, on which negatives are strongest, followed by verbs like *wish,* which is typically counterfactual, as in (4), but not always:

(10)
I wish you would help me tomorrow.
(Compatible with your actually helping)

(11)
I wish you to obey my orders.

Lower on the lexical dimension, we find conditionals (*if* ___) and modals like *could, might.* These space-builders impose counterfactuality in some grammatical constructions, suggest it in others, and also obviously set up ordinary noncounterfactual hypothetical situations:

(12)
John could have been somebody else.

(13)
If John had been somebody else, I would miss him.

(14)
Max could be in New York.
(Counterfactual: . . . instead of here)
(Possible: . . . he may be in New York)

(15)
If the Redfords were home, the lights would be on.
(Counterfactual interpretation: . . . but they're not)
(Inductive reasoning: . . . and indeed they are)

The second formal dimension along which counterfactuality varies is grammatical. Consider the effect of tense variation for the space-builder *if:*

(16)
If Boris comes tomorrow, Olga will be happy.

(17)
If Boris came tomorrow, Olga would be happy.

Table 4.1

	Tense of protasis	Status of protasis B
(16)	present	B or B?
(17)	past	B? or $\sim B$
(18)	past perfect	$\sim B$

Table 4.2

Hypothetical value of tense	+	Time value	=	Surface tense
present	+	past	=	past
past	+	past	=	past perfect
past perfect	+	past	=	past perfect

(18)
If Boris had come tomorrow, Olga would have been happy.

All three sentences express the same "logical" connection between "Boris coming tomorrow" (the protasis B) and "Olga being happy" (the apodosis O). (16) can be used either if B is taken to be valid (we know for sure that Boris is coming, and if he's coming, Olga will be happy; see section 3.2.2, example (10)) or if B is undetermined with respect to the parent space (B?R) at that point in the discourse. (16) cannot be used if $\sim B$ has been established:

(19)
Boris is not coming; if he comes, Olga will be happy.

(17) can be used if B is undetermined or if $\sim B$ is established (counterfactual). It cannot be used if B has been established. (18) can only be used counterfactually; it entails $\sim B$. This distribution of tenses is given schematically in table 4.1.

If B itself refers to a past state or event, then tense also serves to indicate the time relation.[1] The hypothetical value of the tense and the time value combine as shown in table 4.2 to yield the actual surface tense. This implies that, with past time reference, the past perfect is ambiguous between strong counterfactual and weak counterfactual interpretations:

(20)
If Boris had come, Olga would have been happy.
(B?: . . . and she is, so maybe he's around)
($\sim B$: . . . but she's sad)

In cases like (20), where the time reference is past, the weak and strong counterfactual readings merge for purely grammatical reasons. The same phenomenon occurs with modals:

(21)
Boris could have come tomorrow.

(22)
Boris could come tomorrow.
(*B?:* . . . and he will)
(*~B:* . . . but he won't)

(23)
Boris could have come yesterday.
(*B?:* . . . let's see if he did)
(*~B:* . . . but he didn't)

In such examples, lexical and grammatical characteristics bear on whether the protasis or modalized proposition is counterfactual. Notice that there is no strong entailment of counterfactuality with respect to the apodosis: in (16), (17), (18), it may well be the case that Olga will be happy "anyway."

If Olga's happiness is established independently of the protasis for any of these examples, speakers find it helpful to add implicature-canceling *but*'s and *anyway*'s:

(24)
If Boris comes, Olga will be happy; *but* she will be happy *anyway*.

(25)
If Boris came tomorrow, Olga would be happy; *but* she will be happy *anyway*.

(26)
If Boris had come tomorrow, Olga would have been happy; *but* she will be happy anyway.

It has been argued (e.g., by Karttunen (cf. Brée (1982))) that the falsehood of the consequent in counterfactuals is an implicature, not a presupposition or an entailment. (25) and (26) make the same point, but the examples suggest that the implicature is not directly linked to counterfactual conditionals, but rather to conditionals in general.

Cornulier (1983) provides a general solution to the problem. Analyzing the various readings of (27),

(27)

You can sit here if you are invalid $\begin{Bmatrix} \text{and} \\ \text{or} \end{Bmatrix}$ (if) you are over 70.

he sets up an elegant argument showing that *if* cannot be viewed as ambiguous between a one-way conditional and a biconditional; rather, the use of *if* in "*Q, if P, and if R, and if S...*" indicates (on one reading) that each of *P, R, S,...* is a sufficient condition for *Q*. This basic meaning is supplemented with the Gricean implicature that normally all relevant sufficient conditions are specified. In the special case where only one condition, *P*, is mentioned ("*Q, if P*"), this analysis yields the required biconditional since *P*, being the only sufficient condition, is therefore also necessary.

Cornulier is able to unify many superficially different uses of *if* by giving a single minimum interpretation for "*Q, if P,*" amounting roughly to "in all situations (cases) for which *P* is valid, *Q* is valid." By itself, this does not say that there is actually any link between *P* and *Q*, since of course *Q* might be valid in other situations, for example "*~P*"-situations. But if it is assumed that all relevant situations in which *Q* might be valid are specified, *Q* will be taken to arise only in *P*-situations; this corresponds to the implicature on relevant sufficient conditions mentioned above. We can then take *anyway* or *still* to be devices that cancel this exhaustivity implicature, as suggested also by the possible appearance of implicature-canceling *but*'s and *although*'s:[2]

(28)
If you are good, Jesus will love you, *but* if you are bad,

$\begin{bmatrix} \text{Jesus will } \textit{still} \text{ love you} \\ \text{Jesus will love you } \textit{anyway} \end{bmatrix}$.

The first half of (28) carries the implicature (invited inference; Geis and Zwicky (1971)) that only in situations such that "you are good" will Jesus love you. *Still* or *anyway* in the second half cancels this implicature; other situations allow *Q* = "Jesus will love you." In fact, in (28), the overall effect is that *Q* holds in all situations—*P* and *~P* alike. The first half implicates a logical link between *P* and *Q*. The second half ultimately cancels the idea of such a link.

These general properties of conditionals allow for a simplified description of counterfactuals. Suppose a discourse is in process and the current space is R. An utterance of the form "If P, Q" sets up space H in which P and Q hold. Suppose $\sim P$ holds in R; then "P" in the utterance must be marked grammatically *past* or *past perfect* as in (17) or (18); this is a grammatical constraint. Cornulier's implicature that Q is valid only in P-situations implies in turn that Q is not valid in R— that is, that Q, like P, is "counterfactual."

Moreover, according to the treatment of presuppositions in chapter 3, $\sim P$ is an explicit presupposition in R. It follows, then, from general properties of conditionals, that in "counterfactuals" ("If P, Q"), $\sim P$ is typically presupposed and $\sim Q$ is implicated.

This is true as a discourse phenomenon: one must be careful to distinguish various grammatical issues relative to the sentence form actually used. If P has present or future time reference and past-perfect marking, then counterfactuality is grammatically imposed: either $\sim P$ has already been established in parent space R, or it is established at the time of the utterance. This is a semantic property of the construction (cf. (18)). If, on the other hand, P is marked *past* with present or future time reference (17) or *past perfect* with past time reference (19), the semantic constraint is weaker: we know only that P is not established in R. If $\sim P$ is independently established, or presupposed, in R, the result is a counterfactual, with the implicature $\sim Q$. If not, there is no such implicature, as predicted by Cornulier's account: see the interpretation of (19) where Olga is indeed happy, or the inductive reasoning interpretation of (15).

All this can be schematized as follows:

(29)

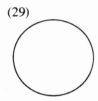 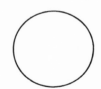

Parent space R Hypothetical space H
Space-builder: *if P*
Holds in H: Q

Semantics: Q holds in all P-situations.
(Cancellable) implicature: Q holds only in P-situations.

Grammar:

P past perfect and nonpast time:	$\sim P/R$
corollary by implicature:	$\sim Q/R$
P past and nonpast time *or*	
past perfect and past time:	$\sim P/R$ (and $\sim Q/R$
	or by implicature)
	$P?R$
P present and nonpast time *or*	
past and past time:	P/R ⎫ no implicature for *Q*
	or
	$P?R$ ⎭

Q anyway (or *still, nevertheless, . . .*): Implicature is reversed; *Q* is satisfied in other situations.

Notice that *anyway, still* do not cancel an implicature within the expression "If *P, Q* anyway," but rather a previous implicature to the effect that *Q* did not hold in *P*-situations. It therefore makes no sense to ask about the logical values of such expressions in isolation, as Lewis (1973) seems to do, or to ask whether they contrapose, on the basis of their linguistic surface form.

In practice, we can distinguish two cases: increasing the sufficient conditions and destroying the logical link.

The first case is exemplified by (30):

(30)

a. If <u>Boris had come</u>, <u>Olga would have come</u>.

            T   *Q*

    But . . .

b. If <u>you had talked to her</u>, <u>she would have come</u> anyway.

               P   *Q*

Anyway in (30b) cancels the implicature that *T* is the only sufficient condition. Assuming that *T* and *P* are invalid in *R* (i.e., that both hypothetical spaces are counterfactual), we now have the implicature that *P* and *T* are the only sufficient conditions and therefore that *Q* is also counterfactual (invalid in *R*): Olga did not come. The contraposition of (30b), with assumption $\sim Q$, is acceptable, and could come out in English as (31):

(31)

Since Olga didn't come, you didn't talk to her.

In the second paradigmatic case, P, the protasis, is the negation of T:

(32)

a. If Boris comes, Olga comes.

$$T = \sim P$$

But . . .

b. If Boris had not come, Olga would have come anyway.

$$P \qquad\qquad\qquad Q$$

P and $\sim P$ cannot both be counterfactual, so if we take P in (32b) to be counterfactual, then $\sim P$ is satisfied in R, and Q is "true" (satisfied in R), by (32a).

Cases like (32) reduce formally to $P \rightarrow Q$ and $\sim P \rightarrow Q$. Contraposition then yields an obvious contradiction: $\sim Q \rightarrow \sim P$ and $\sim Q \rightarrow P$. Viewed from this narrow perspective, Q is simply a tautology.

Nevertheless, counterfactuals involving $\sim Q$ are easily constructible in the same context:

(33)

If Olga had not come, I would have been miserable.

This brings us back to the *construction problem* for hypothetical spaces. If the protasis P is not counterfactual with respect to parent space R, hypothetical space H can easily be constructed by adding P to the structure of R; this ensures optimal fit of H and R. But H may also include only part of the structure of R as long as it fits R. Compare (34) and (35):

(34)

If Peter comes, we'll drink champagne, my sister will sing *Carmen*, and Harry will drive down from Mazatlán.

(35)

If this gas is heated, the pressure will increase.

H for (34) includes counterparts of Peter, my sister, Harry, Mazatlán, etc. But insofar as (35) is independent of my having a sister or Harry's being alive, the corresponding space H will not be specified for these elements (although it may be later in the discourse).[3]

Informally, the general idea is that space *H* is complemented with as much of the structure of parent space *R* as is necessary to carry out the reasoning. This contrasts with an approach seeking to find that space (world, etc.) most similar to *R* but compatible with *P* and *Q*, as in Goodman's (1947), Lewis's (1973), or Goldstick's (1978) treatments.[4] What these treatments probably underestimate is the uncommon flexibility of counterfactuals in ordinary usage:

(36)
If Napoleon had been the son of Alexander, he would have been Macedonian.

(37)
If Napoleon had been the son of Alexander, he would have won the battle of Waterloo.

(38)
If Napoleon had been the son of Alexander, he would not have been Napoleon.

(39)
If Napoleon had been the son of Alexander, Alexander would have been Corsican.

(40)
If Napoleon had been the son of Alexander, he would have had different genes.

It would not make sense to evaluate the "absolute" truth of any of these statements, but they can all be used to make some point, which requires only very partial structuring of *H;* in carrying out such reasonings, one may import into *H* both general "laws" deemed valid in *R* (which are often narrowly prototypical) such as "same nationality for father and son" (36), (39), "different parents, different genes" (40), "different parents, different offspring" (38), "tel père, tel fils" (37) and more specific information such as "Napoleon was Corsican" (39), "Alexander was Macedonian" (36), etc.

Such examples suggest that there is no general *linguistic* algorithm for going from *R* to *H;* but at the same time, it is clear that specific pragmatic situations will impose further constraints on the structural dependencies of *H* with respect to *R*. For example, if the argument is mathematical, then *all* the laws of mathematics (in *R*), and not just a few, remain in effect in *H*, although *H* itself may be a contradictory space (as in proofs by reductio ad absurdum) and therefore contain false mathematical statements (to which true laws can apply).[5] If the counterfactual is meant to deal with chains of states and events in time, of the form (41),

(41)

$$E_0 - E_1 - E_2 \begin{cases} E_3 - E_4 - ... \quad \text{Real events} \\ E'_3 - E'_4 - ... \quad \text{Possible but nonactual events} \end{cases}$$

a plausible implicit constraint is that H differs from R only with respect to events (states) following E'_3 (the first alternative), that is, that prior events/states are not modified by later ones.[6]

Goodman's famous contrast between (42) and (43) illustrates this type of constraint (Goodman (1947)):

(42)
If the match had been struck, it would have lit.

(43)
If the match had been struck, it wouldn't have been dry.

(42')

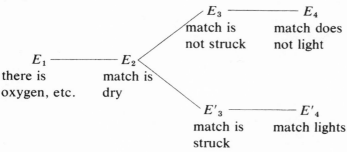

(43')

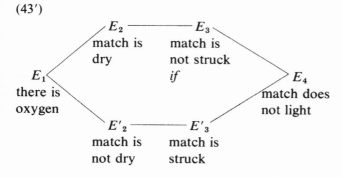

(43') amounts to keeping a later event E_4 constant and modifying earlier events (E'_2) to yield a consistent chain.

The strategy of preferring (42') to (43') (modifying later events rather than earlier ones) seems dominant in the case of causal chains, but if only the logical links between chains are at issue, it is possible, as Goldstick indicates, to override the strategy by explicitly keeping E_4 in R and H, and questioning E_2. This is clear for ordinary hypotheticals: given "There was no light," then

(44)

Either the match was not struck *or if* the match was struck, it wasn't dry.

(44) seems perfectly adequate. Suppose it turns out that the match was not struck; then (43) sounds fairly acceptable as a consequence of (44).

The fact remains that there is a strong tendency to interpret (43) according to the causal event strategy (as in (42)); the striking of the match is then understood to modify a prior state of the match (dryness), which is pragmatically implausible. In the different context of a wet matchbox, (43) would be fine as a causal chain.

The above discussion still leaves apparently unresolved a class of cases where prior states/events seem to be counterfactually modified. Consider the following situation, studied by Brée (1982) and inspired by an experiment of Wason (1968):[7]

Each card has a digit on one side and a letter on the other. The cards have been numbered and lettered in such a way as to obey the rule:

[45]

If the digit is even, then the letter is a vowel.

Suppose a card is drawn and has a B on it. We infer that the digit is odd, and it would be all right to say,

(46)

If the digit had been even, the letter would have been a vowel.

(46) is constructed straightforwardly by assuming that (45) holds in H (imported from R). But the relevant (counterfactual) event is not drawing the *same* card with a different number on it, but rather drawing a *different* card with a different number. Linguistically, this is possible because *the digit, the letter, the card,* etc., are definite descriptions pointing to roles (chapter 2) and may therefore identify different values in R and H, corresponding to different events E_3, E'_3. So the alterna-

tive events do not occur after the state of the card has been fixed: (46) is consistent with the constraint on prior events.

Suppose now, as in Brée's example, that a card is drawn with a *3* and an *A* on it. Then (47) (Brée's S.16) is appropriate:

(47)
If the digit had been even, the letter would *still* have been a vowel.

The counterfactual space *H* contains "the digit be even" (protasis) and the law (45), from which follows "the letter be a vowel." *Still*, like *anyway*, suspends the implicature that different situations lead to different results; it is also anaphoric, referring back to the first situation. *Again* would serve roughly the same purpose in such cases:

(48)
a. I drew a 7, and the letter was a vowel.

b. Then I drew a 10, and the letter was $\begin{Bmatrix} \text{again} \\ \text{still} \end{Bmatrix}$ a vowel.

Other continuations of (48a) are as follows:

(49)
Then I drew a 10, and *this time* the letter was a consonant.

(50)
?*Then I drew a 10, and *this time* the letter was a vowel.

(51)
Then I drew a 10, $\begin{Bmatrix} \text{and this time again, the letter was a vowel} \\ \text{and this time, the letter was still a vowel} \end{Bmatrix}$.

This time, by itself, strongly suggests a change of result. *Still* and *again* force the "same result" interpretation.

As mentioned earlier, there cannot be any general linguistic algorithm for structuring a space *H* counterfactual with respect to *R*, since very partial correspondences are commonly used. However, it remains an interesting problem to find out how *H* *could* be made optimally consistent with *R*. This kind of prototypical counterfactuality is the one discussed in the philosophical literature, and some proposals, such as Goldstick's (1978), are easy to recast in space terms.

Goldstick's algorithm (see the Appendix to this chapter) can be reinterpreted as a set of instructions for transforming the origin space *R* into the counterfactual space *H*. Take a counterfactual of the form "If *A*, then *C*." What the algorithm (viewed in space terms) seeks to do is essentially this: Starting with propositions that express relations in R, discard propositions to achieve consistency with A (the counterfactual protasis), and eliminate propositions that were in part or in toto consequences of $\sim A$. Then discard further propositions to achieve consistency with A and C. Then add A to the set of propositions. The space defined by these propositions is H. The counterfactual is "true" if C is satisfied in H.

As noted in the Appendix, there are problems with this procedure and others like it, but they do not seem insurmountable: it is not unreasonable to think that for *prototypical* counterfactuals, a suitable algorithm can be devised for constructing and evaluating H, with additional heuristic strategies (e.g., stability of prior events as in (42′), or the tendency to preserve laws, rather than particular propositions).

What might be the psychological reality (or plausibility) of such a procedure?

First, the notion of logical consequence used in the algorithm is clearly much too powerful psychologically: not all consequences of all combinations can be considered. This point was already made in chapter 3, note 3, and the notion "logical consequence" replaced by the weaker "accessible consequence."

With the strong notion of consequence, reductio ad absurdum would reduce to absurdity, as noted by F. Recanati (personal communication): take A to be a true mathematical statement to be proved, P the set of mathematical laws and axioms; reductio consists in building up H $\{\sim A, P\}$ and showing that H is ill formed (e.g., contains contradictions). But the algorithms would first make P compatible with $\sim A$, by reducing P—that is, eliminating the very axioms that allow the proof of A—and we would have a consistent, but useless, counterfactual space.

What happens instead is this: it is not known whether P is consistent with $\sim A$—that is, A is a logical consequence of P, but not an accessible consequence (at that point in the discourse)—so H is built up and processed in spite of its logical inconsistency, and in the hope that this inconsistency will reveal itself. This seems to be a common feature of counterfactual reasoning in standard (nonmathematical) discourse as well: we explore counterfactual spaces in order (among other things) to discover possible inconsistencies; we do not (and cannot) eliminate all inconsistencies before setting up the space. Furthermore, we count as true correct deductions carried out within an inconsistent space. This conception of truth would be undesirable from a purely logical standpoint.[8]

The algorithms can be viewed as ideal strategies that can only be used in simplified circumstances: for example, if the partitioning of the parent space R is trivial, that is, if the speaker knows (or thinks he knows) which aspects of R are independent of $\sim A$ and which ones dependent on it. The latter can then be suppressed directly (equivalent of G_1) without elaborate computation; this is in fact the case in examples (I), (II), and (III) reviewed in the Appendix. If the partitioning is not so obvious, or even virtually undecidable, space H can be set up anyway with the protasis A and the structure imported from R that is required to deduce C: the Napoleon examples (36)–(40) are constructed according to this strategy. The building up of counterfactual space H may of course (and in fact typically will) continue after the counterfactual sentence sets it up. In that case, more structure from R may be brought in progressively: if inconsistencies arise (and are accessible), either a patch-up attempt will be made or space H will be entirely discarded.[9]

(52)

A: If Napoleon had been Alexander's son, he would have won the battle of Waterloo.

B: But he would have died long before that.

A: Well, suppose he lived a very long life, without ever aging, or that Alexander was resurrected in Corsica in the eighteenth century . . .

(52) is a typical instance of the structure of H being negotiated.

The prototype and idealized status of the algorithms from a linguistic point of view (pragmatic construction of spaces) should not be confused with their status within a theory of truth. Philosophers such as Goodman, Lewis, and Goldstick were concerned with determining under what strict conditions a counterfactual should count as true (especially in complete, fully specified, decidable contexts). The algorithms can, in principle at least, serve this purpose. It does not follow that their full power is actually used, or even could be used, in processing the corresponding sentences semantically (i.e., linguistically).

The excuse for belaboring this somewhat obvious point is the recent tendency for proselytizing philosophers and generous (but gullible?) linguists to identify linguistic semantic theory with a theory of truth. The impact of this view is actually far from negative, given the considerable overlap of concerns and relevant phenomena in the two domains. Nevertheless, the fundamental goals are different in several important respects: types of significant generalizations, criteria for empirical adequacy, psychological implementation, to name just a few. The above discussion of counterfactuals shows the difference between saying that an algorithm accounts correctly for the truth conditions of counterfactuals and saying that it accounts for their semantics.

In the same way, some scholars concerned with the theory of truth (and with metaphysics) (e.g., Kripke (1980), Vendler (1975)) can say that (36)

(36)
If Napoleon had been the son of Alexander, he would have been Macedonian.

does not correspond to a possible world.[10] Whether they are right or wrong will not modify the linguistic status of (36)—such counterfactuals are easy to construct, to understand, and to evaluate—but could remove it from the realm of sentences having a determined truth value. The same is true for reference: though we may agree with Kripke that there is no possible world in which Hesperus is not Phosphorus, we achieve greater linguistic generality by assuming that two elements, Hesperus and Phosphorus, in some space, may have a single counterpart (Venus) in another (see section 5.2). Whatever may be the metaphysical validity of Kripke's thesis, it does not govern linguistic mental construction (and there is no a priori reason why it should).

We return to hypothetical spaces, the central theme of this section: using a minimal characterization of hypotheticals ("In situations such that P, Q"), a suspendable implicature of exhaustivity of situations, as suggested by Cornulier, and strategies for constructing hypothetical spaces, we obtain a minimal and unified account of conditionals, whether they be noncounterfactual (16), weakly counterfactual (17), or strongly counterfactual (18), whether they have a single logical link (35), a series of logical links (30), or no logical link (28).

The widespread (but, it turns out, mistaken) view that logical connection is an essential component of the meaning of *if* renders puzzling all the cases where there is no such connection. We have seen how forms like "if P, Q anyway" could occur to cancel the implicature "only if $\sim P, Q$," thereby effectively entailing the absence of a logical link between P and Q.

The "fridge and beer" cases (*If you're thirsty, there's beer in the fridge*) are another famous class of exceptions to the "logical link" thesis. Sakahara (1983) studies examples like (53):

(53)

If <u>you need an interpreter</u>, <u>John speaks German</u>.

              A   *B*

He notes that although there is no link between *A* and *B*, the hearer is invited to draw an implicit conclusion *C*, using *A* and *B* as premises, something like (54):

(54)

If *A* (you need an interpreter), then given *B* (John speaks German), *C* (you might hire John).

But, as Sakahara also notes, hidden conclusions are also commonly suggested in ordinary dialogues or sequences of sentences:

(55)

Dialogue:

X: I need an interpreter. (*A*)

Y: John speaks German. (*B*)

Hidden conclusion (*C*): You might hire John.

(56)

Monologue (X wants to help Y, who is having trouble communicating with German friends):

X: <u>You need an interpreter</u>. <u>John speaks German</u>.

              A   *B*

C is implied.

C in (55) and (56) is just a benign conversational implicature. But, as in (53), it is also the main point.

Accordingly, we can view sentences like (53) as setting up a hypothetical space *H*, for the purpose of drawing the relevant implicature *within H*. Notice that this remains consistent with Cornulier's minimal characterization *(MC)* (Cornulier (to appear)):

(57)

MC: In all *A*-situations ("such that you need an interpreter"), *B* ("John speaks German").

Since *B* is true in all situations, it is true in *A*-situations, and so *MC* is "true." Pragmatic knowledge that *B* (John's knowing German) is independent of *A* (somebody needing an interpreter), plus the grammatical

present tense *(speaks)* suggesting that *B* is valid in *R*, prevent the implicature that *"B* only in *A*-situations." Within *H*, we have *A* and *B*, from
which the hidden conclusion *C* follows. Since space *H* corresponds to
"in all *A*-situations," the trivial (53), with no link between *A* and *B*,
yields the nontrivial hidden conditional:

(58)
If you need an interpreter, you might hire John.

Notice that *C*, as opposed to *B*, holds only in *H*, that is, only in
A-situations.

It is interesting that overt and hidden logical links are both derived
from the same minimal characterization of *if A* as a space-builder for
A-situations and that this characterization in itself does not involve a
"logical link" meaning for *if*.

As noted above for *speaks*, grammatical tense may indicate whether
the consequent *B* is valid in *R* or in *H*. Given a present tense protasis,
the present progressive in English will typically relativize *B* to *R* (giving
a "fridge and beer" reading), whereas future relativizes *B* to *H*, giving a
classical interpretation:

(59)

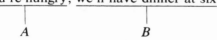

If you're hungry, we're having dinner at six.
       A   *B*

(Suggests: We're having dinner at six, whether you're hungry or not.
Hidden conditional: "If you're hungry, join us for dinner at six.")

(60)

If you're hungry, we'll have dinner at six.
       A   *B*

(Future tense: *B* is valid in *H* (*A*-situations). By implicature, there is
a link between *A* and *B*.)

If *B* itself has future time reference, future tense may be compatible
with validity in *R*, and the conditional sentence will be ambiguous:

(61)
If you're interested, Prof. Murgatroyd will speak tomorrow at five.
(Either the professor speaks anyway and "if you're interested, you
should come," or the professor will speak only if you show interest.)

Here too, the progressive unambiguously relativizes B to R:

(62)

If you're interested, Prof. Murgatroyd $\left\{ \begin{array}{l} \text{will be speaking} \\ \text{is speaking} \end{array} \right\}$
tomorrow at five.
(Only the "fridge and beer" reading)

4.2 Comparatives

Consider the following sentence:

(63)
In that picture, Alice is taller than Lewis.

There are (at least) two possibilities for the interpretation of (63): either Alice and Lewis are both in the picture, and given the optical conventions for evaluating the representation, Alice in the picture is taller than Lewis in the picture; or Lewis is not in the picture, but modulo the representation conventions, the height of Alice in the picture is greater than the height of Lewis (for example, Alice, having just eaten the right kind of mushroom, is as big as a house; the picture represents Alice and the house; and since Alice is the same size as the house, it follows that she is taller than Lewis).

This double possibility is a consequence of the space configuration corresponding to (63), which is given in figure 4.1. We know (by simple application of the ID Principle) that $Alice$ can identify a or a' and $Lewis$ can identify l or l'. (63) can therefore express one of the following relations:

(64)
a. a' taller than l'
b. a' taller than l
c. a taller than l'
d. a taller than l

Relations (64a) and (64b) correspond to the two possibilities noted at the outset. (64d) is ruled out because it contains no element of M.[11] And (64c) is blocked by the additional constraint that in constructions $[SB_M, S]$ like (63), the grammatical subject of S typically identifies an element of M (compare, in a museum setting, the two statements "In that picture, Mona Lisa is observing us," "*?In that picture, we are being observed by Mona Lisa").[12]

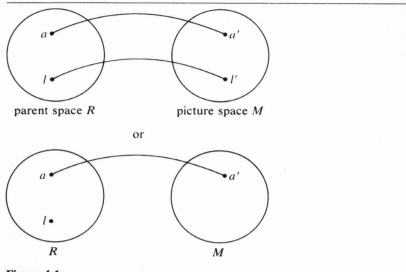

parent space *R*   picture space *M*

or

R   *M*

Figure 4.1

Incidentally, neither interpretation requires that *a'* actually have a counterpart in *R*; interpretation (64a) does not require *l'* to have a counterpart in *R*, and interpretation (64b) is easier if *l* does not have a counterpart in *M*.

The double processing possibility for (63) implies that comparative relations can operate across spaces: relation (64b), *a' > l*, operates on elements *a'* and *l* in different spaces. As expected, we find the same double reading phenomenon for spaces of different kinds:

(65)
Lucy believes that Alice is taller than Lewis.
a. Lucy believes of Alice and of Lewis that the first is taller than the second: *a' > l'*.
b. Lucy has never heard of Lewis; she believes Alice to be 6' tall. The speaker holds Lewis to be 5'10": *a' > l*.

(66)
Last year, Alice was taller than Lewis.
a. Alice-last-year was taller than Lewis-last-year.
b. Alice-last-year was taller than Lewis now.
(Compare: "Last year, Alice was taller than that little boy over there.")

(67)

In that movie, Charlton is stronger than Hercules.
(Hercules may or may not be a character in the movie.)

(68)

Lucy would like her son to be taller than Wilt Chamberlain.
(Possibly, Lucy has never heard of Wilt Chamberlain, but would like her son to be 7'3", which the speaker takes to be taller than Wilt Chamberlain.)

(69)

In Martian chess, gouglons are more powerful than castles.
(Either Martian chess has both gouglons and castles, gouglons being the more powerful, or it doesn't have castles at all: the gouglons in Martian chess are being compared to the castles in Earth chess.)

The analysis lets the comparative relation hold between elements of spaces. Whether or not this is ultimately entirely correct, it is certainly true that comparatives also apply to other things such as states and events:

(70)

John walks faster than Peter runs.

(71)

More people left than stayed.

Such comparatives involve two clauses and a certain amount of syntactic deletion, and perhaps movement as well. The syntactic details need not really concern us here,[13] but I will assume, at least for expository purposes, that forms like (70), (71) can be related to intermediate syntactic forms, something like (70'), (71'):

(70')

(John walks x fast) more than (Peter runs x' fast)

(71')

(x people left) more than (x' people stayed)

(Informally, and simplifying a great deal, we can derive (70) and (71) from (70') and (71') by letting *more* go into the x position and deleting x' *fast* and x' *people* under identity with x *fast* and x *people*, respectively.)

Normal forms like (70′), (71′) have a simple semantics: taking x, x' to be on some scale (degree, number, etc.), they have the interpretation $x > x'$, with "$x = \iota z(\text{John walks } z \text{ fast})$," "$x' = \iota z(\text{Peter runs } z \text{ fast})$." More generally, we can take simple comparatives like (70), (71) to involve two states/events E, E' and some scale Sc on which they can be compared (height, velocity, number, beauty, meanness, etc.). This type of comparative relation can be schematized as in (72):

(72)
E more than E'/Sc
(E is above E' on scale Sc; in (70), E = "John walks," E' = "Peter runs," Sc = velocity (fast).)

In such comparatives, E and E' are relative to the same space. It follows that comparison of E with E (itself) will lead to either contradiction or tautology:

(73)
*E more than E/Sc

(74)
Tautology: E as much as E/Sc

(75)
*The train goes faster than it goes.

(76)
The train goes as fast as it goes.

But comparisons can also occur across spaces, as for Alice and Lewis; that is, E and E' can be relativized to different spaces M and M', and this may be indicated explicitly by the corresponding space-builders, SB_M and $SB_{M'}$:

(77)

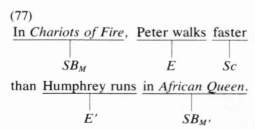

The general form of transspatial comparatives is as follows:

(78)
E/M more than $E'/M'/Sc$

If two spaces are involved, then a state/event E in one may be compared to its counterpart in the other; this yields a comparison between two entities with the same linguistic description:

(79)
In *Chariots of Fire*, Peter runs faster
$\qquad\qquad\qquad\quad \overline{\phantom{\text{Peter runs}}}$
$\qquad\qquad\qquad\qquad\quad |$
$\qquad\qquad\qquad\qquad\; E/M$

than Peter runs in *African Queen*.
$\quad\; \overline{\phantom{\text{Peter runs}}}$
$\qquad\; |$
$\qquad E/M'$

(Standard anaphora and deletion processes will often reduce such forms:

(80)
a. In *Chariots of Fire*, Peter runs faster than *he* runs in *African Queen*.
b. In *Chariots of Fire*, Peter runs faster than he *does* in *African Queen*.
c. In *Chariots of Fire*, Peter runs faster than in *African Queen*.)

This analysis is directly applicable to other types of spaces and space-builders. Suppose for instance that M is the speaker's "reality" (SB_M = *in reality*) and M' is George's beliefs ($SB_{M'}$ = *George believes _____*); then (78) will surface linguistically (after syntactic reduction) as (81):

(81)
In reality, Peter runs faster than George believes he does.
$\;|\qquad\quad |\qquad\qquad\qquad\quad |\qquad\qquad\quad |\qquad\quad |$
$SB_M\qquad E/M\qquad\quad Sc\qquad\qquad SB_{M'}\qquad\; E/M'$

If the parent-space space-builder is not expressed, the result is (82):

(82)
Peter runs faster than George believes he does.
$\;|\qquad\qquad\qquad\qquad\quad |\qquad\qquad\quad |$
$E/M\qquad\qquad\qquad SB_{M'}\qquad\; E/M'$

And if we want to express that E/M' is higher than E/M, the same procedure yields (83a) or, without SB_M explicitly, (83b):

(83)

a. George believes that Peter runs faster than he does in fact.

    $SB_{M'}$ E/M' E/M SB_M

b. George believes that Peter runs faster than he does.[14]

    $SB_{M'}$ E/M' E/M

(83b) is the form that has intrigued linguists, because it admits another parsing in which the comparative relation lies entirely within the belief space:

(84)

George believes that [Peter runs faster than he does].

    $SB_{M'}$ E/M' E/M'

This interpretation, with the events relative to the same space ("George believes ____") is simply a case of (73), like (75) or (85) with an explicit space-builder for the single relevant space:

(85)

*In reality, the train goes faster than it goes.

    SB_M E/M E/M

The two configurations that converge superficially to yield (83b) = (84) are as follows:

(86)

$(E$ more than $E)/M'$

(87)

E/M' more than E/M

In one sense, this contrast is consistent with the observation (Postal (1974), Abbott (1976)) that *more* (in the form ____*er*) has wide scope in (83b) and narrow scope in (84). At the same time, the two possibilities (86), (87) follow directly from the general principle that comparison may apply within one space or across spaces. As in other space-related phenomena (opacity, specificity, time reference, role-value distinctions, etc.; see chapters 1 and 2), it is inappropriate to try to mirror these space-inclusion contrasts structurally by means of deep semantic (or logical) underlying forms.

In fact, for comparatives, Reinhart (1975) has shown that a scopal analysis would be wrong in any event. She considers sentences of the form (88):

(88)
Her headache prevented Rosa from answering more questions than she did.

A scopal representation of (88) would amount to something like (89):

(89)
"the number of questions that Rosa was prevented from answering *exceeds* the number of questions that she answered"

But in fact (88) can be true if Rosa answered ten questions and missed two because of her headache. All (88) does is set up a counterfactual situation ("no headache") in which Rosa *would* have answered more questions than she *actually* did. The space configuration is the same as for (83b), namely a form of (78), where E' is the counterpart of E:

(90)
Her headache prevented Rosa from answering more questions
$SB_{M'}$ E/M'
than she did.
E/M

E/M' is the counterfactual event: Rosa answers x' questions. E/M is the actual event: Rosa answers x questions. The comparative expresses $x' > x$. This does not imply that the number of questions she was prevented from answering (perhaps $x' - x$) is greater than the number of questions she answered, x.

Notice that, as we expect, other counterfactual spaces would yield the same sort of interpretation:

(91)
If Rosa had been well, she would have answered more questions
$SB_{M'}$ E/M'
than she did.
E/M

(92)

I wish Rosa had answered more questions than she did.

   $SB_{M'}$ E/M' E/M

In particular, this type of fact confirms that negation sets up counter-factual spaces (see sections 1.6.4, 3.2.2.7, 4.1):[15]

(93)

Rosa did not answer more questions than she did,

        $SB_{M'}$ E/M' E/M

because she had a headache.

In the counterfactual space set up by *not*, "Rosa answers more questions than she does (in reality)."

The one thing to remember about this range of superficially complex examples is that when viewed in space terms, they are no different from innocuous cases like (94):

(94)

On Thursday, Rosa answered more questions

     $SB_{M'}$ E/M'

than she did on Wednesday.

   E/M SB_M

However, a different and perhaps more difficult kind of complexity stems from another feature of such examples. Consider (95):

(95)

Rosa did not answer *three questions*.

(95) has two interpretations, (I_1) and (I_2):

(I_1)

The number of questions answered by Rosa is less than three.

(For example, situation 1: there are four questions altogether, and Rosa answers two of them.)

(I_2)
There are three questions that Rosa does not answer.
(For example, situation 2: there are eight questions altogether, and Rosa answers five of them.)

(I_1) is false in situation 2, and (I_2) is false in situation 1.

The double possibility follows from the properties of indefinites (like *three questions*) studied in section 2.4: if M is the parent space and M' the counterfactual space (corresponding to *not*), the indefinite identifies an element in M' either by pointing directly to it ("nonspecific") or by pointing to its counterpart in M ("specific"). With respect to (95), these two possibilities are as depicted in figures 4.2 and 4.3. So far, we have a familiar situation—the one rendered in predicate logic by letting the scopes of negatives and quantifiers vary with respect to each other. Notice that even though a' is not the counterpart of b, the event "answering a''' in M' is the counterpart of the event "answering b" in M—in the configuration shown in figure 4.2. In figure 4.3, the counterpart of "answering b" is "answering $a' + b'$." As noted in section 4.1, counterfactual spaces are only partially specified: a' is specified only for number (3), which must be greater than the number of b, to ensure lack of fit between M and M' in figure 4.2. In figure 4.3, a' is the

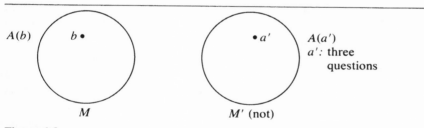

Figure 4.2

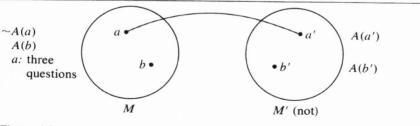

Figure 4.3

counterpart of a (same questions, hence same number); a' has property A (in M'), so its counterpart a does not have the property in M: $\sim A(a)/M$.

The comparatives we have studied present the same potential ambiguity. Taking (90) as an example, recall that the counterfactual event is E': "Rosa answers x' questions." In the analysis of (89), we took "x' questions" to be nonspecific, that is, originating in M'. If instead we take "x' questions" to originate in M, the result is a configuration like figure 4.3, with the following properties:

(96)
a. $a = a' = x'$ questions $\sim A(a)/M$ $A(a')/M'$
b. $b = b' = x$ questions $A(b)/M$ $A(b')/M'$
c. $x' > x$

This corresponds to the reading for which the number of questions not answered exceeds the number of questions answered. (97) has this interpretation:

(97)
Rosa did not answer more questions than she answered.

(In the predicate logic representation, this is the reading where *more* has wide scope over *not*.) Interestingly, however, (93) does not have this interpretation. This is because it also involves verb phrase deletion ("Rosa did not answer more questions than she *did* . . ."). The relevant verb phrases are *answer x questions* and *answer x' questions*. They will count as "identical" for the purpose of deletion if they correspond to events that are counterparts in M and M'. As we have seen, this is precisely the case in the configuration in figure 4.2; but in figure 4.3, the counterpart in M' of the event "answering x questions" in M is the event "answering $x + x'$ questions." The verb phrases count as different: we can have (97), but no further reduction as in (93) or (98):

(98)
Rosa did not answer more questions, because she had a headache.
(Only one reading, as in (93))

The same phenomenon was pointed out by Abbott (1976) for the counterfactual *prevent*:

(99)
Rosa was prevented from answering more questions than she answered by . . .

(99) has the three readings: the obvious "contradictory" one, the "non-specific" reading of (90), and the "specific" reading of (97). Further syntactic reduction can apply only if the events are counterparts, yielding (100) or (101):

(100)
Rosa was prevented from answering more questions than she did by . . .
(Two readings: contradictory or (90))

(101)
Rosa was prevented from answering more questions by . . .
(One reading: (90))

Finally, we must note that comparatives also give rise to role-value distinctions of the sort studied in chapter 2. Comparing two states (or events) is to compare their degrees on some scale. (72) can be paraphrased by (102):

(102)
the degree to which E more than *the degree to which E'*

But "the degree of E" is a role r (in the sense of chapter 2), which takes different values $r(M)$ in different spaces M.

The copula *be* can stand for metonymic relations in general (chapter 5) and in particular for the relation between a role and its value:

(103)
<u>Mitterrand</u> is <u>the president.</u>

   value a role r

We note the attribution of a value a to a role r with an arrow: $r \rightarrow a$.

(104) and (105) are standard sentences involving roles and values:

(104)
The president is the president.

(105)
The president is the president, because 52% of the people voted for him.

Assuming these statements are relative to space R, with r as the role "the president" and a the value of that role in R ($a = r(R)$), (104) has three interpretations:

(106)
a. $r = r$
b. $r(R) = r(R)$
c. $r \rightarrow r(R)$

The first two are clearly tautological; the third however is not, even if it is uninformative by itself. $r(R)$ picks out the value, a, of role r in R; interpretation (106c) expresses that role r takes value a, which is not a tautology since r might have taken other values, and presumably does in other spaces. (105) illustrates this contingency: *him* points to value a (identified by property r), so that (105) yields a new property of a ("52% of the people voted for a"), and this property is presented as the reason why a is the value of role r. In other words, nothing prevents the identification $r(R)$ from being used for a, even when we talk of a's relation to role r.

Single space comparatives of equality have the same property in this respect:

(107)
Jack is as tall as he is.

(108)
Jack is as tall as he is, because he loves spinach.

Taking E = "Jack is tall" and r = "the degree of E," (108) has the same role-value interpretation as (105)—that is, $r \rightarrow r(R)$—and if a is Jack's height, then $r(R)$ is simply a. Thus, interpretation (106c) is the same as $r \rightarrow a$. (106a) is uninformative by itself, since it tells us nothing new about a, but (105) and (108) are informative, since they give us new, nontautological information about the link between r and a. The same is true, mutatis mutandis, for examples like the following:

(109)
I'm surprised that Jack is as tall as he is.

(110)
She's sorry that Jack is as tall as he is.
(Compare: "She's sorry that the president is the president.")

(111)
The fact that Jack is as tall as he is disturbs Mary.

(112)
The possibility that Jack was as cruel as he was never occurred to us.

(This last case also involves an extra possibility space.)

Cases of tautological relative clauses would be handled in the same way:

(113)
John eats what he does.

(114)
John eats what he does because he's on a diet.

(115)
I'm surprised that John eats what he does.

Appendix: Space Version of Goldstick's Algorithm

For this space adaptation of Goldstick's algorithm, I have used the presentation in Brée (1982).

Given the counterfactual

CF = if A, then C

with space-builder *if A* setting up space H in which A is satisfied. To construct H from R, start with H as a replica of R, then:

(G_1)
Discard propositions satisfied in H (that is, suppress the relations in H expressed by these propositions) until the following conditions are satisfied for all conjunctions K of subsets of remaining propositions:
a. K is consistent with A.
b. If K is derivable from O & $\sim A$, then it is derivable from O alone, where O is any of the remaining valid propositions.
The remaining valid propositions form set S.

(G_2)
Discard propositions from S until the following conditions are satisfied for all conjunctions K' of subsets of remaining propositions:
a. K' is consistent with A & C.
b. K' is consistent with $\sim C$.
The remaining propositions from S plus A form S', the set of propositions satisfied in H.

Appropriateness of the counterfactual:
CF is appropriate if C is derivable from S' (satisfied in H).

As Brée points out, there is a problem with this procedure at step (G_2b). Suppose that Olga's reason for going to the party is that Alex goes; suppose further that Alex goes and not Boris. Then (i) is appropriate, given that Alex goes regardless of what Boris does:

(i)
If <u>Boris had gone to the party,</u> <u>Olga would still have gone.</u>

$$A \qquad\qquad\qquad\qquad\qquad C$$

Call D the proposition "Alex goes." Then at step (G_2) in the procedure, C is removed and D is removed (because C is a consequence of D and therefore D is not consistent with $\sim C$). The absence of D in H incorrectly prevents C from being derived (from S'), as the appropriateness condition would require.

It may be, however, that (G_2b) can be entirely dispensed with, given an adequate formulation of (G_1b). (G_1a) eliminates propositions incompatible with A. (G_1b) eliminates propositions compatible with A, but actually derived from a combination of $\sim A$ and something else in R ("O"). If the consequent of the counterfactual, C, or one of its causes is satisfied in R by virtue of some link to $\sim A$, it will be eliminated by (G_1b). If it is satisfied independently of $\sim A$, it will remain and in the absence of (G_2b) will end up in H: the counterfactual will count as appropriate, which seems exactly right.

As an example, consider three situations corresponding to the utterance of (i):

(I)
Structure of R:
1. $\sim A$ (Boris didn't go)
2. $D \rightarrow C$ (If Alex goes, Olga goes)
3. C (Olga went)
4. D (Alex went)

Step (G_1a): Eliminates $\sim A$ $\left\{\begin{array}{l} D \rightarrow C \\ C \\ D \end{array}\right\}$

Step (G_1b): Applies vacuously
Step (G_2a): Applies vacuously $(D \rightarrow C, C, D$ all compatible with A & $C)$

Final structure of H:

$D \rightarrow C$

C

D

A

C is valid in H: CF is appropriate.

($D \rightarrow C$ and D play no role in this procedure; sentence (i) is really only taken to mean that Boris's presence is not linked to Olga's, whatever other reasons Olga may have for going. Step (G_2b) of the original algorithm would discard C and either D or $D \rightarrow C$; C would not be derivable in H.)

(II)

Structure of R:

1. $\sim A$ (Boris didn't go)
2. $\sim A \rightarrow C$ (If Boris doesn't go, Olga goes)
3. $D \rightarrow C$ (If Alex goes, Olga goes)
4. C (Olga went)
5. D (Alex went)

(By 2 and 3, C follows both from 1 and from 5.)

Step (G_1a): Eliminates $\sim A$

Step (G_1b): Eliminates C, since C follows from 2 and $\sim A$ but not from 2 alone

Step (G_2a): Applies vacuously

Final structure of H:

A

$\sim A \rightarrow C$

$D \rightarrow C$

D

C is derivable from 3 and 5 by modus ponens: CF is appropriate.

(III)

Structure of R:

1. $\sim A$ (Boris didn't go)
2. $\sim A \rightarrow C$ (If Boris doesn't go, Olga goes)
3. C (Olga went)
4. D (Alex went)

Step (G_1a): Eliminates $\sim A$

Step (G_1b): Eliminates C (as in (II))

Final structure of H:
A
$\sim A \to C$
D

C is not derivable in H: CF counts as inappropriate.

(A good result, since this time Olga's presence has been linked to Boris's absence but to nothing else.)

A similar (perhaps conceptually simpler) procedure would consist in first giving a *"normal" form* of R: (a) proposition $\sim A$ and (b) a minimum finite set P of propositions that are not consequences of $\sim A$, such that none is a consequence of the others combined with $\sim A$. (All the original propositions valid in R will then be consequences either of P, of $\sim A$, or of P & $\sim A$.) P is then reduced to P' as in (G_1a) to be consistent with A. The final structure of H is $\{P', A\}$.

In the case of (I), this would yield the following partitioned normal form of R:

$\sim A \qquad D \to C \qquad$ (C is discarded as being a consequence of P)

$\qquad\qquad D$

$\qquad\quad \underbrace{\qquad\qquad}$

$\qquad\qquad P$

Structure for H: $\{A, D \to C, D\}$
C is derivable in H by modus ponens.

(II) works the same way.

In (III), C is eliminated because it is a consequence of P & $\sim A$, given the partitioning of R:

$\sim A \qquad \sim A \to C$

$\qquad\qquad D$

$\qquad\quad \underbrace{\qquad\qquad}$

$\qquad\qquad P$

The result is the same inappropriate structure for H as before: $\{A, \sim A \to C, D\}$.

Chapter 5
Transspatial Operators, Philosophical Issues, and Future Perspectives

"Le rendez-vous est dehors," dit Théodule. "Voyons la fillette."

Et il s'avança sur la pointe de ses bottes vers l'angle où Marius avait tourné.

Arrivé là, il s'arrêta stupéfait.

Marius, le front dans ses deux mains, était agenouillé dans l'herbe sur une fosse. Il y avait effeuillé son bouquet. A l'extrémité de la fosse, à un renflement qui marquait la tête, il y avait une croix de bois noir avec ce nom en lettres blanches: Colonel Baron Pontmercy. On entendait Marius sangloter.

La fillette était une tombe.

Victor Hugo, *Les Misérables*[1]

5.1 Transspatial Operators

5.1.1 Be
Many verbs, perhaps a majority, establish relations within spaces. Others (for example, *believe, paint, prevent, look for, wish*) set up new spaces.

The verb (or copula) *be* has special properties. First, it can be used very generally to link a trigger and its target, when the relevant pragmatic function (connector) is known:

(1)

Plato is the red book; Homer is the black book.
(Connector: "writers → books")

(2)

The gastric ulcer is Peter Smith.
(Connector: "illnesses → patients" (in a hospital))

(3)

We are the first house on the right.
(Connector: "people → houses they live in")

(4)

I'm the ham sandwich; the quiche is my friend.
(Connector: "customers → food they order")

(5)

Getty is oil, Carnegie is steel, Vanderbilt is railroads. (cf. Fife (1979))
(Connector: "magnates → product controlled")

(6)

In that picture, Lisa is the girl with blue eyes.
(Image connector: "models → representations")

(7)

In that movie, Cleopatra is Liz Taylor.
(Drama connector: "characters → actors")

"I am the state," "Life is love," "Our future is science," etc., are probably also examples of this type. A pragmatic function can operate within a space (extended metonymy), as in (1) through (7); in that case, *be* stands grammatically for the metonymic link. But a pragmatic function (connector) can also operate from one space to another (chapter 1); in that case, *be* links elements that are counterparts in different spaces. This is what happens in (6) and (7), and it also happens for the other types of spaces. Consider conditionals: "If A, then B." We have seen, among other things, that they set up a hypothetical space H in which the relations expressed by A, and by B, are satisfied. As it stands, however, this formulation is inadequate in some cases involving the copula *be:*

(8)

If <u>Jerry was Napoleon,</u> <u>he wouldn't make so many mistakes.</u>

$\qquad\qquad\quad A \qquad\qquad\qquad\qquad\qquad B$

The counterpart of element a (Jerry) of space R is element a' (Napoleon) of hypothetical space H. If A expressed an internal relation within space H, its noun phrases would identify elements of H, possibly by way of the ID Principle; *Napoleon* identifies a' directly, *Jerry* points to a and identifies its counterpart a'. The relation expressed by A would be *"a' is a',"* which is tautological and therefore inadequate.

But of course A does not express a relation within H in (8): it sets up the link between a and a', that is, a relation between an element of R and an element of H. This is the sense in which *be* is transspatial: when the pragmatic connector is known, *be* can be used to link elements of different spaces.[2]

The same reasoning applies to (7): if the clause following the space-builder *in that movie* expressed an internal relation within the "movie space," it would reduce to the tautological "Cleopatra is Cleopatra." What the clause actually does is to explicitly associate an element of *R*, the actress Liz Taylor, to an element of the movie space, the character Cleopatra. The same is true of (9):

(9)
Dean thought that Jerry was Napoleon.

(9) does not express a relation between "Jerry" and "Napoleon" in the space "Dean thought ____," but rather a counterpart relation between an element of the parent space ("Jerry") and an element of the space "Dean thought" ("Napoleon"); otherwise, the complement of *thought* would reduce after application of the ID Principle to *"a' was a'."*

The transspatial property of *be* that stems from these observations can be formulated as follows:

(10)
Given a configuration
SB_M S
where SB_M is a space-builder and S a grammatical clause of the form
$S = NP_1$ be NP_2
and given the connector *F* linking space *M* to its parent space *R*,
if NP_1 (or NP_2) points to *a* in *R* and NP_2 (or NP_1) points to *a'* in *M*,
then S may express that
a' in M is the counterpart of a in R, that is
$a' = F(a)$

In other words, even though a simple clause usually expresses relations within a space, those of the form *NP be NP* may establish a counterpart relation between elements of different spaces. As opposed to many other verbs, *be* may express transspatial links: this is a consequence of its general metonymic function and of the metonymic nature of pragmatic connectors in general, and of interspatial ones in particular.

However, in the same configurations, there is another interpretation of *be* that is not transspatial. In section 2.2, we saw that the link between a *role* and its *value* is itself a pragmatic function (a connector), *F*, defined as follows,

(11)
$F(m, r) = r(m)$

where m represents the relevant contextual parameters, and in particular the space in which r takes its value. So there is also a metonymic link between a role and its value; and, like the others, this link can be expressed grammatically with the copula *be:*

(12)

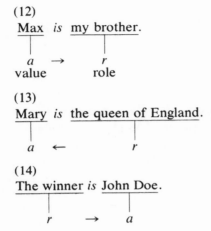

(13)
Mary *is* the queen of England.

(14)
The winner *is* John Doe.

The pragmatic function F, which *be* stands for, is "the attribution of a value to a role," →, mentioned in section 4.1. In space diagrams, like figures 2.5 and 2.6, this link between role and value was represented by a dotted arrow. The role-value relation links two elements *within* a space, a role and a value. (13), for example, gives us a property of Mary—being queen of England—and a property (in the same space) of the role "queen of England"—having Mary as its value.

This means that there will be configurations formally analogous to those in (10), that is,

(15)
$SB_M S$ with $S = NP_1$ be NP_2

where S will express a relation internal to space M, namely the attribution of a value to a role, and not a transspatial link:

(16)
If Mary was the queen of England, everything would be fine.

(17)
George thinks that Mary is the queen of England.

(16) attributes the value "Mary" to the role "queen of England" in the hypothetical space H set up by *if:* this interpretation does *not* make Mary a counterpart of Elizabeth. Similarly, in (17), the role "queen of England" is attributed to Mary in George's beliefs: this is an internal relation within the space "George believes ____."

Such interpretations imply that NP_1 identifies a value and that NP_2 identifies a role:

(18)

$$SB_M \qquad NP_1 \quad be \quad NP_2$$

space M a $\leftarrow$ r

             value   role

However, it happens that a noun phrase that can identify a role in a grammatical construction can also identify the corresponding value, in virtue of the "trigger-target" link between role and value. Consequently, cases like (16), (17) remain potentially ambiguous between a role-value interpretation and a transspatial one: noun phrases like *the queen of England* in (16) and (17) can identify the role "queen of England" or its value, say, Elizabeth. The second strategy, and that one only, implies a transspatial use of *be*. For pragmatic reasons, (19) might be understood in this way:

(19)
If Mary was the queen of England, she would have a sister, Margaret, and a son, Charles.

(The properties mentioned happen to depend more on the person Elizabeth than on the role "queen of England.") The noun phrase *the queen of England* points to the role "queen of England" and identifies its value a' in the hypothetical space H. *Mary* identifies a in R. The protasis of the conditional construction establishes the transspatial relation $a' = F(a)$ by means of the copula *be*.

An extra twist comes in if a proper name functions as a role (see section 2.5). For example, a recent French literary prize (the Goncourt) was awarded to Emile Ajar, pseudonym of a writer whose identity was then unknown, for the novel *La vie devant soi*. A statement such as (20)

(20)
If Romain Gary is Emile Ajar, he's very clever.

could then be interpreted equally well as a transspatial or a role-value statement (with Emile Ajar = "the author of *La vie devant soi*"), with no difference in meaning. This accidental convergence comes about because the role happens to be the only known property for Emile Ajar.

Another, more classical case where a transspatial configuration is understood as a role-value relation involves predication with indefinites:

(21)
If my VW was a Rolls, I would go a lot faster.

A strict application of the characterization of indefinites in chapter 1 sets up a new element *w* (property "Rolls") for *a Rolls* in the hypothetical space *H*. The copula *was* operates transspatially to link element *a* (my VW) in *R* to element *w* (a Rolls) in *H*. In this case, because "Rolls" is the only property of *w*, it amounts to the same thing to establish *w* as a counterpart of *a* or to presuppose that *a* has a counterpart *a'* in *H* and to assign the property "Rolls" to *a'*. This means that (21) is equivalent to an assignment of the property "Rolls" to the counterpart of "my VW" in hypothetical space *H*.

From this point of view, then, (22) and (23) would be analyzed differently, but the meanings would be close:

(22)

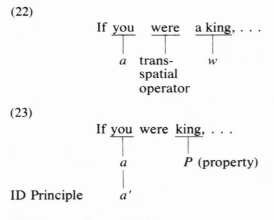

(23)

5.1.2 Other Transspatials
The copula *be* can explicitly link two elements of different spaces. Other verbs or verbal expressions also operate on several spaces, but start with only one element; in this case, one effect is to set up for this element of space *M* a counterpart in another space *M'*.

The most obvious example is perhaps *exist*. Suppose we are talking about the mythical horse Pegasus within a mythological space M. Then, to say (24):

(24)
Pegasus exists (in reality).

is to set up a counterpart of the mythical Pegasus in space M', "in reality ____" (the speaker's "reality"). *Exist* may set up counterparts in all kinds of spaces:

(25)
Pegasus exists *in your imagination*.

(26)
For small children, Santa Claus exists.

(27)
This house exists *on paper*.

(28)
That hotel still existed *in 1929*.

(29)
I wish Santa Claus existed.

(30)
D'Artagnan only existed *in Dumas's books*.

(31)
Pegasus *might* have existed.

(32)
D'Artagnan *may* have existed.

Another series of verbs has the effect, among other things, of copying relations or elements from the speaker's reality (R) to the "reality space" of the grammatical subject of the verb (R_s):

(33)

$$\text{Luke} \begin{cases} \text{knows} \\ \text{understands} \\ \text{has guessed} \\ \text{has learned} \\ \text{realizes} \end{cases} \text{that Mary hates him.}$$

Here the two spaces correspond to the speaker's reality (R) and "Luke's reality as conceived of by the speaker," space R_S included in R. The relation "Mary hates Luke," satisfied in R, becomes satisfied in R_S for the counterparts of "Mary" and "Luke" in that space. The factivity of these verbs is a direct consequence of this transspatial property: the complement clause is "true" in classical terms, because it expresses a relation valid in R; furthermore, the constructions are presuppositional in the sense of chapter 3. The fact that two spaces are involved explains why the usual opacity/transparency phenomena occur with such verbs, in spite of their factivity:

(34)
Oedipus realizes that his mother hates him, but he doesn't know that she's his mother.

The noun phrase *his mother* points to an element a ("Jocasta") in R and identifies its counterpart a' in R_S (Oedipus's reality); a is the value of the role "mother of Oedipus" in R, but its counterpart a' is not the value of the role "mother of Oedipus" in R_S.

Another interesting case of a possible transspatial operator is the verb *find*. We would say that *find* involves two spaces: on the one hand, reality in the wide sense, with objects, relations, etc.; on the other, a perception space of the subject, which may, depending on the circumstances, correspond to what that person can see, touch, or take, and more metaphorically to what that person can apprehend, understand, be conscious of, etc. Again, we use the notation R_S for this space.

Furthermore, the verb *find* can be used with or without the presupposition that the subject was looking for what he found. When present, this presupposition sets up a third space linked to *look for,* as in utterances like "Luke is looking for a car" ($SB_M = Luke\ is\ looking\ for$ ___).

In both cases, with or without the presupposition, *find* would have the effect of setting up a counterpart in R_S for the element of R associated with its direct object. Therefore, linguistic "ambiguities" will appear if the descriptions in R and in R_S are different for the counterparts:

(35)
Toto found *a car*.

(Context: Toto is a baby playing with a cardboard box, which he "takes" to be a car)

(36)

George has found *heaven* at last.

(Context: George has found a place, which "for him" is heaven)

(37)

Don Quixote found *the giants,* but they were windmills.

The force of these examples is reduced by the fact that space R_S may be set up pragmatically, that is, without an explicit space-builder:

(38)

Toto is driving a car.

(39)

George is in heaven.

(40)

Don Quixote is fighting giants.

Accordingly, the transspatial analysis of *find* remains speculative. It would have the advantage of linking up naturally with the use of *find* in paradigm (33):

(41)

Copernicus *found* that the earth revolved around the sun.

Find also has uses similar to those of *invent, make,* etc., where it would be an ordinary space-builder: *find an idea, find a new engine,* etc.

And if *find* is used with the presupposition "look for," there will be ambiguities comparable to specific-nonspecific, even though the existence of the object found is always implied (as opposed to the existence of the object looked for):

(42)

He found *a watch.*

(. . . that he had lost: it's the watch he was looking for)

(43)

He found *a watch.*

(. . . he was looking for a suitable present)

Notice also expressions like "find a friend," "find a master," where the characteristic property of the object ("friend," "master") only appears when it is found as such. The object may have been perceived, or accessible to consciousness, for a long time, but what counts is its conception in terms of a new role. Here again, R_S can be invoked if we note that the new property is in turn often transferred to R: once we find a friend, there is a chance that he will in fact be one.

5.2 Philosophical Issues

As mentioned before, there are differences between the objectives and adequacy criteria of the research carried out here and those usually adopted in philosophical investigations of the same phenomena. In particular, two crucial questions from a standard philosophical point of view, truth and reference, have not played a central role in the study of mental spaces. It has not been my prime concern here to discover under what conditions an utterance would count as true in a certain state of a real or fictional world. Linguistic expressions help to set up and identify space elements, but do not *refer* to them. Reference would be another connection, presumably relating space elements and real (or perhaps fictional or possible) entities.[3] The study of this connection is complicated by the fact that one cannot *talk* about it without setting up corresponding spaces in the philosophical discourse. Of course, in prototype cases such as describing a real-world situation, there seems to be a pretty good fit between the mental space constructed and the domain of reference, but this is no longer obviously so in complex cases: beliefs, counterfactuals, optatives, etc.

The construction of spaces should not be overinterpreted. They are not representations of reality or of partial "possible worlds." In particular, a belief space ("Max believes ____") is not a belief or state of belief; at most, it is a way of talking about beliefs.

The construction of spaces represents a way in which we think and talk but does not in itself say anything about the real objects of this thinking and talking. This point is obvious in the case of metaphors: detailed studies (for example, Lakoff and Johnson (1980)) show how the vocabulary of moving objects applies to "time" in a coherent and subtle way. This way of talking is probably not without influence on our conceptualization of time, and even on the physical theories that deal with it; but we do not see it as divulging an actual physical property of "time" in the universe. Similarly, it is convenient to say (and perhaps to think) in daily life "The sun rises, sets, moves across the sky, etc.," regardless of the particular knowledge one has of physics.

In epistemology or metaphysics, there may be a tendency to have language tell us more than it can: the fact that we talk in a certain way about what is believed, or about counterfactual situations, does not necessarily tell us much about the nature of beliefs or of possible worlds.

One must also bear in mind that in most philosophical analyses, the description of language is not an ultimate goal; it is meant to support claims linked to other subjects (including truth and reference). As long as the analysis works locally and serves the main objectives, it fulfills its goal. But if the mechanics of language become the main objective, there will be further criteria of elegance and maximal generalization. In the present study, this leads to a regrouping at a certain level of time, images, propositional attitudes, modal operators, etc. A philosophical analysis, on the other hand, might start by carefully distinguishing these notions, given the obvious disparity of their domains of reference.

As a specific example, consider Kripke's work on names and descriptions (Kripke (1980)), which is well known and bears on some of the phenomena discussed here. I am not directly concerned with the philosophical, or metaphysical, "rigidity thesis": this thesis short-circuits the linguistic or psychological functioning of nouns, in order to directly raise the problem of their reference in the actual world or in possible worlds (or "counterfactual situations"). For the question to be asked in these terms, possible worlds must be available as domains of reference; this constitutes a "metaphysical" choice and is quite acceptable as such. Spaces, on the other hand, are constructions linked to a discourse; they are part of the description of cognition but do not imply any corresponding metaphysical object.

According to Kripke, a name is rigid because it refers to the same individual or object, regardless of what possible world the utterance it appears in is relative to, as long as the individual exists in that possible world. In particular, the name does not abbreviate a property, or set of properties, of the individual (or object). An immediate consequence is that identity of objects is a necessary "property." If Hesperus is Phosphorus in reality, there is no world in which Hesperus is not Phosphorus; if the object *a* that I call *Hesperus* or *Phosphorus* turns up in another possible world, it will still be *a*. Of course, *a* may not have the name *Hesperus* or *Phosphorus* in that world. Conversely, a world with two objects called *Hesperus* and *Phosphorus* and having (perhaps in combination) the properties of *a* is not a world in which our Hesperus (*a*) is different from our Phosphorus (*a*); it is a world with two new objects (b and c) that happen to have the properties assigned to a in our world.

At first blush, this point of view runs counter to the space correspondences we have observed: two elements b and c in a certain space may well have the same counterpart in another space (section 2.1). This is the case, for instance, in the interpretation of (44) and (45):

(44)
Luke believes that Hesperus is not Phosphorus.

(45)
If Hesperus was not Phosphorus, . . .   (counterfactual)

What this reveals is that strictly speaking, Kripke's "metaphysical" question about identity in possible worlds is different in nature, and independent, from the question of space counterparts. The construction of successive spaces is epistemic or doxastic; it is linked to successive conceptions of reality for the speaker and for those he speaks of. Such conceptions do not correspond to possible worlds in Kripke's sense; however, since this point is often misunderstood, I will try to say more about the differences and also the analogies between the two systems.

First, there is a sense in which rigidity has an equivalent in space construction. In a single space, the identity relation expressed by *be* can never be satisfied by two distinct elements; if a is different from b and if we have "d_a be d_b," the only interpretation is metonymic: role-value assignment, pragmatic connection, etc. There will therefore only be identity, or at least the semblance of identity, if *be* operates transspatially as in section 5.1 to set up a link. Consider (46):

(46)
In fact, Hesperus is Phosphorus.

This utterance is relative to a space R_0 ("accepted view of reality until then"); in R_0, there are two elements b and c named *Hesperus* and *Phosphorus*, respectively. The space-builder *in fact* sets up a new space R, which will be the new "accepted reality." What does (46) tell us—or rather, what does it construct given this bispatial configuration? *Phosphorus* points to c in R_0; in virtue of the ID Principle, it identifies the counterpart c' in R. *Hesperus* points to and identifies b in R_0. Since *be* is transspatial, the relation obtained, "b be c'," expresses that c' is the counterpart of b in R (see figure 5.1). So the final effect of (46) is to replace two elements in the origin space R_0 by a single one in the target

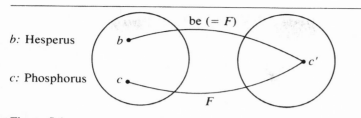

b: Hesperus

c: Phosphorus

Figure 5.1

space *R*. In the example, the space-builder *in fact* indicates explicitly the new reality space *R*. But we know that this explicit indication is not necessary (the spaces can be set up pragmatically). Hence, the same analysis is possible for naked forms like (47):

(47)
Hesperus is Phosphorus.

To repeat, one never establishes identity between two elements of a space: one space is followed by another, in which the two elements of the first have a single counterpart. Language freely allows such substitutions; their function may be to move us closer to truth (as in (46) and (47)) or to set up counterfactual situations ("If I was Queen Elizabeth, . . ." "If Dracula had been born twins, . . .").

In spite of this "multiple counterpart" feature, there is another respect in which something like the rigidity thesis holds for spaces: definite descriptions first point to roles, and then to values, by way of the ID Principle. Names, on the other hand, point to values directly, in the absence of special contextual stipulations (section 2.5).[4] From this point of view, a description, as role, will change values from one space to the next, whereas a proper noun, used transparently, will identify the counterparts of the value that it names. This accounts easily for the phenomena discussed by Kripke: the scope of a description depends on which space the element described belongs to (with subsequent application of the ID Principle); its rigidity depends on whether it is interpreted as a role or as a value.

It is another matter to show that all this bears on the philosophical thesis itself. In his presentation, Kripke never says how important the linguistic data actually are or how they would support particular claims; but he certainly gives the impression that they play a part in the argument. Maybe this is an effect of the a priori judgment that the semantics of sentences consists in the characterization of their truth conditions with respect to possible worlds.

Once this a priori assumption is dropped, as here, the relationship between the linguistic data and the philosophical claims needs to be reexamined.

An example discussed elsewhere by Kripke (Kripke (1979)) brings this out clearly. He studies in great detail the following situation: Pierre, brought up in France, has heard about the city of Londres and has been led to believe "Londres est jolie." Later, life leads him to England, where he speaks English and lives in the city known to him by the name *London*. He forms the belief "London is ugly," while continuing to believe "Londres est jolie." This belief is not contradictory, since Pierre takes the cities known to him as *Londres* and *London* to be distinct. Under such conditions, is (48) true or false?

(48)
Pierre believes that London is pretty.

Kripke shows in minute detail that there is no answer, no matter what theory of reference is adopted: that is the puzzle, which then extends to common nouns (at least those that apply to natural kinds, and perhaps others as well; cf. Putnam (1979)).

What is the situation in terms of spaces? We do not ask about the truth conditions of the "proposition" /Pierre believes that London is pretty/; we do not open up Pierre's head to look at his "beliefs." What is at issue is the spatial configuration associated with utterance (48) under the specified contextual conditions. There is nothing paradoxical about this construction: it involves parent space R (speaker's "reality") in which one element, a, has the names *London* and *Londres*, and space M, set up by *Pierre believes* ____ in which two elements, b and c, are called respectively *London* and *Londres;* the relations "b is ugly" and "c is pretty" are satisfied in M. Furthermore, if Pierre's "mistake" is known to the discourse participants, a in R has been connected to b and c in M. This is a common configuration of multiple connection, analogous to the ones in section 2.1; it is depicted in figure 5.2. The ID Principle applies in the interpretation of (48): *London* points to a in space R and must identify its counterpart in space M. The only special feature of figure 5.2 is that a happens to have two counterparts, so that there are two possible ways of applying the ID Principle: from a to b or from a to c. Depending on the strategy adopted, (48) may therefore construct a relation "b is pretty" in M or a relation "c is pretty." This

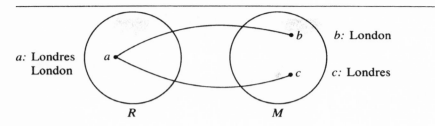

Figure 5.2

effectively corresponds to the two possible understandings of (48) in the particular situation: either, *for Pierre,* the city he knows as *London* is pretty or the city he knows as *Londres* is pretty.[5] The first understanding happens to correspond to something false, the second to something true. Of course, it would be misleading under such circumstances for the speaker to use (48); but, as Ch. Travis points out (personal communication), further specification of context might make it clear which counterpart, *b* or *c*, is relevant—that is, in what sense Pierre believes London to be pretty. The existence of this double strategy is the reason why (48) does not have a truth value in the classical sense.

Should we say, then, that Kripke's puzzle merely stems from a simple ambiguity? That formulation, too, would be misleading. First, there is of course no grammatical (or structural) ambiguity in sentence (48). Second, I have repeatedly stressed the difference between the usual notion of ambiguity and the multiple strategies of spatial construction. Finally, there is an extra factor involved in this particular case: in many examples, the strategic choice depends on which principles apply. Does the ID Principle apply? Role-value assignment? Floating of presuppositions? In example (48) and the corresponding configuration given in figure 5.2, this is not the case: there is no choice between role and value, and the ID Principle applies regardless of the interpretation.[6] The double possibility appears *within* a mode of spatial construction, and not because there might be several modes. That is the special feature, and it explains why (48) does not lend itself to the classical oppositions such as opaque-transparent, de re-de dicto, referential-attributive, etc.

It may be worth emphasizing, however, that in the situation imagined, (48) raises no particular theoretical problem: its properties are automatic consequences of the general laws of spatial construction, and of their being underdetermined. There is no semantic paradox; there is only a paradox if we try to find truth conditions for (48), in the relevant situation, using the classical distinctions.

The fact that (48) does not lead to a semantic paradox, but appears paradoxical with respect to a theory of truth, illustrates the specific character of the latter and also perhaps suggests that its objectives be reassessed.

Let me be more explicit. In order to avoid likely misunderstandings, I emphasized at the outset that the study of mental spaces did not, per se, constitute a theory of reference. The space elements are not referred to by expressions of language; they are set up, identified, etc., and may then be used for purposes of reference (or possibly purported reference). However, this distinction has an obvious and yet nontrivial consequence: theories of reference based on the use of language cannot bypass mental spaces; they will have to forsake the idea of a direct link between linguistic structures and referents and take into account the important intermediate process of space construction. In that sense, the analyses in this book can be regarded as part of the solution to classical philosophical queries. The guiding thought in approaching philosophical puzzles from the mental space perspective is that before truth paradoxes can be exhibited, we must sort out the space constructions involved. In some respects, the mistake of trying to provide truth conditions for sentences directly is comparable to the direct use of surface structures for building inference schemata (e.g., syllogisms).

Many of the linguistic (and in my view cognitive) issues raised in the mental space framework are thus relevant to concerns in the philosophy of language. This was clear, presumably, for the opacity-transparency phenomena that are recast as part of a more general question, namely, that of space connectors and identification. Notice that the mental space perspective accounts not only for why linguistic expressions have the properties observed but also, as a by-product, for why a direct assignment of truth conditions to expressions would face the problems it does: for example, no substitution salva veritate on certain readings, superficial contradiction ("The rich duke was actually broke," "The castle was a shack"). The same is true for intentional identity (section 2.4), proper names (section 2.5), presuppositions (chapter 3), "cross-world identification" (sections 2.1, 5.1, 5.2), and "rigid designators" (section 5.2).

To say that the mental space perspective offers solutions for philosophical puzzles is not, however, totally accurate. What it shows is a certain organization of linguistic phenomena and why such phenomena might appear puzzling from a direct truth-conditional viewpoint. What this actually amounts to is a rejection of the way in which the problems are standardly put; that is, we replace certain problems by others. And this strategy is possible only if we bring in the cognitive interface between expressions of language and the world.

Consider finally the referential-attributive distinction introduced by Donnellan (1966); this is another area where important philosophical observations can be recast profitably in broader mental space terms. As readers have no doubt already noticed on reading chapter 2, Donnellan's distinction follows from the difference between role and value, and the link between them. Consider a standard example:

(49)
Caesar's murderer is insane.

If the description *Caesar's murderer* is constructed (or processed) according to principle (51) of chapter 1, Definite Interpretation, a space element e is identified directly and endowed with the property "insane."[7] If e then refers to some individual (say, Brutus) who has the required property, (49) will be deemed true. As Donnellan has crucially observed, Brutus might in fact not be "Caesar's murderer": as long as reference of e to Brutus is intended (and perhaps recognized as such), (49) can count as true, in spite of discrepancies between real properties of Brutus and identifying properties of e. This is of course the "referential" use of definite descriptions.

If *Caesar's murderer* is understood as a role r, then "insane" is a property of that role and of its value in the relevant space. If there is no such role, there will a fortiori be no values, and nothing will be referred to (in the "real" world). Still, if the speaker thinks Caesar has been murdered, and we know that he takes Brutus to be the murderer, then even if he speaks under the role interpretation (i.e., attributively), we may understand him to imply that Brutus is insane, and this could be true. This is irrelevant to the question of truth conditions for (49), but shows that cognitively, we can take into account implications of making statements "without truth value," which is also perhaps another way of viewing the mistaken, but successful, referential use of (49). If there is a real equivalent for role r—that is, if somebody has in fact murdered Caesar—then the properties of the value (or values) may be truth-conditionally relevant, but the simplicity of Donnellan's example obscures the fact that this is by no means necessary. In the case of (49), if murdering Caesar is a sign of insanity, then people who do it are insane: if the role has the property, the values should have it too. But consider other cases of the kind "The president is over 21." Here the verification might consist in looking up the Constitution (no president has yet been elected, and perhaps none will be for another hundred years, or ever). Or, as in chapter 2, "The president changes every four years"; the corresponding individuals do not necessarily change. So the way in which a property of a role relates to the values of that role varies with the kinds of roles and properties involved. In effect, Donnellan makes the same point, when suggesting that someone who says in 1960 "The Republican presidential candidate in 1964 will be a conservative" does not refer to Goldwater, who in fact turned out to be the Republican candidate in 1964 (and who was also a conservative, which made the statement true). The example sentence, uttered in the appropriate conditions, would set up a "1964" space in which the role "Republican presidential candidate" would take a value with the property "conservative" and would be undetermined as to other aspects. Notice also that if we elect a different chairman every week, the statement "In 1964, the chairman will be Irish" indicates a property of the role, which in practice may cover fifty-two values.

Since roles are space elements, their identifying descriptions could differ from reality as in the referential uses. Searle (1979) corroborates this "prediction": the attributive use of (49) could count as true if Caesar had undergone an almost, but not quite, deadly assault; the improper characterization of the role as "the murderer" would be a "near miss" but would not prevent the construal "whoever assaulted Caesar is insane."

The role-value interaction also explains why the referential-attributive contrast can be felt, even when the corresponding readings are truth-functionally equivalent. Consider the old favorite "This morning, I spoke to a logician": if a $logician$ sets up a new element w directly, by principle (50) of chapter 1, Indefinite Interpretation, we have something akin to the "referential" use; if a $logician$ sets up a role r (section 2.4), then the role, rather than its value, is in the limelight. Two different space constructions are thus possible in connection with the example. However, they happen to be indistinguishable truth-conditionally: if the sentence is true under the role interpretation, there must be a value of that role satisfying the relation "this morning, I spoke to ____," and vice versa. The same is true for examples like "John married a $girl$ his $parents$ $disapprove$ of" (Partee (1970)); of course, truth-functional equivalence is lost in other environments (cf. "John tried to marry a girl his parents disapprove of"—other spaces come into play).

Naturally, what makes this account of the philosophical observations interesting is the fact that the space construction of roles and values was introduced and motivated on very general grounds (recall chapter 2: multiple connectors, discourse quantification, interpretation of indefinites, proper names, theatrical situations, etc.). This means in turn that the role-value account of attributivity is a by-product, among others, of the general perspective.

No doubt this section, focusing somewhat arbitrarily and by way of illustration on Kripke and Donnellan, has been too brief to meet all demands for philosophical clarification. The general account of *be* as linking triggers and targets, elements and their counterparts across spaces, roles and values is also quite important and would lead to a reassessment of basic issues concerning sense and reference. In short, a serious discussion of the incidence of the mental space approach on problems and methods in the philosophy of language could easily take up another book.

Let me, however, repeat the general thesis: mental space construction is (an important) part of natural language semantics and pragmatics. Theories of truth based on linguistic phenomena cannot avoid taking it into account, and indeed, apparent paradoxes of direct truth and reference assignment often arise from the failure to take into account properties of the intermediate space constructions.

5.3 More Questions and Some Speculations

This book has focused on the elementary principles of space construction. The emerging perspective suggests, I believe, that we take another look at several more or less traditional questions. Each one would require a lengthy exposition and careful analyses that I will not attempt here; still, I offer some possible orientations, briefly sketched, with no serious argumentation.

We have seen that spaces can be introduced explicitly by space-builders or implicitly on pragmatic grounds (e.g., fiction, theater, free indirect style, or (more simply) cases when change of time or belief is not formally marked, as in the dialogue between Jim and Huckleberry ("since the night I got killed") or in Victor Hugo's expression ("the girl was a tomb") (see the epigraphs that opened this book and the present chapter)). In a speech situation, the fact that something is said is pragmatically salient; the space of "what is said" is set up. But an explicit space-builder for that space would be *I say that* ___. In terms of truth conditions, the equivalence between *"X"* and "I say that *X"* is problematic; many analyses of performatives center on this problem. But in space terms, we could view the phenomenon as just another case of presence or absence of an explicit space-builder. Ross's famous syntactic observations (Ross (1970)) about phenomena that occur with or without an explicit performative would then simply reflect that the same space is set up in both cases.[8] The same would apply to other performatives. For instance, *Caesar orders* ___ is a space-builder, as shown by the opaque, transparent, specific, nonspecific, etc., interpretations of "Caesar orders us to attack a village"; the corresponding space is a projection, similar to wishes, counterfactuals, possibilities, etc. The performative effect would then stem somewhat trivially from the power that we may have to transmit the orders we set up. (Transmitting orders is of course different from having them acknowledged as legitimate, which is different in turn from having them obeyed.) If the speaker himself happens to be in command (or to think he is), he can therefore set up his own orders by saying "I order . . . ," an instance of explicit space-building. But "The troops will attack at dawn," without an explicit space-builder, said by Caesar (at the right time, in the appropriate circumstances), would be relativized to the same space, thereby counting as an order, simply in virtue of the role occupied by Caesar in the ordering "(sub)ritual" that sets up the required space pragmatically.[9]

This is similar to the view that satisfaction conditions should be relativized to the relevant social rituals (Fauconnier (1981)). But instead of using the misleading expression "true with respect to some ritual," one should speak of "satisfaction" in the corresponding space. Social rituals, in this broad sense, have properties of prototypes, frames, ICMs, etc.

Another vast topic is discourse reference. Research on mental spaces was first motivated by technical difficulties in finding coherent logical representations for pronominalization phenomena. On the one hand, it was clear that pronouns are similar in several respects to the bound variables of ordinary logic; on the other hand, treatments of pronouns as variables also raised insurmountable difficulties. In particular, it is always possible for an anaphor outside the logical scope of the operator to bind its antecedent:

(50)

If a man owns a donkey, he beats *it*.   (Geach (1962))

(51)

Mary did not manage to catch a fish; otherwise she would have cooked *it*. She might have given *it* to her children.   (Fauconnier (1976))

(52)

Nancy wants to write a short story and hopes she can get *Playboy* to accept *it*.   (McCawley (1978))

(53)

Mary firmly hopes to catch a fish, and I will try to cook *it*.   (Fauconnier (1976))

(54)

If John wants a hamburger, he will order *it*.   (Fauconnier (1979))

In space terms, there is no technical problem of anaphors and logical scope; all the relevant noun phrases correspond to elements, which can be triggers or targets. For example, in (54), *if*, *John wants*, and *he will order* are space-builders.[10] The most likely pragmatic interpretation is that in which *a hamburger* sets up a role; the configuration is given in figure 5.3. If its antecedent is *a hamburger*, a pronoun can then link to *r* or to *r'*, in virtue of general properties of open connectors. Similarly, in (51) *a fish* sets up a role (or an element) in the counterfactual space established via negation, so that ulterior pronominalization in discourse is possible, *as long as* the targets are in appropriate spaces. This notion of appropriate space constitutes the real semantic problem, and I have not dealt with it. I have only given examples: in (53), an element set up in the space "Mary hopes ____" has a counterpart in a "future" space; in (54), an element set up in a "want" space has a counterpart in a space "order ____"; in (50), there is no problem since trigger and target are the same, both in the hypothetical space set up by *if*. Defining the conditions under which an element can have counterparts in other spaces is a complex question that probably involves implicatures, prototypes, and schemata for the unfolding of scenarios (see McCawley (1978) for some interesting suggestions and observations in this respect). Notice that such counterparts can also be introduced explicitly, as in "I have exactly the dress you're looking for—here it is."

Sloppy identity is another phenomenon that might be looked at in terms of roles and spaces. In (55), for example,

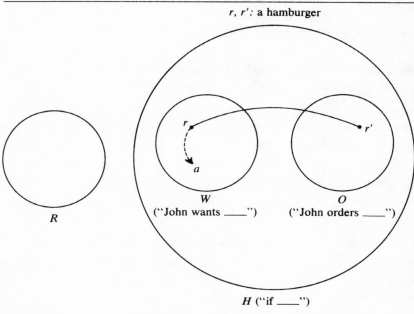

Figure 5.3

(55)

This tree has lost *its leaves;* that one still has *them.*

its leaves and the pronoun *them* point to a role, "leaves of tree," which is the "same" for each tree. The values are identified after pronominalization has operated on the roles. This sort of treatment would involve "mini-spaces" linked to an object or individual and part of its environment; a detailed study should reinterpret in space terms the λ-notation, used with some success by Sag (1975) and Williams (1977).

Another controversial question in linguistics, linked to the preceding one, is the status of logical forms. It is of course possible to provide notational systems for representing linearly the spatial configurations we have discussed. Kuroda's "Indexed Predicate Calculus" (Kuroda (1982)) might be interpreted in this way. What would be the role of such a representation within a linguistic theory? Or again, can we go directly from grammatical structures to spaces, or do we need another intermediate formal structure such as Kuroda's? Throughout this book, I have defended the idea that the constructions proceed directly, and will be multiple for a given grammatical form, because the relevant processes are underdetermined. The indexed calculus technique will require specific linguistic justification and perhaps also some elaboration to deal with the more complex spatial configurations.

Another area that should have been dealt with but was not (except for implicit remarks in sections 2.2 and 2.4), is quantification. A promising idea is to associate universally quantified expressions with mini-spaces in which a new, unspecified element would correspond to the quantified phrase (e.g., *each one*). That element would be the counterpart of all elements in the origin space that belong to the domain of quantification; its properties in the mini-space would thereby be transferred to all its counterparts. And the notion of "fit" of the mini-space with the origin space would require a precise, more than intuitive characterization. Ioup's examples (section 2.4) were analyzed in this spirit. The two configurations for "Each boy danced with a girl" would be something like those shown in figures 5.4 and 5.5. These figures correspond respectively to the logical transcription shown in (56) and (57):

(56)

$\forall x \ (x = \text{boy}) \ \exists y \ (y = \text{girl}) \ (x \text{ danced with } y)$

(57)

$\exists y \ (y = \text{girl}) \ \forall x \ (x = \text{boy}) \ (x \text{ danced with } y)$

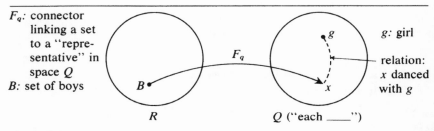

F_q: connector
linking a set
to a "repre-
sentative" in
space Q
B: set of boys

g: girl

relation:
x danced
with g

Figure 5.4

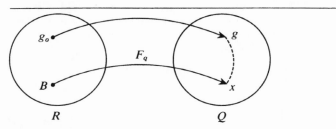

Figure 5.5

x and g in figure 5.4 would function like roles: when x is "filled in" by one of its counterparts in B, g takes on some value in R. In figure 5.5, g has a counterpart g_o in R (once and for all) and therefore a fixed value, whence the interpretation "same girl for all boys." Observations by O. Dahl (Workshop on Recent Trends in Semantics, Urbino, July 1983), in Fauconnier (1978a), and in section 2.2 above could support this kind of approach. Needless to say, all the work remains to be done.

The same idea of an independent space would apply for "generics"; as J. Thorne notes (personal communication), they can come with explicit space-builders, such as *in general, normally, usually*. This is why singular indefinites can have a "universal" interpretation:

(58)
In general, a Frenchman is trustworthy.

(59)
Normally, a bird has wings.

(60)
Usually, a child starts to talk around two.

The indefinite article is used here as elsewhere to set up a new element in a space. Because the space is "generic," the element will be linked to sets of the origin space (by a connector similar to F_q). As usual, the space-builder need not appear explicitly, and we can have the corresponding "simple" statements:

(61)
A Frenchman is trustworthy.

(62)
A bird has wings.

(63)
A child starts to talk around two.

Speech acts, discourse reference, quantification, and generics are traditional problem areas for which the mental space perspective suggests fresh research orientations. One could also investigate reported speech, the multiple spatial layers used to construct narratives, the social schemata that structure spaces and set up certain pragmatic connectors rather than others, or the effects of a gestural modality, instead of an oral one, on the implementation of space phenomena.[11]

The last point is especially interesting, because sign language seems to have ways of setting up spaces and elements (i.e., abstract referential domains) using body-shift and three-dimensionality.[12] The mental construction, which remains the same regardless of the modality involved, can be reflected concretely by very different codes, adapted to that modality.[13]

Notes

Introductory Note

1. Steve Tesich, "Focusing on Friends," *New York Times Magazine,* December 4, 1983. This wonderful example (especially "The very Atlantic I had flown over . . .") was noticed and kindly brought to my attention by James McCawley.

2. This implies metaphysical choices about what can be referred to (objects, individuals in possible worlds, etc.). See chapter 1, note 5; section 4.1; and section 5.3.

3. Cognitive scientists (Kugler, Turvey, and Shaw (1980)) have pointed out the *first-order isomorphism fallacy* (FOIF), which consists in attributing to an organism internal structures analogous to the external structures of its outputs. Kugler, Turvey, and Shaw give many examples. For instance, termites build architecturally complex arches and pillars; the FOIF would consist in endowing the termites with some "mental program" for building arches and pillars. But in fact the termites "obey" a very simple rule in depositing glutinous sand flavored with pheromone: they follow a path of increasing pheromone density and deposit when the density gradient inverts. The fact that this behavior leads to the formation of arches and pillars is part of physics, not a property of termites.

The analogy—which I don't want to push—between that situation and natural language logic would be the following: we use relatively simple principles for space construction, but their iteration can produce complex configurations; the utterances corresponding to a grammatically simple sentence may set up many different spatial configurations. Mutatis mutandis, the FOIF would consist in trying to reflect in the structure of the sentence itself the complexity and diversity of the potential configurations to which it may give rise.

4. The speaker-listener does not consider all the interpretations of a sentence and then discard the inappropriate ones. He sets up a space configuration starting from the configuration already available at that point in the discourse. There will of course be choices and strategies, but the potential of a sentence, given a previous configuration, is always far less than its general potential for all possible configurations. (A brick could theoretically occupy any position in

a wall, but at any stage of the actual building process, there is only one place for it to go.)

5. J. P. Changeux (1983) writes,

L'encéphale de l'homme que l'on sait *contenir,* dans l'organisation anatomique de son cortex, des représentations du monde qui l'entoure, est aussi capable d'en *construire* et de les utiliser dans ses calculs.

Chapter 1

1. On frames and scenarios, see Fillmore (1982). On literal metaphor as a structuring of conceptual networks, see Lakoff and Johnson (1980), Lindner (1981), Brugman (1981), Vandeloise (1982). On accounting for presuppositions in terms of linked discourse worlds, see Dinsmore (1981b). On "scopal" phenomena as referential correspondence between concrete or mental images, see Jackendoff (1975), Fauconnier (1978b).

2. See Nunberg (1978, 1979). The relevant phenomena and their theoretical importance had already been pointed out by Borkin (1984). Also see Bolinger (1968).

3. However, as P. Encrevé points out (personal communication), discourse reference to the omelet (the trigger) is not precluded:

(i)
The mushroom omelet left without paying. *He* complained that *it* was inedible.

Let us say only for present purposes that the *target* is a *foremost* antecedent. The trigger cannot be an antecedent for grammatical anaphoric processes: reflexivization, relative pronouns (cf. ex. (26)).

4. See note 3. As mentioned below in the text, the "openness" of connectors is variable.

5. Deciding what is thereby "referred to" is a different matter. If the informal presentation at this point were interpreted in standard terms of "reference," I would seem to be saying that *Lisa* has multiple reference (like *the mushroom omelet*). But, to quote Charles Travis (personal communication):

Someone might say: *Lisa* always refers to Lisa. The variation is that "is smiling" sometimes ascribes a property of smiling simpliciter, and sometimes one of smiling in such and such a picture.

This point is even more obvious in the later examples (36) and (37), where *mind* replaces *picture:* we would not want to say that there are many Lisas — one in reality, one in Len's mind, one in Sue's mind, etc. To quote Travis again:

Many philosophers will want to say that we don't want to take the metaphor "in the mind" too seriously. Since the mind is not a place, it's not possible to refer to any objects in there, so not possible to have them stand in relation under pragmatic connector functions.

I am in complete agreement with these points. What is at issue in the present language-oriented study is not the deep nature of Lisa, or Len's beliefs, or mental and concrete images, but rather how we talk about them; and here metaphors do need to be taken seriously. The view that will unfold in the text is *not* that we refer to many Lisas, or that the mind is a place with pictures; rather, in order to talk about Lisa, in various circumstances and from different points of view (including cameras and retinae), we indulge in mental construction of spaces containing, among other things, elements and their counterparts. It is *not* the case that the word *Lisa* refers to such elements: it helps to set them up, and it is then the mental elements themselves that may refer to "real Lisa."

6. However, the use of the word *refer* in this connection leads to the problems mentioned in note 5. What I shall say later, using the terminology of section 1.4 and following, is that, mentally, two spaces are set up, one for "reality" and one for the picture, with counterparts corresponding to Lisa in each, which may satisfy different relations. The effect of the ID Principle is that a description of one counterpart may identify another.

7. See notes 5 and 6. The presentation in the text is admittedly very loose at this point: we do not know what it means to "talk as if Lisa has a counterpart in Len's mind." One might say that the clarification of such notions is the subject matter of the rest of this book.

8. As G. Lakoff has noted in discussion, the idea that we may conceptualize pictures and beliefs or understanding in similar ways is corroborated by the extensive use of vision terms to talk about both:

(i)
I *see* what you mean.

(ii)
My *image (impression)* of her is different.

(iii)
In Len's *view,* metaphysics is part of geometry.

(iv)
She showed a lot of *vision* and *insight.*

(v)
I get the *picture.*

9. Again, this preliminary presentation is likely to raise premature "philosophical" objections: whether the speaker is right or wrong amounts to whether what he says is true or false. So a direct truth-conditional account does not have to worry about his mental representations. However, for reasons that I hope will become clearer as we go along and that will be spelled out explicitly in chapter 4, I believe direct truth-conditional accounts are misguided, at least to do the linguistic job at hand. To capture the relevant generalizations, we need to take into account what the utterance, true or false, represents mentally for the speaker.

The term *mental representation* should be interpreted in a weak and general sense: I make no claims about neurological organization or mental images. The construction of mental spaces argued for in later sections represents a minimal characterization of something happening at some cognitive level.

10. J. McCawley points out (personal communication) that the individuation of the image units is given entirely by the interpretation put on the painting, not by

any physical individuation of the paint (e.g., in one of Jean Cocteau's carica-tures, a single wiggly line may be both a person's ear and some of his hair).

11. I use "sets" here to give a first explicit characterization of mental spaces, mainly because sets are familiar, and handy for explicitness and formalization. Mental spaces may turn out to be endowed with a different and/or richer kind of structure than sets can have (e.g., image schemata or nonpropositional prototypes).

12. The general idea that indefinites in some sense add new elements to a context is certainly neither surprising nor original. For instance, Donnellan (1978) writes,

One would like to say that the initial sentences in these examples, the ones containing the indefinite description, serve to introduce a particular thing, a man, a suitcase, or whatever, and that this is what justifies the subsequent use of a pronoun or definite description.

13. Some nouns can have an "invisible" second argument. For example, in (i) N = friend, "N"(w) = "w is a friend of Bill."

(i)
Bill talked to *a friend*.

14. This is a temporary simplification: S may also indicate connection between spaces ("In the movie, Elizabeth Taylor is Cleopatra"). See chapter 5.

15. Things are actually slightly more complex because "quarterback" can also be a description in R of the property that holds in M (through the ID Principle applied to properties—see section 3.4).

16. Third, irrelevant reading: "Ari covers the tanker with paint."

17. Space-builders like *paint, envision, imagine*, etc., can be followed by a noun phrase, instead of a full clause, in which case an element is introduced with no additional relation. Compare with (i):

(i)
Ari painted a tanker crossing the channel.

18. Lexical decomposition of the type "seek = try to find" will not save (58).

19. There is a major difference here with previous approaches, whether logi-cally based (McCawley (1970), Postal (1974)) or interpretive (OBC).

20. The spaces can be part of the discourse, without being signaled in every sentence by a grammatical space-builder.

21. The parent space here, as often, is determined pragmatically.

22. See section 3.3 for more readings of (64).

23. How H relates to R, and how this relation determines the "logic" of hypo-theticals, is discussed in chapter 4.

Chapter 2

1. Cross-world identification is often assumed in philosophical or linguistic discussion of these matters (e.g., Lewis (1968), Kripke (1980), Kuroda (1982)),

even if it is characterized in very different ways (similarity of counterparts, rigidity, etc.).

2. Peter Gärdenfors informs me that a similar and even more intricate situation occurs in a film of Rainer Werner Fassbinder's.

3. Some speakers accept (7) with the required interpretation by "looping" from x_2 to x_3 in M via x_1 in R. But double looping from y_1 to x_2 is still ruled out.

4. Strictly speaking, the universal quantifier is too strong in any case, since there may be "exceptions" to lawlike, or generic, statements:

(i)
She likes to tie her hat with a string, but not *that* one.

(ii)
The president lives in the Elysée Palace, but Mitterrand chose to keep his own apartment rue de Bièvre.

5. There should be more even in the prototype case; Goffman (1974) uses the terms *play, playing, production,* and *run,* and points out other distinctions (see below in the text).

6. (121) is fine with other interpretations, such as $L(c, e)$ ("Golda in the play looks like Ingrid") or $L (d, e)$ ("Ingrid in the play looks like Ingrid in real life"). Figure 2.21 remains a simplification: the play starring Ingrid Bergman (more than one performance: a "run") would constitute a fifth space, as in "Ingrid is good in that play, but not tonight."

7. I am indebted to Erving Goffman for pointing out in private conversation that there might be connections between "sociological" frames and "linguistic" spaces. Also, I am grateful to James McCawley for reminding me of their importance with respect to the present section on names and drama.

Chapter 3

1. On the negation test, see for example Wilson (1975), Atlas (1979). For an excellent general presentation of presupposition, see Ducrot (1972).

2. The paraphrases such as {Max smoked before} are meant to stand for the corresponding relations of elements, which may well themselves be relative to some other space (e.g., "before").

3. Not all "logical" consequences of A can count as later presuppositions; knowing the axioms does not imply presupposing all the theorems. The accessible consequences are the ones obtained with minimal processing. This is evidently a fuzzy notion: the same consequence is more accessible in some contexts than in others, more accessible for some people than for others, etc. More will be said in chapter 4.

4. Implicit = not explicit, *explicit* being defined by D_1.

5. Assertions too can float by optimization and implicature, as in (i):

(i)
My mother told me she was ready → my mother was ready

Chapter 4

1. Langacker (1978) uses the word *distal* for the simple past, to reflect its distance-marking function, either in time or with respect to reality.

2. *But* may also indicate only the contrast between the two hypothetical situations:

(i)
If you are good, Jesus will love you, but if you are bad, he will punish you (*anyway).

3. A "law" like (35) is never universal; it holds under certain assumptions (e.g., that the volume of gas remains the same). This amounts to importing into *H* some properties satisfied in *R*.

4. The principal aim of such approaches is not to explain the linguistic phenomenon, but to assign truth conditions; I return later to the difference between these goals.

5. One can also test the completeness or consistency of a system by explicitly adding or removing laws in the counterfactual space.

6. I use the terms *states* and *events* intuitively and for convenience, hoping nothing serious hinges on this possible malapropism. Adjacent events in the chain are allowed to be simultaneous.

7. More elaborated experiments of the same kind are presented in the very interesting study by Evans (to appear).

8. Either because proofs from false premises are rejected, or because $A \rightarrow B$ counts as true if A is false under any deduction procedure, or again because the notion of correct deduction does not make sense in an inconsistent space.

9. The discarded space H is not entirely forgotten: incompatibilities have been established, possibilities have been eliminated, etc.

10. Ironically, this position itself is often defended by invoking more or less directly laws like (38), "different parents, different children."

11. In a construction SB_MS, S must involve at least one element of space M (chapter 1).

12. But this is not true of all types of relations:

(i)
On television, *we* love Sinatra.

(ii)
In that painting, *I* was struck by the dancer.

13. Several syntactic analyses could be compatible with the relevant space construction.

14. With adverbial space-builders, the two spaces must usually be indicated explicitly:

(i)
In that movie, Peter runs faster than he does $\begin{Bmatrix} *\emptyset \\ \text{in real life} \end{Bmatrix}$.

15. Speakers normally do not say "Rosa didn't answer more questions than she did" (any more than "He does what he does"), because they are uninformative. But perhaps on a par with "I know what I know," one could say "I don't know more than I know."

Chapter 5

1. Thanks to F. Recanati, who provides this example from Victor Hugo. Théodule believes that Marius is about to meet a girl (*fillette*) and give her the flowers. He follows Marius and finds him crying over a tomb: "The girl was a tomb."

2. The transspatial properties of *be* were already used in the analyses of section 2.5. Recall in particular examples like (i):

(i)
Ben thought that Henry was George.

3. Metaphysical choices are involved in deciding what there is to refer to; there is no reason to think that space construction is metaphysically constrained.

4. Except that names like *Hamlet* can also identify theatrical roles, in which case they behave like other linguistic roles:

(i)
Laurence Olivier was Hamlet in 1935. He was a splendid Hamlet. He played Hamlet well.

5. This is clearer if London happens to have a third name, say *Lunduna,* known by the speaker but not by Pierre. Then (i)

(i)
Pierre believes that Lunduna is pretty.

has the two interpretations mentioned in the text.

6. Or rather, in the context at hand, the construction for which the ID Principle does not apply is not distinguished, since Pierre and the speaker agree on the name *London* for one of the elements. In the example with *Lunduna* (note 5), the ID Principle must apply.

7. Again, this way of putting things is open to superficial objections: it is certainly not element *e* (qua mental construct) that is or is not insane. But recall that this category mistake is like the confusion between Mona Lisa being enigmatic and the corresponding patch of paint being enigmatic.

8. This idea is due, in good part, to G. Lakoff (personal communication).

9. More generally, the speaker may present someone else's orders in the same way (e.g., "Caesar orders you to leave"). Whether this is taken as mere information or as an actual transmission of the orders will depend in particular on the speaker's own role within the situation; when orders are known through certain channels, they count as transmitted; through others, they do not; and some cases are undecided. This is social convention, not natural logic.

   Agents have social power to establish certain (social) relations and can do so by setting them up in the common mental "reality" (space *R* built by each participant): "The meeting is open," "I apologize," etc. Of course, if the situation is legitimate, establishing the relation is enough to make it true ipso facto—a side effect of the special conditions for establishment.

In a sense, this approach to performatives and speech acts would be a paradoxical reconciliation of performative prefixes (Searle (1969)), self-verification (Benveniste (1966), Cornulier (1980)), and sociological analyses (Bourdieu (1982)). Also see Recanati (1981) and Diller (1982).

10. Strictly speaking, *he will order* sets up two spaces: future "he will ____," containing in turn "he order ____."

11. On reported speech, see de Fornel (1980), Darde (1982).

A remarkable paper by Vuillaume (to appear) provides a host of examples concerning multiple spatial layers, and an analysis of them in terms of levels. In Fauconnier (1984), I attempt to show that five general spaces are set up in connection with the sort of narrative Vuillaume discusses, and possibly for stories in general.

On social schemata, see Encrevé and de Fornel (1983).

12. On sign language, see Bellugi and Klima (1979). Body-shift and three-dimensionality have been studied at the Salk Institute by U. Bellugi, C. Padden, and R. Lacy. They may prove critical for establishing a general cognitive basis for the semantics of reference.

13. There are a number of other recent studies that point out problems of standard truth-conditional semantics and/or suggest approaches in terms of mental models. The following are especially relevant for the phenomena considered in this book: McCawley (1978), Johnson-Laird (1981), Dahl (1975), Reichgelt (1982), Shadbolt (1983), Stenning (1977), Travis (1981), Rivara (1978), Saarinen (1977).

References

Abbott, B. (1976). In defense of certain scopes. In *Proceedings of the 12th Meeting of the Chicago Linguistic Society.* University of Chicago.

Atlas, J. (1979). How linguistics matters to philosophy: Presupposition, truth and meaning. In Oh and Dinneen, eds. (1979).

Baker, C. L. (1966). Definiteness and indefiniteness in English. M.A. thesis, University of Illinois.

Bellugi, U., and E. Klima. (1979). *The Signs of Language.* Cambridge, Mass.: Harvard University Press.

Benveniste, E. (1966). *Problèmes de linguistique générale.* Paris: Gallimard.

Bien, J. (1982). Computational explication of intensionality. *IInf UW Reports,* University of Warsaw.

Bolinger, D. (1968). Judgments of grammaticality. *Lingua* 21, 34–40.

Borkin, A. (1984). *Problems in Form and Function.* Appendix A. Norwood, N.J.: Ablex.

Bourdieu, P. (1980). *Le Sens Pratique.* Paris: Editions de Minuit.

Bourdieu, P. (1982). *Ce que parler veut dire.* Paris: Fayard.

Brée, D. S. (1982). Counterfactuals and causality. *Journal of Semantics* 1.2.

Brugman, C. (1981). Story of *over.* M.A. thesis, University of California at Berkeley.

Brugman, C. (1988). The syntax and semantics of *have* and its complements. Doctoral dissertation, University of California at Berkeley.

Brugman, C. (To appear). Mental spaces and constructional meaning. In Fauconnier and Sweetser, eds.

Carey, K. (1993). The role of pragmatics in the development of *have* constructions in English. Doctoral dissertation, University of California at San Diego.

Changeux, J. P. (1983). *L'homme neuronal.* Paris: Fayard.

Chomsky, N. (1990). On formalization and formal linguistics. Letter to the Editor of *Natural Language and Linguistic Theory* 8.1, 143–7.

Churchland, P. S. (1986). *Neurophilosophy.* Cambridge, Mass.: MIT Press.

Coleman, L., and P. Kay. (1981). Prototype semantics: The English verb *lie.*

Cormack, A. (1987). Review of *Mental Spaces, Linguistics and Philosophy* 10.2, 247–260. Language 57.1.

Cornulier, B. de (1980). *Meaning Detachment.* Amsterdam: John Benjamins.

Cornulier, B. de (1983). *If* and the presumption of exhaustivity. *Journal of Pragmatics,* 7, 247–249.

Cornulier, B. de (To appear). *Pour la pragmatique.* Paris: Le Seuil.

Cutrer, M. (1994). Time and tense in narratives and everyday language. Doctoral dissertation, University of California at San Diego.

Dahl, O. (1975). Individuals, subindividuals, and manifestations. *Logical Grammar Reports,* University of Göteborg.

Damasio, A. (1989). Time-locked multiregional retroactivation: A systems-level proposal for the neural substrates of recall and recognition. *Cognition 33,* 25–62.

Darde, J.-N. (1982). Le journal *l'Humanité* et les événements du Cambodge de 1975 à 1979: Les stratégies discursives d'une palinodie. Thèse de doctorat, Université de Paris VIII.

Darde, J.-N. (1984). *Le ministère de la vérité.* Paris: Le Seuil.

Den, Y. (1990). Towards a formalized theory of mental spaces. In Sakahara, ed.

Diller, A.-M. (1982). Interrogation directe et indirecte en français. Thèse de doctorat, Université de Paris VIII.

Dinsmore, J. (1979). Pragmatics, formal theory, and the analysis of presupposition. Doctoral dissertation, University of California at San Diego.

Dinsmore, J. (1981a). Review of Oh and Dinneen, eds. *Journal of Pragmatics* 5.4, 335–364.

Dinsmore, J. (1981b). *The Inheritance of Presupposition.* Amsterdam: John Benjamins.

Dinsmore, J. (1986). Spaceprobe: A system for representing complex knowledge. In *Proceedings of the First International Conference on Methodologies for Intelligent Systems.* New York: Association for Computing Machinery, 399–407.

Dinsmore, J. (1991). *Partitioned Representations.* Dordrecht: Kluwer.

Dominicy, M. (1991). *Histoire, Epistemologie, Langage.* TK:TK.

Donnellan, K. (1966). Reference and definite descriptions. *Philosophical Review* 60, 281–304.

Donnellan, K. (1978). Speaker references, descriptions, and anaphora. In P. Cole, ed., *Syntax and Semantics.* Vol. 9: *Pragmatics.* New York: Academic Press.

Ducrot, O. (1972). *Dire et ne pas dire.* Paris: Hermann.

Eco, H. (1978). Possible worlds and text pragmatics: Un drame bien parisien. *VS* 19/20. Bompiani.

Edelman, G. (1992). *Bright Air, Brilliant Fire: On the Matter of the Mind.* New York: Basic Books.

Ejerhed, E. (1980). Tense as a source of intensional ambiguity. In *Ambiguities in Intensional Contexts.* Dordrecht: Reidel.

Encrevé, P. (1988). "C'est Reagan qui a coulé le billet vert" *Actes de la Recherche en Sciences Sociales 71/72.*

Encrevé, P., and M. de Fornel (1983). Le sens en pratique. *Actes de la Recherche en Sciences Sociales 46.*

Evans, J. St. B. T. (To appear). Heuristic and analytic processes in reasoning.

Fauconnier, G. (1976). *Aspects logiques et grammaticaux de la quantification et de l'anaphore.* Paris: Champion.

Fauconnier, G. (1978a). Is there a linguistic level of logical representation? *Theoretical Linguistics* 5.1.

Fauconnier, G. (1978b). Espaces référentiels. In *Sull'Anafora,* Accademia della Crusca. Firenze.

Fauconnier, G. (1979). Mental spaces. Ms., University of California at San Diego and Université de Paris VIII.

Fauconnier, G. (1981). Social ritual and relative truth in natural language. In K. Knorr-Cetina and A. Cicourel, eds., *Advances in Social Theory and Methodology*. London: Routledge and Kegan Paul.

Fauconnier, G. (1984). *Espaces mentaux*. Paris: Minuit.

Fauconnier, G. (1986). Roles and connecting paths. In C. Travis, ed.,' *Meaning and Interpretation*. Oxford: Blackwell.

Fauconnier, G. (1990a). Domains and connections. *Cognitive Linguistics* 1.1.

Fauconnier, G. (1990b). Invisible meaning. *Berkeley Linguistic Society 16*.

Fauconnier, G. (1992). Galilée, les étoiles, et la Grande Syntaxe. In A. Hertz and L. Tasmowski, eds., *De la musique à la linguistique*. Communication and Cognition Series, New York: Plenum.

Fauconnier, G. (To appear). *Cognitive Mappings for Language and Thought*. New York: Cambridge University Press.

Fauconnier, G., and M. Turner. (1993). Conceptual projection and middle spaces. Manuscript, University of California at San Diego.

Fauconnier, G., and E. Sweetser, eds. (To appear). *Spaces, Worlds, and Grammar*. Chicago: University of Chicago Press.

Fife, J. (1979). The meanings of *be*. Ms., University of California at San Diego.

Fillmore, C. (1982). Towards a descriptive framework for spatial deixis. In R.J. Jarvella and W. Klein, eds., *Speech, Place and Action*. London: Wiley.

Fillmore, C. (1985). Frames and the semantics of understanding. *Quaderni di Semantica 62*. 222–53.

Fillmore, C. (1988). The mechanisms of construction grammar. *Berkeley Linguistic Society* 14.

Fodor, J. D. (1970). Non-specific NP's in English. *Harvard Computational Laboratory Report NSF 20,* Harvard University.

Fornel, M. de (1980). Attributivité, discours rapporté et espaces référentiels. *Semantikos* 4.2.

Fujii, S. (1992). English and Japanese devices for building mental spaces. Manuscript, University of California at Berkeley.

Fujimura, O. (1973). *Three Dimensions of Linguistic Theory.* Tokyo: TEC.

Gazdar, G. (1979). *Pragmatics, Implicature, Presupposition and Logical Form.* New York: Academic Press.

Geach, P. (1962). *Reference and Generality.* Ithaca, N.Y.: Cornell University Press.

Geach, P. (1972). *Logical Matters.* Berkeley, Calif.: University of California Press.

Geis, M., and A. Zwicky. (1971). On invited inferences. *Linguistic Inquiry* 2.4.

Goffman, E. (1974). *Frame Analysis.* New York: Harper and Row.

Goldberg, A. (in press). *Constructions.* Chicago: University of Chicago Press.

Goldstick, D. (1978). The truth conditions of counterfactual conditional sentences. *Mind* 87, no. 345.

Goodman, N. (1947). The problem of counterfactual conditionals. *Journal of Philosophy* 44.

Grice, P. (1975). Logic and conversation. In P. Cole and J. Morgan, eds., *Syntax and Semantics.* Vol. 3: *Speech Acts.* New York: Academic Press.

Gross, M. (1975). *Méthodes en Syntaxe.* Paris: Hermann.

Gross, M. (1979). The failure of generative grammar. *Language,* 55.4, 859–85.

Hofstadter, D. R., G. A. Clossman, and M. J. Meredith (1982). Shakespeare's plays weren't written by him, but by someone else of the same name: An essay on intensionality and frame-based knowledge representation systems. Bloomington, Ind.: Indiana University Linguistics Club.

Ioup, G. (1977). Specificity and the interpretation of quantifiers. *Linguistics and Philosophy* 1, 233–245.

Jackendoff, R. (1975). On belief contexts. *Linguistic Inquiry* 6.1.

Jackendoff, R. (1983). *Semantics and Cognition.* Cambridge, Mass.: MIT Press.

Jacob, P. (1980). *L'Empirisme logique.* Paris: Minuit.

Johnson-Laird, P. N. (1981). Comprehension as the construction of mental models. In *Philosophical Transactions of the Royal Society of London*, B295.

Kamp, H. (1984). A theory of truth and semantic representation. In J. Groenendijk, T. Janssen, and M. Stokhof, eds., *Truth, Interpretation, and Information*. Dordrecht: Foris.

Karttunen, L. (1973). Presuppositions of compound sentences. *Linguistic Inquiry* 4.2.

Karttunen, L., and S. Peters. (1979). Conventional implicature. In Oh and Dinneen, eds. (1979).

Keenan, E. (1971). Two kinds of presupposition in natural language. In C. Fillmore and D. T. Langendoen, eds., *Studies in Linguistic Semantics*. New York: Holt, Rinehart and Winston.

Kinsui, S., and Y. Takubo. (1990). A discourse management analysis of the Japanese demonstrative expressions. In Sakahara, ed.

Kripke, S. (1979). A puzzle about belief. In A. Margalit, ed., *Meaning and Use*. Dordrecht: Reidel.

Kripke, S. (1980). *Naming and Necessity*. Oxford: Blackwell.

Kugler, P., M. Turvey, and R. Shaw. (1980). Is the cognitive penetrability criterion invalidated by contemporary physics? *Behavior and Brain Sciences*. Vol. 2.

Kuroda, S.-Y. (1977). Description of presuppositional phenomena from a nonpresuppositionalist point of view. *Linguisticae Investigationes* 1, 63–162.

Kuroda, S.-Y. (1982). Indexed predicate calculus. *Journal of Semantics* 1.1.

Lakoff, G. (1982). Categories and cognitive models. Ms., University of California at Berkeley.

Lakoff, G. (1987). *Women, Fire and Dangerous Things*. Chicago: University of Chicago Press.

Lakoff, G. (To appear). Multiple selves. In Fauconnier and Sweetser, eds.

Lakoff, G., and M. Johnson. (1980). *Metaphors We Live By*. Chicago: University of Chicago Press.

Lakoff, G., and M. Turner. (1989). *More than Cool Reason*. Chicago: University of Chicago Press.

Langacker, R. (1978). The form and meaning of the English auxiliary. *Language* 54, 853–882.

Langacker, R. (1987). *Foundations of Cognitive Grammar.* Vol. I. Stanford, Cal: Stanford University Press.

Langacker, R. (1992). *Foundations of Cognitive Grammar.* Vol. II. Stanford, Cal: Stanford University Press.

Langacker, R. (1993). Reference point constructions. *Cognitive Linguistics* 4-1, 1–38.

Langendoen, T., and H. Savin. (1971). The projection problem for presuppositions. In C. Fillmore and D. T. Langendoen, eds., *Studies in Linguistic Semantics.* New York: Holt, Rinehart and Winston.

Lewis, D. (1968). Counterpart theory and quantified modal logic. *Journal of Philosophy* 65.5.

Lewis, D. (1973). *Counterfactuals.* Cambridge, Mass.: Harvard University Press.

Lindner, S. (1981). Lexico-semantic analysis of verb-particle constructions with *up* and *out.* Bloomington, Ind.: Indiana University Linguistics Club.

Magnini, B., and C. Strapparava. (1990). Computational representation of mental spaces: A functional approach. IRST-Technical Report # 9004-01. Trento, Italy.

Maida, A. (1984). Belief spaces: Foundations of a computational theory of belief. CS-84-22, Dept. of Computer Science. Pennsylvania State University.

Mandler, J. M. (1992). How to build a baby II: Conceptual primitives. *Psychological Review 99.*

Marconi, D. (1992). Semantica cognitiva. *Introduzione alla filosofia analitica del linguaggio.* Roma-Bari: Laterza, 431–82.

Matsumoto, Y. (To appear). Abstract change expressions in Japanese. In Fauconnier & Sweetser, eds.

McCawley, J. (1970). Where do noun phrases come from? In R. Jacobs and P. S. Rosenbaum, eds., *Readings in English Transformational Grammar.* Waltham, Mass.: Ginn.

McCawley, J. (1978). World-creating predicates. *VS* 19/20. Bompiani.

McCawley, J. (1981). *Everything that Linguists Have Always Wanted to Know about Logic.* Chicago: University of Chicago Press.

Mejias-Bikandi, E. (1993). Syntax, discourse, and acts of mind: A study of the indicative/subjunctive in Spanish. Doctoral dissertation, University of California at San Diego.

Mejias, E. (To appear). Space accessibility and mood in Spanish. In Fauconnier and Sweetser, eds.

Montague, R. (1974). The proper treatment of quantification in ordinary English. In R. Thomason ed., *Formal Philosophy: Selected Papers of Richard Montague.* New Haven, Conn.: Yale University Press.

Morgan, J. (1973). Presupposition and the representation of meaning: Prolegomena. Doctoral dissertation, University of Chicago.

Nunberg, G. (1978). The pragmatics of reference. Bloomington, Ind.: Indiana University Linguistics Club.

Nunberg, G. (1979). The non-uniqueness of semantic solutions: Polysemy. *Linguistics and Philosophy* 3.2.

Oh, C.-K., and Di. Dineen. (1979). *Syntax and Semantics.* Vol. 11: *Presupposition.* New York: Academic Press.

Omori, A. (1988). Exploration into mental spaces: Where do linguistics expressions come from? *Journal of the English Linguistic Society of Japan.* Vol. 5, 130–149.

Partee, B. (1970). Opacity, coreference and pronouns. *Synthese* 21, 359–385.

Postal, P. (1974). On certain ambiguities. *Linguistic Inquiry* 5.3.

Putnam, H. (1979). Comments on Kripke. In A. Margalit, ed., *Meaning and Use.* Dordrecht: Reidel.

Quine, W. V. O. (1960). *Word and Object.* Cambridge, Mass.: MIT Press.

Recanati, F. (1981). *Les énoncés performatifs.* Paris: Minuit.

Recanati, F. (1983). La sémantique des noms propres: Remarques sur la notion de désignateur rigide. *Langue Française* 57.

Reddy, M. (1979). The conduit metaphor. In A. Ortony, ed., *Metaphor and Thought.* Cambridge: Cambridge University Press.

Reichgelt, H. (1982). Mental models and discourse. *Journal of Semantics* 1.4.

Reinhart, T. (1975). On certain ambiguities and uncertain scope. In *Proceedings of the 11th meeting of the Chicago Linguistic Society.* University of Chicago.

Rivara, R. (1978). Les noms propres et la référence. *Sigma* 3. Montpellier.

Ross, J. (1973). Nouniness. In Fujimura, ed.

Ross, J. (1975). Where to do things with words. In Cole and Morgan eds., *Syntax and Semantics: Speech Acts.* Vol. 2. New York: Academic Press.

Ross, J. R. (1970). On declarative sentences. In R. Jacobs and P. S. Rosenbaum, eds., *Readings in English Transformational Grammar.* Waltham, Mass.: Ginn.

Rota, G. C. (1990). Mathematics and philosophy: The story of a misunderstanding. *Review of Metaphysics* 44, 259–271.

Rubba, J. (To appear). Alternate grounds in the interpretation of deictic expressions. In Fauconnier and Sweetser, eds.

Ruwet, N. (1991). A propos de la grammaire générative. Quelques considérations intempestives. In M. Dominicy, ed.

Saarinen, E. (1977). Intentional identity interpreted: A case study of the relations among quantifiers, pronouns and propositional attitudes. *Reports from the Department of Philosophy* no. 5, University of Helsinki.

Sag, I. (1975). A logical theory of verb phrase deletion. In *Proceedings of the 11th meeting of the Chicago Linguistic Society.* University of Chicago.

Sakahara, S. (1983). La chaîne de prémisses et la chaîne d'inférences, ou "on trouve tout à la Samaritaine sauf le 'si d'énonciation'." *Semantikos* 6.1–2.

Sakahara, S., ed. (1990). *Advances in Japanese Cognitive Science.* Vol. 3. Tokyo: Kodansha Scientific.

Sakahara, S. (To appear). Roles and identificational copular sentences. In Fauconnier and Sweetser, eds.

Sanders, J., and G. Redeker. (To appear). Perspective and the representation of speech and thought in narrative texts. In Fauconnier and Sweetser, eds.

Schiebe, T. (1975). *Über Präsuppositionen zusammengesetzter Sätze im Deutschen*. Stockholm: Almquist & Wiksell.

Searle, J. (1969). *Speech Acts*. Cambridge: Cambridge University Press.

Searle, J. (1979). *Expression and Meaning: Studies in the Theory of Speech Acts*. Cambridge and New York: Cambridge University Press.

Sereno, M. (1990). Language and the primate brain. *Center for Research in Language Newsletter*, Vol. 4, no. 4, University of California at San Diego.

Seuren, P. (1984). *Discourse Semantics*. Oxford: Oxford University Press.

Shadbolt, N. (1983). Processing reference. *Journal of Semantics* 2.1.

Shepard, R. (1978). The mental image. *American Psychologist*, Feb., 125–137.

Shepard, R., and J. Metzler. (1971). Mental rotation of three-dimensional objects. *Science* 171, no. 3972.

Soames, S. (1982). How presuppositions are inherited: A solution to the projection problem. *Linguistic Inquiry* 13.3.

Stenning, K. (1977). Articles, quantifiers, and their encoding in textual comprehension. In *Discourse Processes: Advances in Research and Theory*. Norwood, N.J.: Ablex.

Sweetser, E. (1981). The definition of *lie*. Paper presented at the 8th meeting, American Anthropological Association.

Sweetser, E. (1989). Role and individual interpretations of change predicates. Manuscript, University of California at Berkeley.

Sweetser, E. (To appear a). Mental spaces and the grammar of conditional constructions. In Fauconnier and Sweetser, eds.

Sweetser, E. (To appear b). Reasoning, mappings, and meta-metaphorical conditionals. In M. Shibatani and S. Thompson, eds., *Topics in Semantics*.

Sweetser, E., and G. Fauconnier (To appear). Cognitive links and domains. In Fauconnier and Sweetser, eds.

Takubo, Y. (1990). On the role of the hearer's territory of information. In Sakahara, ed.

Takubo, Y., and S. Kinsui. (1992). Discourse management in terms of mental domains. Manuscript, Kyushu University.

Talmy, L. (1985). Force dynamics in language and thought. *Papers from the Parasession on Causatives and Agentivity.* Chicago: Chicago Linguistic Society.

Talmy, L. (1991). Path to realization: A typology of event conflation. Manuscript, University of Buffalo.

Tarski, A. (1944). The semantic conception of truth and the foundations of semantics. *Journal of Philosophy and Phenomenological Research 4,* 341–375.

Travis, C. (1981). *The True and the False: The Domain of the Pragmatic.* Amsterdam: John Benjamins.

Turner, M. (1991). *Reading Minds.* Princeton: Princeton University Press.

Vandeloise, C. (1984). Description of space in French. Doctoral dissertation, University of California at San Diego.

Van Hoek, K. (1991). *Paths Through Conceptual Structure: Constraints on Pronominal Anaphora.* Doctoral dissertation, University of California at San Diego.

Van Hoek, K. (To appear). Conceptual locations for reference in American sign language. In Fauconnier and Sweetser, eds.

Vendler, Z. (1975). The possibility of possible worlds. *Canadian Journal of Philosophy* 5.1.

Vuillaume, M. (To appear). Grammaire temporelle des récits de fiction. *Semantikos.*

Wason, P. C. (1968). Reasoning about a rule. *Quarterly Journal of Experimental Psychology* 20, 273–281.

Williams, E. (1977). Discourse and logical form. *Linguistic Inquiry* 8.1.

Wilson, D. (1975). *Presupposition and Non-Truth-Conditional Semantics.* New York: Academic Press.

Index

16432392R00145

Made in the USA
San Bernardino, CA
02 November 2014